The Universe Is on Our Side

The Universe Is
on Our Side

Restoring Faith in American Public Life

BRUCE LEDEWITZ

OXFORD

UNIVERSITY PRESS

OXFORD
UNIVERSITY PRESS

Oxford University Press is a department of the University of Oxford. It furthers
the University's objective of excellence in research, scholarship, and education
by publishing worldwide. Oxford is a registered trade mark of Oxford University
Press in the UK and certain other countries.

Published in the United States of America by Oxford University Press
198 Madison Avenue, New York, NY 10016, United States of America.

CIP data is on file at the Library of Congress
ISBN 978–0–19–756393–9

DOI: 10.1093/oso/9780197563939.001.0001

1 3 5 7 9 8 6 4 2

Printed by Sheridan Books, Inc., United States of America

To my wife, Patt, with all my love. Always marry an editor.

"This underlying order, further honed by selection, augurs a new place for us—expected rather than vastly improbable, at home in the universe in a newly understood way."

Stuart Kauffman, *At Home in the Universe* (1995)

Contents

Acknowledgments

When you write during a pandemic shutdown, you have the impression you are working on your own. But this is an illusion. My friend and teacher, Robert Taylor, often tells the story of the novice who arrives at the temple, seeking spiritual enlightenment. The master asks him, "How did you come here?" The novice replies, "By train." "Fool," responds the master, "the whole world brought you here." So, I have many thanks to give.

Foremost, to Patt Risher Ledewitz, my wife. She edited every word for content and clarity and shared her deepest responses. I suppose I could have written this book without her, but I'm glad I didn't have to.

Then, to my talented research assistant, Diana Bruce. By email, she molded the work into a form acceptable to a publisher.

Also, to my editor at Oxford University Press, Cynthia Read. My book proposal had been making the rounds for quite some time before she rescued it.

By the time Cynthia Read saw it, that proposal had been sharpened under the careful eye of my friend Eugene Mazo, who helped me as he has helped so many others. He is the best model I know of what the academy needs—the generous teacher-scholar.

These were just the immediate help. In the longer term, I have benefited for forty years from the resources of Duquesne University School of Law. The law library, under the direction of Frank Liu and with the able assistance of Tsegaye Beru, provided the materials I needed for this book. Our dean, April Barton, like her predecessors, has been immensely supportive. My colleagues at Duquesne have always been a community tolerant of new ideas. My students have always been sympathetic to a professor whose first commitment is to constitutional democracy. And my administrative assistant, Nicole Pasqualino, always finds whatever mistakes I miss.

I have also benefited from living across the street from the Monterey Pub, surrounded by close friendships that one does not usually encounter this late in life.

Recently, I have had the opportunity of trying out my remedies for public life in the actual political sphere, as a regular contributor to the *Pennsylvania Capital-Star*. The editor-in-chief there, John Micek, has kept my thinking closely tied to solutions for the problems of the day.

But for all that, there is still the actual train that brought me to writing this book. There were many persons on that train: teachers from the New Haven

Hebrew Day School and Northfield Mt. Hermon, friends at Congregation Dor Hadash, my synagogue before I left Judaism, now known to all because of a gunman in 2018, and Gertrude Falls, who, even more than my parents, reared me and, before I could speak, showed me the love of God. Above all, there is the engineer who has driven that train for forty years, Robert Taylor. He and his wife Nancy have been a haven for learning, whatever the chaos of our time.

To each and all, my gratitude. I hope this book is worthy of you.

Prologue

I am writing this book on the eve of the 2020 presidential election, a few months away, and in the shadow of the Covid-19 pandemic. But you, the reader, will not read this book until much later.

I will do a minor rewrite after the election, but not much in the book will change regardless of how the election turns out.

Given the partisan temper of our time, it may seem surprising that I can say that. After all, this is a book about the brokenness of American public life. Donald Trump and Joe Biden are very different people, with quite different characters, who will pursue vastly different agendas if elected. The policy implications of the various possible combinations—Republican majorities in both houses of Congress, Democratic majorities in both houses, divided government, all of which can be matched with either presidential winner—will yield a greatly different tone and content to American public life. Am I suggesting that none of that matters?

That would be an absurd claim. Of course it matters a great deal, in many ways, which political party dominates American public life. And I have strong preferences personally in those choices. Given our partisanship, the reader must be informed that I am a registered Democrat who has not voted for a Republican candidate for any office in years.

But in another sense, no, it does not matter at all who wins in 2020.

No matter the election outcome, in America and in all the world, the forces of progress will continue to be in decline.

That is not a partisan statement. By progress, I am not referring to policy disagreements over things like the tax rate, or government regulation of business, or even important foreign policy issues, like participation in the Iranian nuclear agreement.

Instead, by progress, I am referring to confidence in the promise of freedom and democracy, of the importance of limited government and the rule of law, of the potential for reasoned debate to reach fair and convincing conclusions. I am talking about the inspiration of the American Revolution creating the experiment of self-government and the commitment, exemplified by Abraham Lincoln, that government of the people, by the people, for the people, shall not perish from the Earth. I am pointing to the establishment of universal human rights—the great accomplishment of the post-WWII international order.

The forces of progress in this sense are in decline all over the world. And, no, I don't think the outcome of the November 2020 election in America will change that.

Even to call these forces by a traditional name, the party of humanity, seems more like a joke today than a claim.

The strongmen of the world—Putin, Modi, Erdogan, Xi—are ascendant. Though any one of them may fall at any time, the trend they embody away from liberal regimes will continue. Their successors will also be authoritarian.

The decline in the forces of progress did not happen because of a counterargument about human nature, government, or the universe. The strongmen did not win some intellectual contest. Instead, one day, almost out of the blue it seemed, people no longer had confidence in the various national forms of constitutional democracy. These political structures no longer seemed to represent hope for the future. Certainly, their apparent inevitability, so obvious in the 1990s that some thought history had come to an end, evaporated.

What the strongmen offered has not in any sense become more convincing. They are just picking up the pieces from something that failed.

The descent of the American response to the coronavirus into absurd partisan bickering is a perfect symbol of our decline. Imagine a country that could not plan for a serious threat to public health and then, afterward, in the reopening, could not enter into a rational discussion of the proper trade-off between the requirements of public health and the need to avoid economic disaster. Many Americans decided that even minor impositions, like wearing a mask in public, were grave threats to liberty. Other Americans decided that deaths due to Covid-19 were to be treated as entirely different from other risks to life and health that we run every day. Any trade-off was considered homicide.

Listening to this back-and-forth was like living in a world of fantasy.

At one time, an emergency like the coronavirus would have elicited broad American consensus. This time, Covid policy became a matter of party politics. For weeks, President Trump dithered over the seriousness of the threat, instead of planning to meet it. But when he did act decisively, as in banning travel from China to the United States, he was criticized by Democrats.

There must be something deeper going on than our usual categories of political opposition to explain a national failure as momentous as dueling narratives describing hundreds of thousands of American deaths. American failure that enormous at the levels of functioning institutions and national solidarity must have an explanation that goes beyond economic inequality, or racism, or technology, or prejudiced media, or the character of particular politicians and their coalitions.

The decline of the forces of progress worldwide must have a fundamental explanation, exemplified most dramatically in one key player—the United States.

Even if this explanation turns out to be an irreversible, cyclical movement of history, it will still be something unexpected, unaddressed, and unsurpassed.

That is why this book, which is about American public life, discusses our politics only in passing. That is why it can be written on the eve of the 2020 election and in the shadow of the pandemic, without knowing how these things will turn out.

When did the American decline begin? With government mendacity in Vietnam? With a malaise at the time of President Jimmy Carter? With the greed of the 1980s? With the hyper-partisanship, and poor character traits, of the Clinton years? With the defense of torture after 9/11? With the wearying, endless, pointless wars that followed? With the growing divide between the 1 percent and the rest of us? With bloated government bureaucracies that stifled innovation? Certainly, by the time of the opioid crisis, the rot, whenever it started, was well advanced.

Or maybe all this is the final reckoning for enslaving Africans and murdering native people, that only looks like decline. When dealing with fundamental change, one must look for fundamental explanations.

One reason for the atmosphere of fatalism in America is that no institution feels like a source of renewal. What intellectuals are offering hope? Which universities are addressing decline? What religious traditions are beacons of salvation?

Of course, there are individual exceptions in all these realms. But in terms of American society as a whole, all institutions have failed.

Even science, regarded as a great success story, now is mired in untestable mathematical cosmic schemes and addresses the colonization of Mars not as an opportunity to gain knowledge, but as a getaway route.

If either political party could gain real power, what would it actually do? What could be worse than an era of partisanship in which we don't even have enough confidence in our own side to vote *for* our candidates? As Ezra Klein showed in his recent book *Why We Are Polarized*, we are often voting *against* the other candidate.

Remarkably, all of this is occurring at a time that is not characterized by worldwide depression, war, or famine. In fact, there is a group of thinkers who rightly point out that the condition of humanity as a whole has never been better than in these early years of the 21st century. Their metrics, whether deaths by violence or available calories or life expectancy, are accurate. The coronavirus is only a temporary interruption of these trends.

So, why is there decline? This should be an age of joy. But it's not.

Even in the particular national example of this book, the United States of America, times have not been terrible, Covid-19 notwithstanding. Economic stagnation is not the same as economic disaster. Economic inequality is not impoverishment. Nor does anything prevent the application of solutions to the problems that we do have. Certainly, nothing prevents creative thought from attempting to create solutions. The objective situation does not justify fatalism. Yet, here we are.

It has seemed to me for years that the decline in America is spiritual, by which I mean occurring at the level of consciousness. We are different. We are not up to challenges that our forbears would have surmounted. We are not worthy of the traditions that were bequeathed to us.

We are anxious, fearful, heedless of giving offense, and ready to take offense. We lack the resiliency that Americans had before.

Why should all this be?

This book is an attempt to answer that question. We are not in the hands of some arbitrary historical epoch. We are not subject to some angry deity. Rightly seen, where we are is not a mystery. It is the working out of a centuries-long event. That event is the Death of God. We had a story about the meaning of life and now we do not. How we come to terms with that event will determine our future.

Introduction

In 1972, the Canadian Jesuit theologian and philosopher Bernard Lonergan asked a question, in two parts, that he thought every human being must ultimately answer:

> Is the universe on our side, or are we just gamblers and, if we are gamblers, are we not perhaps fools, individually struggling for authenticity and collectively endeavoring to snatch progress from the ever-mounting welter of decline? . . . Does there or does there not necessarily exist a transcendent, intelligent ground of the universe?[1]

This book is an argument that the American people—ordinary people, leaders, thinkers—must ask this question, and then attempt to live according to our answer, in order to heal our broken public life. This question must become a focus for our society.

That is an extraordinary claim. We are awash in books, articles, and opinions about what went wrong in American public life. Yet the failure to ask a question like this is not among any of the usual explanations. In addition, the question itself is extremely problematic for our age.

On the one hand, for religious people, the answer is obviously, *yes*, the universe is on our side. Among theists—particularly Jews, Christians, and Muslims—God is the creator of the universe and has our good as His aim. Among nontheistic religious people, the answer is not as direct, but there is believed to be a structure to reality that humans can come to know and, in that process, live in harmony with divine order. So, still, for most religious people, the answer is, *yes*, the universe is on our side.

Genuinely religious people have no problem asking and answering this question.

But how many genuinely religious people are there? And what is their influence on this culture? At the level at which this question is asked—at the level of thinking—we are secular. And that includes a lot of people who nonetheless attend religious services.

---

[1] BERNARD LONERGAN, METHOD IN THEOLOGY 102 (2d ed. 1973).

The Universe Is on Our Side. Bruce Ledewitz, Oxford University Press. © Oxford University Press 2022. DOI: 10.1093/oso/9780197563939.003.0001

On the other hand, for most self-consciously nonreligious people, the "universe" is a collection of forces and matter that does not have an aim, whether for or against humanity. So, beyond the obvious fact that humans are here, and thus the universe permits the establishment and continuation of human existence, the question is meaningless. Certainly, the deeper, metaphysical implications that Lonergan clearly had in mind are considered just empty categories.

Insofar as the question could be answered, the universe, in Sam Harris's memorable phrase, "sustains us, it would seem, only to devour us at its leisure."[2] So, it is obviously, at the very least, not on our side.

For the rest of us, neither genuinely religious nor self-consciously nonreligious—the vast majority of people—it would be unprecedented to ask this question, let alone to live by one's answer to it. Most people do not ask questions like this.

This introduction, then, must amount to a preliminary presentation of the book's entire argument in order to show that Lonergan's question, and our answer to it, are crucial in healing American public life.

To begin, we have to ask, as the theologian Tom Berry used to do, "What is the source of the difficulty?" We know that American public life is broken, and we do not lack for suggestions for what went wrong and what to do about it. Daniel Drezner refers to this as the "21st-century cottage industry of books devoted to how things went off course."[3] These usual explanations diverge, of course, according to the political party membership or more generally to the "side" to which an author belongs.

Americans do not disagree entirely about the nature of the problems, though. We just assign blame and causation differently.

Most Americans, for example, lament the increase in partisanship and the decrease in civility in the public square. We mourn the disappearance of reasoned discourse leading to reliable conclusions upon which rational policy can be based. We would like the two major political parties to work together in Washington and our state capitals to address and solve the nation's problems. But we don't have much hope that any of this will occur.

The reasons for our fatalism do not differ in form, just in content, depending on our side. We say that the other side is unreasonable. They hate us and our way of life. They stop at nothing to gain and maintain power. They care nothing about the welfare of this country. They are not even above manipulating elections and

---

[2] SAM HARRIS, THE END OF FAITH 36 (2004).

[3] Daniel W. Drezner, *America Has Gone off the Rails. Steven Brill Sees Ways to Get It Back on Track*, NEW YORK TIMES (July 2, 2018), https://www.nytimes.com/2018/07/02/books/review/steven-brill-tailspin.html.

refusing to accept the outcome. The real problem is that our side is too nice. We have to begin to play hardball.

Democrats say this about Republicans and Republicans say this about Democrats. Word for word, the very same thing. Believe it or not.

I don't mean that the two sides are the same or equivalent. I do maintain, however, that blaming the other side will not solve our problems. We already know the result when politics becomes war. If the only way to a healthy political life is the defeat of 45 percent of the American people—roughly each side—then America will not have a healthy political life.

Even if one side does really well in an election, the experience of Obamacare, with the constant efforts to undo it, shows that the American structure of government does not work effectively when the two parties are toxic to each other, even if one party has temporary dominance.

Americans on both sides also believe that the reason public life does not improve is that the other side has a stranglehold on the organs of debate. For the Left, this refers to the power of big money, the mendacity of corporations, and the paraphernalia of right-wing media. For the Right, this refers to the power of the establishment media, the left-wing domination of universities, and the prejudices of the knowledge classes generally.

Each side maintains that, because of this stranglehold, its message cannot get out and the American people, who would overwhelmingly agree with it, never really get to hear what it has to say.

In addition, if we are candid, we also believe that a large number of the members of the other side are too stupid or too corrupt to make reasoned decisions.

So, despite strong national preferences otherwise, we end up with both increasing economic inequality and increasing governmental size and power. Political passions increase in ferocity and yet, it seems, nothing can be done. Nothing really changes.

If we look below the surface, we see another common characteristic among many Americans—a lack of trust. Americans do not trust our institutions to tell the truth, to be nonpartisan, or to proceed in an objective way to serve the common good.

We certainly do not trust our political opponents. But, often, we do not even trust the leaders that we vote for. We believe that everybody is tainted, that no one in public life is honest.

This lack of trust is not just political. It is ontological. That is, our lack of trust is really about the fundamental nature of things. We don't any longer have a story in common that makes sense of reality—that answers the question, "What's it all about?" We no longer expect progress. We don't trust the future to be better than the past. We have no hope.

In the context of the West, there is a name for our condition that the philosopher Friedrich Nietzsche well knew—nihilism. It is the final working out of the Death of God that Nietzsche announced in 1882.

The final and full expression of the Death of God occurred in a moment at the beginning of the 21st century in the rise of the New Atheist movement. Three books can be considered the trilogy of those years. The verve and acidic wit of Christopher Hitchens got most of the headlines, with his monumental blockbuster of 2007, *God Is Not Great: How Religion Poisons Everything*. Richard Dawkins had the scientific grounding in his book *The God Delusion*, of 2006.

But the thinker who ended up with the greatest influence by far was Sam Harris, in *The End of Faith* in 2004. It was Harris who understood that the issue was not primarily about God or religion, but more generally about how we know things. This is called epistemology. This is the reason that the subtitle of Harris's book used an epistemological term: *Religion, Terror, and the Future of Reason*. Harris's argument went beyond not believing in God and not being religious. He argued that we should rely on evidence and reason in all the areas of life. Thus, his subject was not the end of faith in God. It was the end of faith, period.

Harris knew, but failed to take into account sufficiently, that faith, or you could say, warranted trust, is at the heart of all truth-seeking. As Lonergan wrote in a different context, the scientific investigator does not actually recheck all of the results of prior investigations. Instead, there is reliance on trusted sources. This is true in all areas of life.

Faith is a necessary ingredient for any healthy human society.

Harris and his band unintentionally put the final nail in the coffin of the acceptance of truth.

Harris did not cause the resulting catastrophe. But he was its herald. Over the next fifteen years, the trends of nihilism and relativism, which had been present for years, accelerated in disciplines such as law, history, and the social sciences. The findings of the natural sciences were increasingly greeted with skepticism from both the Left and the Right, depending on the political context. Even religion was warped by the death of truth.

Worst of all, in politics itself, outrageous and nonsensical assertions were routinely accepted. Even absurd allegations of murder. Policy descended into deranged nonsense and wishful thinking.

This pathological condition was absolutely not the property of one political side. There are climate change deniers and anti-vaxxers. There are tax cut supply-siders telling us that taxes can always be cut, and there are deficit-increasing modern monetary theorists telling us that spending can always be increased.

And, as we know, even discussion of how to address a natural threat that was no one's fault—the coronavirus—became completely politicized.

Not surprisingly, the debasement of discourse in the era of the death of truth led to what this book calls the Age of Evasion. If nothing can really be decided, then at a certain stage, serious questions cease to be asked. At this point, which is the point American society has reached, public life is best described as unserious. Irony replaces reason and passion replaces planning.

And if you think unseriousness is the property only of your opponents, note that some on the Right actually believe we can take off our masks and some on the Left actually believe we can disband the police. Those suggestions are theater, not policies.

The movements described above did not proceed sequentially. Actually, all of these trends had been going on, and continued to unfold, at the same time and were mixed up with each other. They all culminated and became unmistakably visible, however, at the time of the pandemic.

All of these trends share a common provenance in the Death of God. That is why Part I of the book is called, *The Death of God Comes Home to Roost*. This is the fundamental explanation of how things came to be the way they are in American public life.

This is also why there is no obvious way forward out of our morass. Nietzsche knew that the Death of God was a monumental event with far-ranging consequences. God would not be easily buried. It may not prove impossible to build and sustain a civilization without God, but it is certainly not easy and there is pain. Our situation is proof of that.

The Death of God is not by any means universal. It refers to effects on society as a whole. Vigorous, believing communities remain. Certainly, that is the case for individuals.

But as vibrant as sectors of religion can remain after the Death of God, there is no going back in terms of society as a whole. The God who could found Western civilization is no more. That omnipotent figure who could personally ensure our welfare will not return. That is why no one in public life dared to ask God forthrightly to spare America the effects of the virus. When, in July, Louisiana governor John Bell Edwards called for three days of fasting and prayer to stop the spread of the virus, he sheepishly referred to it as "a little bit unusual."[4] If we are seeking a renaissance in American public life, we will have to proceed in a new way.

---

[4] *Louisiana Catholic Governor Calls for Prayer and Fasting amid Coronavirus*, CATHOLIC NEWS AGENCY (Jul. 17, 2020), https://www.catholicnewsagency.com/news/louisiana-catholic-governor-calls-for-prayer-and-fasting-to-end-coronavirus-88983?utm_campaign=CNA%20Daily&utm_medium=email&_hsmi=91611598&_hsenc=p2ANqtz-9y4i2IJVgNIdlQ1qRpxsuSfU1Po6OLSJK9nAlxD4NBYZirw5YPR_3wtOZQm_LCobk8jXhcuimu5nDhM2R-AX7pdJDUSg&utm_content=91611598&utm_source=hs_email.

That is the role of Lonergan's question, "Is the universe on our side?" In the age of evasion, one needs to ask a real question. It is the only way to clarify the situation we are in and to begin to move forward.

The question must be fundamental. It must be a way to reorient ourselves to reality.

In an age of unseriousness, the question must be serious. It must be one that we can plausibly ask.

And in an age in which religion is in decline, it must be the sort of question that Martin Heidegger had in mind when he said that questioning is the piety of thinking.

Lonergan's question is that sort of question.

Albert Camus, the great postwar French thinker, knew the importance of responding to the Death of God. He anticipated our crisis. Here is a quote from Camus's *Notebooks*, which I found in a 2013 essay by Claire Messud in the *New York Review of Books*. Camus is at a gathering of French intellectuals—Arthur Koestler, Jean-Paul Sartre, Andre Malraux, and Manes Sperber—and he addressed them in these words:

> Don't you believe we are all responsible for the absence of values? And that if all of us who come from Nietzscheism, from nihilism, or from historical realism said in public that we were wrong and that there are moral values and that in the future we shall do the necessary to establish and illustrate them, don't you believe that would be the beginning of a hope?[5]

How, at the level of society, is a question asked? Camus was showing us how we begin. We surround ourselves with others, in a loose organizational sense, and engage in discussion. Camus believed that this activity could change French society—and probably he believed it could change the West as a whole.

Lonergan had a name for this kind of questioning activity. He called it cosmopolis. Cosmopolis is a diffuse array of people in a society in decline, who engage in reason and discussion. They are not a political party. They don't have a program.

Cosmopolis does not stop with questioning but drives toward answers. What is the answer to Lonergan's question?

While the answer I give is *yes*, the universe is on our side, this book first takes seriously the negative response. Most people who ask a question like this are negligent toward the answer. But there are those—we can call them the heroes of the negative—who understand this question and courageously set forth the *no*

---

[5] Claire Messud, *Camus & Algeria: The Moral Question*, NEW YORK TIMES REVIEW OF BOOKS (Nov. 7, 2013), https://www.nybooks.com/articles/2013/11/07/camus-and-algeria-moral-question/.

and then strive to live in accordance with this understanding of reality. One hero of this kind is the thinker John Gray, in particular in his book *Seven Types of Atheism*. And there are others, who also will be discussed in this book.

A courageous and open *no* today would be an improvement in the tone and content of American public life. It might be tragic, but it would be thoughtful. If questioning itself can begin to end the breakdown, then this negative answer would put our nation on a firm path of recovery.

Nevertheless, *no* is not my answer. Nor was it Lonergan's answer. After setting forth the *no*, I try to show in the book that the universe *is* on our side.

Why is it so difficult to make that positive case? The major reason is a lack of vocabulary and categories. To make sense of the question, to treat the matter as one even amenable to discussion, there must be more to epistemology than the senses and more to ontology than mechanistic materialism. Yet these categories of sensation and materialism are so ingrained that it is hard to imagine anything else.

It will be necessary at that point in the argument to introduce the process philosophy of Alfred North Whitehead. Although Whitehead is notoriously hard going for the nonspecialist, popularized presentations of process philosophy exist that demonstrate the possibility of real knowledge beyond sensory perception and validate experiences of, and influences of, ideal, normative categories. Without employing supernaturalism of any sort, we can refer to the good, the true, the beautiful, and the just as a part of the universe. We can understand beneficent purpose and aim as more than just human constructs. We can, in other words, speak meaningfully of living in harmony with a deeper harmony in the ultimately real.

But would even a positive answer to Lonergan's question accomplish the goal referred to in the subtitle of this book—*Restoring Faith in American Public Life*? Bluntly, so what if the universe is on our side? According to the argument in this book, the universe has always been on our side and yet Americans hate each other vehemently.

Understanding the implication of the *yes* to Lonergan's question requires revisiting the argument made in Part I of the book. Why did the Death of God have such a devastating effect on American public life?

America was widely regarded as the Western society most dependent on religious meaning and on the truth of ideas. Unlike other, more homogeneous countries, which could function through neo-ethnic modes of national solidarity, America was founded on the idea of self-evident truth guaranteed by a beneficent universe. This conception was called in the Declaration of Independence "Nature's God."

Despite the continuation of slavery and the genocide of indigenous people, these American conceptions were inherently universal, applying to all human beings. America is thus uniquely vulnerable to the siren call of nationalism. When the divinely inspired nature of public life became implausible, Americans literally turned on each other.

In addition, the vaunted individualism of American public philosophy did not become destructive historically because it was always understood as part of a larger whole. Thus, individual human rights served the cause of justice for all and the invisible hand of capitalism served the common good. Again, these are cosmic understandings.

But when individualism became "Every man for himself" in a cold, indifferent universe in which all claims are equally valid or invalid, the cacophony of American life lost all capacity for harmony.

So, the realization that our original conception of the universe as concerned, beneficent, and directive is still valid, even without the presence of a traditional God, would revive the old faith upon which America was founded. It would restore faith in American public life.

We already know what public life can look like when vouchsafed by a meaning-filled universe because we knew that type of politics for a short, but glorious interval—the civil rights revolution. The power for good that Martin Luther King Jr. brought into public life was premised upon his simple injunction—"that the arc of the moral universe is long, but it bends toward justice."[6] It was this plainly religious understanding, put in secular terms, that not only sanctified suffering for the sake of truth, without the need for retaliation against enemies, but gave hope that today's opponent might, indeed should, be expected to become tomorrow's friend. A universe that is on our side means that truth has the power to persuade. It gives to all participants in public life a realistic hope in the future.

A public life founded on these insights is one that not only functions through the faith of the direct participants in public life, but is one that the public generally can have faith in—thus, the subtitle of this book, and the title of Part II. Restoring faith refers to both these internal and external dimensions.

One question remains at the end of the book. Does all this bring us back to God?

I take up the issue of God in the last chapter of the book. But I do not attempt to resolve it.

---

[6] Martin Luther King Jr., *Address at the Eleventh Annual Convention of the Southern Christian Leadership Conference (Aug. 16, 1967)*, *in* A CALL TO CONSCIENCE 171, 199 (Clayborne Carson & Kris Shepard eds., 2001). Dr. King repeated this injunction on numerous occasions in somewhat different formulations.

I am content to leave the matter of God unresolved because of the immense distance between where the book begins and where it ends. Right now, America is broken. I hope the movement in this book, if followed in good faith, can begin a healing process. That is enough for now. The patient does not have to get out of the hospital bed, immediately ready to go home. Much more treatment will be needed in the future. It is enough for now to stop the bleeding.

PART I
THE DEATH OF GOD COMES HOME TO ROOST

1

The Breakdown in American Public Life

Is There a Breakdown?

Before beginning an investigation into the breakdown in American public life, I have to ask whether there has been any breakdown at all.

Clearly, there is a noticeable level of partisan vituperation in America today. But America has had periods of high partisan conflict in the past—in the gilded age of the late 19th century, for example—without anyone suggesting that the system was broken.

Yes, there are ways in which the system of governance is not functioning well today. The global response to the pandemic is a prime example of a lack of preparation. In fact, the *New York Times* published an extensive treatment of that subject by Thomas Friedman on May 30, 2020, entitled *How We Broke the World*.[1]

Yet America has suffered lapses in preparation for previous emergencies—the failure to anticipate the attack on Pearl Harbor, for example—and the system of governance worked just fine in the war effort that followed.

It is the case that President Donald Trump registered historically low levels of voter satisfaction throughout his first term, and, further, the 2016 presidential election did represent a kind of nadir in American political history because of the unpopularity of the candidates of both major parties. But all that could just be bad luck.

Anyway, Abraham Lincoln was very unpopular at the beginning of his presidential term and yet he is regarded as a pre-eminent American statesman.

So, we should take seriously the possibility that there has been no breakdown.

We begin our consideration with two major issues that are often cited as evidence of breakdown: political polarization and economic inequality.

As Ezra Klein shows in his book, *Why We're Polarized*, the major change in American political life in the latter half of the 20th century was that the two major political parties began to stand consistently for differing policies. Before the 1960s, that was not the case. So, Klein calls his first chapter, "How Democrats Became Liberals and Republicans Became Conservatives."

---

[1] Thomas L. Friedman, *How We Broke the World*, New York Times (May 30, 2020), https://www.nytimes.com/2020/05/30/opinion/sunday/coronavirus-globalization.html.

The Universe Is on Our Side. Bruce Ledewitz, Oxford University Press. © Oxford University Press 2022.
DOI: 10.1093/oso/9780197563939.003.0002

As Klein notes, this change was regarded as a good thing. He tells the story, surprising from our current point of view, of a paper issued by the American Political Science Association in 1950 that called for the two major parties to become more ideologically cohesive. In Klein's description, the paper "laments that the parties contain too much diversity of opinion and work together too easily, leaving voters confused about who to vote for and why." It was difficult at that time for the public to make intelligent policy choices through elections. Thus, Phyllis Schlafly's self-published book, *A Choice Not an Echo*, which helped Barry Goldwater win the Republican nomination for president in 1964, could be regarded as a positive change in American public life.

Those persons who criticize this reorientation of American politics, such as Steven Levitsky and Daniel Ziblatt in their book *How Democracies Die*, are actually criticizing the content of this new Republican Party ideology, which they consider by the time of Richard Nixon's southern strategy in 1968 to be racist, rather than the fact of ideological cohesion itself. If the parties had reoriented themselves around issues of trade policy, for example, Levitsky and Ziblatt would presumably approve. Klein agrees with them that the reorientation ultimately proceeded along racial lines.

Once parties do organize around policy commitments, polarized voting is to be expected. If, for example, voters care deeply about abortion, on either side, their votes in many elections are foreordained for the candidates of one party or the other. The same thing is true about climate change and low taxes, just in different directions.

Furthermore, since parties now pursue policies cohesively, the majority organization of legislative houses is important. Thus, there are many voters in Maine who have to consider Senate Majority Leader Mitch McConnell's judicial candidates in deciding whether to vote for Republican Susan Collins for senator in 2020. Though Collins may oppose some of those judges, her vote as a Republican to organize the Senate Republican majority allows McConnell's judicial project to go forward. Sophisticated voters are aware of these matters.

So, voting against Collins even if a voter agrees with her on many issues is not evidence of breakdown. Rather, this kind of polarized voting could be an attempt to pursue the sort of issue agendas that politics is supposed to allow people to do.

In terms of economic inequality, the question is, what can be done about it? It is certainly the case that such inequality has surged in recent decades. It is also the case that there are simple policies that can have a modest effect on inequality—such as raising the minimum wage, easing restrictions on union organizing, maintaining progressive taxation, and so forth. And it is also the case that these policies have not been enacted. Indeed, to some extent, the opposite has occurred.

But if Democratic majorities are elected in Congress, along with a Democratic president, these modest policies are likely to be enacted. So, all that awaits is a favorable vote by the people.

Beyond these modest changes, however, there is no evidence that the American people favor more dramatic policies to address this issue. The people may prefer inequality to a more government-controlled economy. Inequality has proved a difficult problem to solve, but failing to solve it does not mean that American public life has broken down.

This point can be generalized for other claims that "the system is broken" and that people cannot get what they want.

Sometimes, what people want is just hard to get. And there are often unpopular trade-offs. In addition, sometimes people want contradictory things and cannot have them all.

This latter point is missed by Benjamin Page and Martin Gilens in their influential 2018 book, *Democracy in America?* Page and Gilens use polling data to show what Americans want and then demonstrate that we don't get these policies.

The fallacy at the heart of their book is that government action is often a trade-off. We may want policy A in the abstract, but not if the consequence is also policy B.

In a review of their book,[2] I illustrated this with a reference to a mass transit referendum in Nashville in 2018. Polls showed that the initiative was popular and supporters outspent opponents in the run-up to the vote. Nevertheless, the initiative was overwhelmingly defeated.

What happened was that the Koch brothers paid for a group of volunteers to go door to door in Nashville arguing that the transit spending would be wasteful and would result in unacceptably high taxes. They did not lie about anything. The voters apparently just decided that the benefits of transit did not outweigh the costs.

This probably happens more often than progressives want to admit and may explain why Democrats often underperform in elections.

That is not breakdown.

The other matter often referenced in arguments about the breakdown of public life is the level of anger and name-calling in America today. Later, I do treat this as evidence of breakdown. Here, I just want to make the point that a certain level of this kind of behavior is to be expected because people have strong feelings about many political issues. The question in whether there is a breakdown is, do we go too far today?

---

[2] Bruce Ledewitz, *What Has Gone Wrong and What Can We Do About It?*, 54 TULSA L. REV. 247 (2019).

Social media may only be making angry comments, which were always present, more visible and audible. And certain political figures may just be personally less restrained in their speech.

Again, the mere fact that this occurs is not necessarily evidence of breakdown.

All in all, things may not be as bad as we imagine. Beyond that, there is a lot in America that is actually going very well. In some ways, American public life is not only not broken, it is thriving.

Much Is Going Right in America

On Monday, May 25, 2020, George Floyd, a forty-six-year old black man, died in police custody. Videos showed a Minneapolis police officer with his knee on Floyd's neck shortly before his death.

Floyd's death touched off days of protests, many of which turned violent. In one act of domestic terrorism, which turned out to be the action of a white supremacist, federal officer Dave Underwood was shot from a car while protecting the federal building in downtown Oakland, California. The shooting of Underwood was plainly premeditated murder that had little to do with protests that escalated into mostly minor acts of violence. There was also a lot of looting, some of which probably reflected opportunistic crimes by ordinary criminals.

The protests referenced previous instances of police brutality against African Americans. One protestor, Elizabeth Betts in Washington, DC, told an NPR reporter, "We are at a point where it's the same story, the same things are happening. I'm tired of this."[3]

The profound constitutionalist and giant of the civil rights movement, Charles Black, once told a class I attended that race is the great unfinished business of America. While the tumult and violence of protests are distressing, they are evidence that America is at long last taking up this great unfinished business. What we are witnessing is not evidence of decline, but of arrival.

Unlike 1968, when America was divided over the great issues of war and race, and the cities burned when the angels of peace, Bobby and Martin, were murdered, America today is not really divided concerning George Floyd. No one defends what happened to him. Most of America was in sympathy with the aims of the protestors, but of course not with violence or looting.

Certainly, there was a time, not long ago, when police did mistreat African Americans with impunity. With murder charges pending against the officer who

---

[3] Brakkton Booker et al., *Violence Erupts As Outrage over George Floyd's Death Spills into a New Week*, NPR (June 1, 2020), https://www.npr.org/2020/06/01/866472832/violence-escalates-as-protests-over-george-floyd-death-continue.

killed George Floyd* [Ed. Note: Officer Derek Chauvin was convicted of Floyd's murder in April 2021], and other criminal charges pending against other officers present, that day has clearly passed.

In addition, President Trump's frantic calls to meet the looting that did occur with more violence—the president tweeted in what was hopefully unknowing an echo of Miami Police Chief Walter Headley's racist 1967 threat, "When the looting starts, the shooting starts"—were ignored by local authorities and local police departments.

Not only is this not breakdown, it is evidence of incredible progress. America today is a far less racist country than it was even thirty years ago.

While the election of Barack Obama did not usher in a post-race era, it certainly was a step in that direction.

Nor is race the only arena in which long-needed action is at last taking place. The anger of the #MeToo movement similarly makes it seem like things are getting worse. But, again, what is actually happening is that long-suppressed injustices are finally being addressed.

There may be excesses in such a time. They are, in some measure, the cost of progress.

The same thing can be said about issues of sexual orientation. As late as 1986, the U.S. Supreme Court upheld a law making sexual activity among gay persons a crime. While there remains strong opposition to same-sex marriage in America, there are not many persons today who advocate laws like that.

There is also opposition to accommodations for transgender persons. Nevertheless, there is also a great deal of support, in place of the lonely isolation of years ago.

While President Trump's election can be viewed as a hope by some to turn back the clock in these areas, that attitude does not represent the view of all, or even most, of his supporters. As we will see, a lot of that support viewed itself as defensive—not as an attempt to take anything away, but as an effort to retain something. Many Trump supporters would say they only want to live and let live.

The best example of this benign approach is the goal of religious believers to obtain religious exemptions from generally applicable laws in the field of sexual relations. Such proponents maintain that they only want "to be left alone" and do not profess to want to remove rights that have been won. That is why, while *Roe v. Wade*, the abortion decision, is widely regarded as in danger of being overruled, *Obergefell v. Hodges*, the case protecting same-sex marriage, seems entirely safe.

President Trump himself touted his success in reducing the racial gap in income. Prior to the arrival of the coronavirus and resulting shutdown, President Trump was justly proud of the effect his policies were having on African Americans and low-wage workers. President Trump accomplished more in this regard than progressive policies had ever done.

So, things are not as bad as we fear and are better in some ways than we hoped. Nevertheless, American public life has broken down. We now turn to what that means.

Destructive Partisanship

Partisanship is the tendency to put the interests of one's political affiliation ahead of the interests of the country. Destructive partisanship is a general refusal to co-operate with the other side. Partisanship is a problem today in the United States. Destructive partisanship is where we are headed.

In 2018, former President Bill Clinton and well-known author James Patterson were interviewed on a golf course by Jack McCallum of *Sports Illustrated* about their collaboration on the thriller, *The President Is Missing*. The interview ends with both men musing about the state of affairs in Washington today.

Clinton says, "All this division and personal animosity, character assassination and loss of trust is bad for the country. I think, fundamentally, even the people who currently benefit from the state of affairs can't possibly be happy with it."

Patterson adds, "The book is partly about compromise. We compromise all the time in our lives, with our spouses, with our kids, with our employees. But all of a sudden it's become no compromise about anything."[4]

That is destructive partisanship.

Destructive partisanship is illustrated in the well-known quote by Mitch McConnell in 2010 that "[t]he single most important thing we want to achieve is for President Obama to be a one-term president."[5]

Yet, McConnell in that same quote actually held out the possibility of cooperation with Obama, even if he considered the prospect unlikely. So, even destructive partisanship is not absolute.

Destructive partisanship is the attitude that inspired not a single Republican to vote for Clinton's first budget, before any tarnishing from his improprieties. Similarly, there was only one Republican vote in Congress—in the House—for the Affordable Care Act, though the act was premised on concepts like the individual mandate that numerous Republicans had supported previously.

Destructive partisanship is not an attribute of one party. In August 2019, President Trump reportedly was considering a payroll tax cut to forestall a

---

[4] Jack McCallum, *The President Is Golfing*, SPORTS ILLUSTRATED (June 27, 2018), https://www.si.com/golf/2018/06/27/president-missing-bill-clinton-james-patterson-book.
[5] Glenn Kessler, *When Did McConnell Say He Wanted to Make Obama a "One-Term President,"* WASHINGTON POST (Sept. 25, 2012), https://www.washingtonpost.com/blogs/fact-checker/post/when-did-mcconnell-say-he-wanted-to-make-obama-a-one-term-president/2012/09/24/79fd5cd8-0696-11e2-afffd6c7f20a83bf_blog.html?utm_term=.8d23393ac435.

possible recession. At that time, most economists were predicting a recession by 2021.

It was clear that the Democratic-controlled House was not going to cooperate with any tax-cutting action. At least some Democrats considered a recession before the 2020 election a price worth paying to remove Trump from the White House.[6] The single most important thing for some Democrats was for President Trump to be a one-term president.

Then there was the complete absence of Democratic Party support for the 2017 tax cut even though the heart of that bill, lowering the corporate tax rate, had been proposed earlier by President Barack Obama.

There also were the two votes to remove presidents in recent years. No Democrat voted to remove Bill Clinton from office—not even as a symbolic protest against his immorality and lying. Only one Republican did vote to remove President Trump—Mitt Romney.

That absence of conscience is destructive partisanship.

American government cannot function properly under these circumstances. The two political parties have to be able to work together if America is to progress. Most of the important legislative achievements of recent years, from the Endangered Species Act to the Voting Rights Act, were bipartisan. We are not a parliamentary system that almost always permits effective government action, even with close political division. In our system, divided government, which happens all the time, can prevent government action. We are uniquely vulnerable to partisan deadlock.

It took the unprecedented threat of Covid-19 to get the parties to work together on stimulus legislation. In four weeks, beginning in late February 2020, Congress passed, and the president signed, three stimulus bills with wide bipartisan support. On March 25, 2020, after a voice vote in the House, the third stimulus bill, by far the largest at $2.2 trillion, passed the Senate in a unanimous vote. The bill was signed by President Trump.

But the bipartisanship was temporary, brought on by an unparalleled threat. More reflective of the underlying national condition was the fact that no Democrats were invited to the signing ceremony by President Trump.

The fragile moment of national unity in late March dissipated by late April. By then, President Trump was inconsistently encouraging demonstrations against the shutdown at the same time the executive branch was still issuing guidance that encouraged the shutdown to continue in many states.

---

[6] Jacob Pramuk, *White House Official Denies Administration Is Looking at a Payroll Tax Cut,* CNBC (Aug. 19, 2019), https://www.cnbc.com/2019/08/19/trump-white-house-reportedly-looks-at-payroll-tax-cut.html.

On May 15, 2020, the House passed a fourth stimulus bill. But by then, partisan lines had hardened. There was no immediate response by the Republican Senate. It would take weeks for any further action even to be considered.

Even at the beginning of the crisis, the American response was dominated by partisanship. On January 31, 2020, President Trump issued restrictions on travel from China. At the time, this move was criticized by Democrats and their allies in the press. It was one of the few aggressive actions that the administration took against the spread of the virus and yet he still ran into partisan headwinds.

For that matter, President Trump invited this negative response by repeatedly referring to the virus as the "China virus" in what looked like an attempt to stir up xenophobic and nationalist passions.

By the beginning of June, the partisan deadlock had gotten even worse, with Republican state legislators in some states suing their governors over the shutdown. Even modest restrictions like mask-wearing in stores stirred violent reactions while, on the other side, New York Democratic governor Andrew Cuomo insisted that reopening must not risk a single life—plainly an unrealistic standard.

As stated above, destructive partisanship is never absolute. The government continues to operate despite partisan differences. Democrats and Republicans were able to pass an extension of the Mexico-Canada-U.S. trade deal in early 2020.

Overall, however, in a dangerous world, America is unable to speak with a unified voice. In the spring of 2020, while the United States grappled with over 100,000 dead along with economic devastation from the virus, China, Russia, North Korea, and Iran all tested U.S. resolve in various ways. In none of these instances did America respond effectively. Destructive partisanship is part of the reason that our politics no longer stop at the water's edge.

Destructive partisanship is part of the breakdown of American public life. The next question is, from what does this partisanship stem? In part, the answer is the differences in policy that the parties adopted in the 1960s and 1970s.

But that is not the whole story. In some areas, like policies on China, and trade generally, it is not at all clear what the policies of the two parties are. Those policies change and overlap. In other areas, like foreign and military policy in the Middle East, the parties have changed positions over time.

Domestically, the party coalitions are more stable in terms of policy. But even so, Republican senators Josh Hawley from Missouri and Marco Rubio from Florida can sound like Bernie Sanders, socialist from Vermont, in their criticisms of unbridled capitalism.

The level of mutual hostility that partisanship brings in the United States does not seem commensurate with the differences in policy prescriptions between the two parties. If our acrimony is not based on policy, however, on what is it based?

Partisanship as Distrust

In spring 2020, President Trump insisted that voting by mail would allow Democrats to manufacture votes and steal the 2020 election. Meanwhile, Democrats worried that President Trump's threats to call out the military to suppress domestic protests over police misconduct were just a warm-up to Republican efforts to derail the 2020 election if things looked bad for the president's re-election.

The level of distrust between Democrats and Republicans is very high.

In particular, Democrats regard Republicans as racist. As noted earlier, authors like Ezra Klein, Steven Levitsky, and Daniel Ziblatt view the Republican coalition as essentially based on white supremacy.

Liberal economist Paul Krugman put the matter bluntly in his *New York Times* column on June 2, 2020: "What has Trump really offered to the white working class that makes up most of his base? Basically, he has provided affirmation and cover for racial hostility."[7]

Krugman considers those white Trump supporters to be victims, but only in a sense: "The core story of U.S. politics over the past four decades is that wealthy elites weaponized white racism to gain political power, which they used to pursue policies that enriched the already wealthy at workers' expense."

So, these white voters did not get anything for their support. They were fooled. But, in Krugman's view, they are still racists.

As for Republicans, their distrust of the Left is so great that the 2016 election was called by Michael Anton, in the *Clairmont Review of Books*, "the Flight 93 election":

> 2016 is the Flight 93 election: charge the cockpit or you die. You may die anyway. You—or the leader of your party—may make it into the cockpit and not know how to fly or land the plane. There are no guarantees. Except one: if you don't try, death is certain. To compound the metaphor: a Hillary Clinton presidency is Russian Roulette with a semi-auto. With Trump, at least you can spin the cylinder and take your chances.[8]

Michael Anton is not some wild conspiratorial wacko. In 2017, Anton joined the National Security Council. (He left in April 2018.)

My Democratic friends would be amazed at this essay. Anton says that "our side has been losing consistently since 1988" to the "tsunami of leftism." He is

---

[7] Paul Krugman, *Trump Takes Us to the Brink*, NEW YORK TIMES (June 1, 2020), https://www.nytimes.com/2020/06/01/opinion/trump-george-floyd-police-brutality.html.
[8] Publius Decius Mus, *The Flight 93 Election*, CLAREMONT REVIEW OF BOOKS (Sep. 5, 2016), https://claremontreviewofbooks.com/digital/the-flight-93-election/.

referring as much to the condition of the culture as he is about government policies as such.

Then there was the actual threat, voiced during oral argument in the *Obergefell* same-sex marriage case, that any religious institution of higher education that refused to accept same-sex couples, as many would refuse, in married housing, for example, might face the loss of its tax-exempt status.[9]

We can sum this all up in a phrase used by Robin Olson in a 2018 story by Jennifer Percy about distrust of the federal government in eastern Oregon: "Bottom line is we don't trust you. We don't trust you to look out for our best interests."[10]

This statement was from a conservative in a rural area. But it certainly could have also been uttered by any demonstrator angry about the death of George Floyd upon hearing President Trump call his death "a grave tragedy."

Or it could have been uttered by people on the Left when Republican legislators in Wisconsin forced people to vote in person in the middle of the pandemic. Many thought Republican legislators would risk voters' lives rather than risk losing an election.

This distrust eventually extends to more than just political opponents. Ezra Klein calls this negative polarization. Americans don't even trust the people they vote for.

And distrust can go beyond politicians. In 2019, Monica Potts wrote a beautiful story in the *New York Times Magazine* about the suspicion that greeted support for a county library in rural Arkansas:

> People here think life here has taken a turn for the worse. What's also true, though, is that many here seem determined to get rid of the last institutions trying to help them, to keep people with educations out, and to retreat from community life and concentrate on taking care of themselves and their own families. It's an attitude that is against taxes, immigrants and government, but also against helping your neighbor.[11]

This is a level of distrust that applies to everyone outside of one's immediate circle.

[9] David Bernstein, *The Supreme Court Oral Argument That Cost Democrats the Presidency*, WASHINGTON POST: VOLOKH CONSPIRACY (Dec. 7, 2016), https://www.washingtonpost.com/news/volokh-conspiracy/wp/2016/12/07/the-supreme-court-oral-argument-that-cost-democrats-thepresidency/?utm_term=.02f1dbd52e06 [https://perma.cc/T339-45PZ].

[10] Jennifer Percy, *Fear of the Federal Government in the Ranchlands of Oregon*, NEW YORK TIMES (Jan. 18, 2018), https://www.nytimes.com/2018/01/18/magazine/fear-of-the-federal-government-in-the-ranchlands-of-oregon.html?searchResultPosition=3.

[11] Monica Potts, *In the Land of Self-Defeat*, NEW YORK TIMES (Oct. 4, 2019), https://www.nytimes.com/2019/10/04/opinion/sunday/trump-arkansas.html.

Finally, there is the distrust of the experts. People on the Left imagine that it is conservatives who distrust science. But, actually, it is all of America. There are plenty of Democrats who are generally anti-vaccine despite all the scientific evidence about their effectiveness and safety. Only about half of Americans say they would be vaccinated against the coronavirus if a vaccine were available.[12] That statistic indicates a deep and widespread lack of trust present in America.

The attitude that climate change deniers are different is not justified. In America, scientific consensus is always potentially in question.

This is not shocking since plenty of scientific evidence does in fact turn out to be corporate propaganda, as shown by David Michaels in *The Triumph of Doubt*. If that is not the case about climate change, it is only because there is less money to be made from addressing it than from ignoring it.

Distrust is only the first step, however. The next step in the breakdown in American public life is fear and hatred.

They Want to Destroy Us

That story about eastern Oregon above was headlined with the quote, "They want to destroy us." That is basically how some Americans feel about each other.

The author of the Flight 93 election essay not only distrusted what the other side would do, but also feared and hated what he thought they would do. He felt threatened.

Tom Killian, a millennial supporter of Bernie Sanders, felt similarly, but with regard to a portion of his own side: "I am very aware of the contempt that conservative Democrats hold my generation in and the feeling is definitely mutual."[13] They reject who I am. I reject who they are.

In a review of the movie *The Hunt*—a satire about blue Americans hunting red Americans for sport—A.O. Scott writes, "Rage—shared by characters on both sides, even as they direct it at each other—is what *The Hunt* is all about. Anger is the source of its humor and its horror, both of which are fairly effective."[14]

The Hunt is not a scream of outrage. Scott describes the movie as an attempt to deal with outrage: "The filmmakers aren't inflaming passions so much as soothing them with laughter and mayhem. They're trying to make a movie that everyone will like about how Americans hate one another."

---

[12] Hannah Fingerhut & Lauren Neergaard, *AP-NORC Poll: Half of Americans Would Get a COVID-19 Vaccine*, AP NEWS (May 27, 2020), https://apnews.com/dacdc8bc428dd4df6511bfa259cfec44.

[13] Maggie Astor, *Young Voters Know What They Want. But They Don't See Anyone Offering It*, NEW YORK TIMES (Mar. 22, 2020), https://www.nytimes.com/2020/03/22/us/politics/young-voters-biden-sanders.html.

[14] A. O. Scott, *The Hunt Review: The Culture War, With Heavy Casualties*, NEW YORK TIMES (Mar. 13, 2020), https://www.nytimes.com/2020/03/11/movies/the-hunt-review.html.

This rage that Americans feel does not always have defined targets or clear goals. It is the perfect era for the theatrical version of the 1976 movie *Network*, which opened in December 2018 at the Belasco Theatre on Broadway, starring Bryan Cranston, and played for six months. It was a sensation because, indeed, Americans today are mad as hell and are not going to take it anymore.

It is all diffuse outrage. The "they" that want to destroy "us" do not really have faces.

The narrative about the anger and frustration of the white working class that turned to Donald Trump as an outlet has been articulated in numerous contexts. J. D. Vance captured this feeling in his 2016 memoir *Hillbilly Elegy*, which explained as well as anything else the election of 2016.

Vance insisted that the white working class is fed up with all elites, Republican as well as Democratic.[15] This is a good example of Ezra Klein's concept of negative partisanship. My side is almost as bad as their side.

That diffuse feeling of resentment is also why there is no clear program that emerges from these feelings of anger. Trump received political support as an expression of these feelings, not as a platform or plan. According to Vance, it was precisely the cultural disconnection of Donald Trump that explained his popularity. Trump won their votes because he, like they, did not fit in.

But diffuse anger also describes the protests on the Left after the death of George Floyd. When Elizabeth Betts said, above, "I'm tired of this," she spoke for many, and not just about police reform.

Undoing structural racism is the perfect emblem of this diffuse mood of anger because, by definition, that kind of racism is about the unfairness of everything. That is why there were plenty of white protestors at these demonstrations. Many people identify with this mood of generalized anger and fear.

There is a phrase that was used to describe the anger of the white working class that actually applies across the board to the way Americans feel. Arlie Hochschild set out to understand the Tea Party movement from the inside. She used the image of people cutting in line to explain the anger she found. The people she interviewed felt they followed the rules, but other people, who did not do so, got all the benefits.

She titled her book: *Strangers in Their Own Land*.

Certainly, Hochschild's subjects spoke in terms tinged with racial and immigrant animus. But the feeling that the game is rigged, that other people have unfair advantages, that I will never get what I deserve no matter what I do, while others get undeserved benefits, is not confined to the Right and is not primarily racial. It is exactly how other people feel about the 1 percent. About those parents

---

[15] Tessa Berenson, *J. D. Vance on Why Life Might Get Worse for the White Working Class*, TIME (Nov. 3, 2016), https://time.com/4556065/jd-vance-white-working-class/.

who cheated to get their kids into good colleges. About white privilege. About men. About straights. About all the other people who, one way or another, get things handed to them.

The difference between the two sides may be this: Hochschild was describing people who felt they used to know who they were and what life was about and they resented it when they found out that things had changed.

Whereas, on the Left, people may feel that others have always had special privileges and things have not changed, though there were promises that they would. They resent that.

The members of Hochschild's group have become strangers in their own land. The other group continues to remain strangers in a land that ought to be theirs.

But either way, hopes and dreams are not going to be fulfilled, because of the unnamed "they." The system is set up to benefit the unnamed "they." They want to destroy people like me. I fear them and I hate them.

That describes another view of the breakdown in American public life.

Dueling Narratives

While Americans have been divided before, distrustful, fearful, and angry before, our current dueling narratives, and disagreements over facts, are new.

Nobody ever said slavery was a hoax.

That is actually an exaggeration. There were dueling narratives over slavery. Defenders of the institution portrayed it as a benign kind of trusteeship by a dominant and advanced race over a lesser race of human beings. That is why Senator John Calhoun of South Carolina had to argue that the Declaration of Independence's proclamation that all men were created equal was a lie.

But those dueling narratives about slavery did not remain static, which is why Abraham Lincoln was reported to have said upon meeting Harriet Beecher Stowe, the author of *Uncle Tom's Cabin*, "So you're the little woman who wrote the book that made this Great War?"[16]

The truth of slavery was too awful to remain a lie forever.

But in America today, it is possible for dueling narratives to simply remain in place.

---

[16] As Daniel Vollaro points out, the reason for the popularity of this apochryphal story is that it met "American cultural expectations." Literary exposures of slavery greatly aided abolition. *Lincoln, Stowe, and the "Little Woman/Great War" Story: The Making, and Breaking, of a Great American Anecdote,*   https://quod.lib.umich.edu/j/jala/2629860.0030.104/--lincoln-stowe-and-the-little-womangreat-war-story-the-making?rgn=main;view=fulltext .

This was the case with regard to the pandemic. There was a moment of national unity in late March and early April 2020, when it did not matter which news outlet one watched. All outlets told the same story.

On April 1, President Trump warned us of "a hell of a bad two weeks," with the ultimate number of COVID-19 deaths estimated to be 100,000 to 240,000. The country was unified at that time.

But then, in late April, the narrative shifted and began to diverge. Republicans were more likely to feel that the economy was reopening too slowly. Democrats were more likely to feel that this was happening too quickly.

Suddenly, as is so often the case, it was as if Fox and the mainstream media were covering different events. That was when there began to be talk of the virus as a hoax. And when the efforts to mitigate the spread of the virus, by wearing masks, for example, began to be treated as a form of government tyranny.

On the other side, that was also the time when dire warnings about reopening the economy too quickly became a fixation. The resulting increase in Covid-19 cases was attributed solely to Republican governors opening up too quickly, even though California, with a Democratic governor, suffered the same fate.

When UPMC in Pittsburgh reported in July that the current virus strand had mutated to become more easily transmissible but less lethal, that should have been good news that explained part of the increase in cases. But it was mostly ignored by the national media.[17]

This is all part of what *Time Magazine* announced at the beginning of the Trump administration as "the death of truth."

One aspect of that death was that President Trump simply enunciates falsehoods. In April 2020, the *Washington Post* fact-checker reported 18,000 false or misleading statements by the president during his term in office.[18]

But, in a sense, lies are the least of our problems. Very often, claims by President Trump that are clearly false—for example, winning the popular vote in the 2016 election—are understood to be false and are ignored by almost everyone.

Far worse, and a barrier to effective public policy, is the situation in which a serious policy issue is simply frozen in place because America can no longer come to a consensus on simple facts.

Naturally, there will be disagreement about contestable claims, such as "President Trump rebuilt the military" or "Joe Biden has stood with African Americans."

---

[17] Randy Griffith, *UPMC Doctors: Milder Virus Strain Now Dominant In SW Pa.*, TRIBUNE-DEMOCRAT (July 10, 2020), https://www.tribdem.com/coronavirus/upmc-doctors-milder-virus-strain-now-dominant-in-sw-pa/article_8966ef02-c23d-11ea-b362-33635d1c4557.html.

[18] *President Trump Made 18,000 False or Misleading Claims in 1,170 Days*, WASHINGTON POST: FACT CHECKER (Apr. 14, 2020), https://www.washingtonpost.com/politics/2020/04/14/president-trump-made-18000-false-or-misleading-claims-1170-days/.

But American public life is broken because, for example, we cannot agree whether the world is getting warmer and whether human activity is the cause. This is the sort of simple scientific finding of which it used to be said, in the words attributed to Senator Patrick Moynihan, "Everyone is entitled to his own opinion, but not his own facts."

There is something drastically wrong when there is an ongoing disagreement that refuses to be resolved about something like climate change.

Underlying this inability to agree on the facts is a loss of faith. It is no longer inconceivable to many Americans that a widespread scientific consensus might be fraudulently procured. That loss of faith is the final evidence of the breakdown in American public life.

Loss of Faith in Persuasion, in Institutions, in Everything

On January 19, 2020, two headlines in the published Sunday edition of the *New York Times* seemed to epitomize where we are as a society today—"How Did Americans Lose Faith in Everything?" by Yuval Levin,[19] and "Has Trust Become Irrelevant?" by Laurence Scott.[20]

The authors of these two pieces were commenting on different matters. Levin was concerned that American institutions have lost the capacity to mold character and now focus solely on performance instead. Scott was commenting on the prevalence of surveillance to render trust—and privacy, for that matter—irrelevant.

But the underlying theme of loss of faith and trust seems to me to be the real driver in American public life.

To take an example from my own field of law, the premise of freedom of speech is partly that people have a right to have their say about things, whatever the merits of their views. But the historical justification of freedom of speech was always that, as Shakespeare put it, the truth will out. We discuss matters freely as a society in order to come to the best conclusions.

This is faith in persuasion. This faith used to be at the heart of politics.

That is no longer the case. Most political professionals would say today that attempts at persuading voters who have not made up their minds about who they will vote for is an impractical endeavor. It is much more efficient to tailor a candidate's message to, and devote a campaign's resources to, motivating the candidate's base. It is even called "weaponizing the base."

---

[19] Yuval Levin, *How Did Americas Lose Faith in Everything?*, NEW YORK TIMES (Jan. 18, 2020), https://www.nytimes.com/2020/01/18/opinion/sunday/institutions-trust.html.

[20] Laurence Scott, *How the "Sharing" Economy Erodes Both Privacy and Trust*, NEW YORK TIMES (Jan. 18, 2020), https://www.nytimes.com/2020/01/18/opinion/sunday/privacy-trust.html.

Americans no longer believe that the best arguments win in the long run.

It is a short, albeit dishonorable, step from turning out one's own voters to preventing, or at least making it harder, for the other side's voters to vote. Voter suppression is premised on a lack of faith in persuasion.

In his last book, *Ill Fares the Land*, Tony Judt, the great social democrat, wrote simply, "Clearly, we cannot do without trust." Healthy political life is premised on trust—trust in my opponents to be reasonable and serve the common good, trust in the voters to make wise decisions, even trust in my own allies not to take advantage of the losing side, when we win. Trust, in other words, that we are all in this together.

That is why the statement by Hillary Clinton that "they were never going to let me be president"[21] was so shocking. Nothing prevented Clinton from winning. In fact, she did win the popular vote, quite convincingly. It is fair to say that she was mistreated by FBI director James Comey in the last stages of the campaign, but the race should not have been that close. If Clinton failed to hold enough white voters to win Michigan, Pennsylvania, and Wisconsin, when some of those voters had supported Barack Obama, that was really the fault of her campaign.

It is true that Clinton faced sexism, as every female candidate in America does, but there was no conspiracy of a "they" denying her the presidency.

Yet, though shocking, Clinton's statement makes perfect sense in a culture that expects shadowy forces to control things. That is a culture that has lost faith in institutions and people to act reasonably.

This condition explains why Supreme Court Justice Neil Gorsuch would choose this particular moment to remind us of a story about Benjamin Franklin. Asked upon leaving the Constitutional Convention what form of government America was to have, Franklin is said to have answered: a republic, if you can keep it. That is the title of Justice Gorsuch's recent book: *A Republic, If You Can Keep It*. By using that title, Justice Gorsuch implies that there is again a question about our future.

The science fiction author William Gibson has a phrase for this loss of faith. He calls it "the end of the future." Gibson points out that we don't talk about the 22nd century, in contrast to how people used to talk about the coming 21st century.

This lack of faith in the future is also the reason that space travel is now about having a safe haven for humanity rather than an exciting new vista for knowledge.

The pandemic was just one more piece of evidence that those who fear the coming apocalypse, as Mark O'Connell describes it in his recent book, *Notes*

---

[21] Amy Chozick, *"They Were Never Going to Let Me Be President,"* NEW YORK TIMES (Apr. 20, 2018), https://www.nytimes.com/2018/04/20/sunday-review/hillary-clinton-chasing-hillary.html.

from an Apocalypse, may well be right. The new slogan for our age is: The worst is yet to come.[22]

Despair

What happens to a people who distrust, fear, hate, doubt, and lose faith? They—we—despair. This is the final stage of the breakdown in American public life. In this despair, we see the opioid crisis, angry rather than hopeful demonstrations, political fatalism, and the absence of hope in the future.

We no longer believe that good things are coming. We no longer even have a story to tell ourselves about ourselves in which a better future would make sense.

The *New York Times* unintentionally described our current mood with this headline about a blockbuster video game sequel:

> *"The Last of Us Part II" Is a Dark Game for a Dark Time.*
> *Set in a violent, tribal, pandemic-ravaged world, the long-awaited Naughty Dog epic will leave you damaged—and awed.*[23]

Bleak damage sells.

How did we arrive at this breakdown in American public life? That is the subject of the next chapter.

---

[22] Farhad Manjoo, *The Worst Is Yet to Come*, NEW YORK TIMES (May 20, 2020), https://www.nytimes.com/2020/05/20/opinion/coronavirus-worst-case.html.
[23] Conor Dougherty, *"The Last of Us Part II" Is a Dark Game for a Dark Time*, NEW YORK TIMES (June 19, 2020), https://www.nytimes.com/2020/06/19/business/last-of-us-2-review.html.

2

The Spiritual Dimension of the Breakdown

Americans today are divided, distrustful, angry, and fearful. We cannot agree on what is happening, even at the most basic level. We lack trust in each other, in our institutions, and in the future. Many of us are in despair. While there are many people working hard to make things better by trying to bring Americans together, this sad story is our current state.

Most people would probably agree with that description.

In fact, everyone would probably at least agree that there has been a breakdown, in the sense that the American political system is failing to address our national problems adequately and people are deeply dissatisfied.

We don't lack for explanations for this situation. In fact, we have a surfeit of proposals as to how we arrived at this moment. Many books have been written. Lots of articles. Podcasts. And so forth.

Almost all of these accounts are partisan. They will be read as attacks on one party and its actual or perceived coalition of support, or the other.

In this chapter, I skim through some of those proffered explanations and suggest that they are inadequate. Some of them are referring to symptoms of the breakdown, rather than causes. Others are pointing to serious problems that the breakdown is preventing us from addressing. And yet others are accurate in their analyses, but incommensurate with the depth of the American crisis. Actually, these inadequacies are often mixed together.

As the title of this chapter shows, I regard the breakdown in American public life as a spiritual crisis that affects everyone. By spiritual, I mean that it is a crisis in our national consciousness.

Some of these proposed explanations have a spiritual component. In fact, all of the explanations contain hints of a national spiritual decline. In that way, there is a level of agreement among all these approaches.

The Economy

By far the most prevalent explanation for America's current dissatisfaction is material and economic. People, especially people in the lower economic quadrant,

The Universe Is on Our Side. Bruce Ledewitz, Oxford University Press. © Oxford University Press 2022.
DOI: 10.1093/oso/9780197563939.003.0003

are said to be angry because of long-term wage stagnation, the loss of well-paid, blue-collar jobs, and economic inequality that channels gains in wealth to the top 1 percent.

If you want to know why people are mad, why so many oppose free trade and why immigration is such a tense political issue, look to the economy.

This explanation is so pervasive that an account like *The People vs. Democracy*, by Yascha Mounk, which emphasizes non-economic factors such as the rise of social media and identity politics, also includes economic inequality. Even an influential book about constitutional law, *The Crisis of the Middle-Class Constitution*, by Ganesh Sitaraman, begins with this economic premise.

There is nothing new in this account. Using a phrase from Paul Krugman for its title, Timothy Noah's 2012 book, *The Great Divergence*, explained in an evenhanded way the economic causes of inequality and its effects on government policies. Noah offered some reforms that might address the problem.

Many accounts are much more partisan than his. Our economic condition is often said to stem from intentional policies on behalf of the wealthy. The same Paul Krugman, for example, called the 2017 tax cut "class warfare aimed at perpetuating inequality into the next generation." He continues:

> Taken together, the elements of both the House and the Senate bills amount to a more or less systematic attempt to lavish benefits on the children of the ultra-wealthy while making it harder for less fortunate young people to achieve upward social mobility.
>
> Or to put it differently, the tax legislation Republicans are trying to ram through Congress with indecent haste, without hearings or time for any kind of serious study, looks an awful lot like an attempt not simply to reinforce plutocracy, but to entrench a hereditary plutocracy.

It has been observed that many of the supposed victims of this supposed Republican plot tend to vote Republican. This situation vexes liberals, a vexation parodied in the title of Thomas Frank's 2005 best seller, *What's the Matter with Kansas?* Frank argued that conservatives pulled a fast one, legislating economic benefits for the rich while proclaiming a cultural connection with workers. The solution he proposed was for Democrats to emphasize bread-and-butter issues. This was a page from Bill Clinton's 1990s playbook.

Recently, however, other critics, though accepting this class critique, have subtly altered it. Michael Lind, who is hard to cabin in current political categories, argues in *The New Class War* that it is really the managerial elite associated largely with the Democratic Party that has dispossessed the working class. This theme of cultural disdain by a "knowledge class" has echoes in articles like "How the GOP Became the Party of the Left Behind,"[1] the remark by Hillary Clinton about the "deplorables" who supported Donald Trump, and, for that matter, Barack Obama's earlier comment about people clinging to their guns and Bibles.

My conservative friends love to point out that many people who support extending the pandemic shutdown are part of the class that can work from home and still collect a paycheck.

Richard Rorty is credited with predicting these trends, including these new class divisions, in 1998:

> Members of labor unions, and unorganized unskilled workers, will sooner or later realize that their government is not even trying to prevent wages from sinking or to prevent jobs from being exported. Around the same time, they will realize that suburban white-collar workers—themselves desperately afraid of being downsized—are not going to let themselves be taxed to provide social benefits for anyone else.
>
> At that point, something will crack. The nonsuburban electorate will decide that the system has failed and start looking for a strongman to vote for—someone willing to assure them that, once he is elected, the smug bureaucrats, tricky lawyers, overpaid bond salesmen, and postmodernist professors will no longer be calling the shots.[2]

Needless to say, there is a lot of truth in all of this.

But three cautions about viewing economics as central must be noted. First, the current national divisions seem out of proportion to actual economic conditions. Voters in Europe in the 1930s turned away from democracy and embraced fascism only after Depression and runaway inflation. In contrast, America's economic performance since 1970, while not stellar, was not really that bad. Even with the severe downturn in 2008, growth muddled along at 1.5 to 2.5 percent on average. Wage performance lagged but did not decline for most people.

Second, there are aspects of the breakdown that do not seem to have anything to do with economic conditions. Why should economic dislocation cause Americans to come up with competing narratives about the world? That did not happen during the Great Depression.

Finally, why should economic dissatisfaction linger? The breakdown in public life is not just about what the problems are. It is also about why we cannot address

---

[1] Eduaro Porter, *How the G.O.P. Became the Party of the Left Behind*, New York Times (Jan. 27, 2020), https://www.nytimes.com/interactive/2020/01/27/business/economy/republican-party-voters-income.html.

[2] Sean Illing, *Richard Rorty's Prescient Warnings for the American Left*, Vox (Feb. 2, 2019), https://www.vox.com/policy-and-politics/2017/2/9/14543938/donald-trump-richard-rorty-election-liberalism-conservatives.

them. Why is there no genuinely popular national figure who can speak to our ills the way that FDR and Ronald Reagan spoke to earlier economic dissatisfactions?

The economic accounts, whatever their internal differences, have nothing to say about deadlock and despair. Why don't we do something about all this? That is what needs an explanation.

Big Money

The economic explanation for inaction that goes along with the economic explanation for dissatisfaction is that big money controls the actions of government. That is said to be why we don't get the policies we want.

This is the message of many observers, perhaps most carefully set forth by Page and Gilens in *Democracy in America?* Although, as I described in Chapter 1, while the authors rely on polls to indicate what Americans want rather than trying to ascertain what positions actually win elections, they do convincingly demonstrate the power of money in politics.

Another voice in this field is that of Harvard Law professor Lawrence Lessig, who, after a distinguished career in copyright law, became the leading voice in American law on the subject of the corrupting influence of money in politics. His views are most comprehensively set forth in *Republic, Lost*, in 2011.

In addition, most people are aware of the consistent efforts by progressives to overrule, or limit the impact of, campaign finance cases like *Citizens United*,[3] which are said to be responsible for the power of big money in American politics.

But this explanation does not work. While it is certainly the case that Congress pays more attention to the wishes of the rich than those of the poor, this truism has little to do with the current state of American public life.

Progressives have been complaining about big money for so long that they have failed to notice that the facts on the ground have changed. Barack Obama changed the narrative that Democrats would be consistently outspent by Republicans. And the success of Donald Trump in obtaining the Republican nomination for president in 2016 demonstrated that big money does not always get the candidates that it wants. Bernie Sanders did not get the Democratic nomination in either 2016 or 2020, but big money was not the reason for his failures. Democrats have outspent Republicans in the 2020 cycle.

In policy, there are similar limits on what big money can accomplish. Yes, having money helps. It helps a lot. But, fundamentally, the wishes of the people count more. So, when President George W. Bush wanted to privatize Social Security, that plan went nowhere. Similarly, the Republican Party was committed

---

[3] *Citizens United v. FEC*, 558 U.S. 310 (2010).

to repealing Obamacare, but when it came to actually doing so, the party failed, in part because of popular opinion.

The experience of the Affordable Care Act demonstrates something else as well. When it first passed, Obamacare was so unpopular that Democratic Party candidates for Congress ran away from it. Nevertheless, the party lost control of the House in 2010, in part because of Obamacare.

Since the Affordable Care Act became much more popular later, this political failure has to be attributed to Democratic Party ineptitude rather than the power of big money.

Despite this, big money remains a convenient excuse for the inability of Democrats to translate popular support into actual legislation. The fault is not that of big money.

As I have argued elsewhere,[4] the real problem with money in politics is spending that is independent of the candidate actually running for office. It is independent money that permits candidates to benefit from irresponsible advertising by dark money, the source of which need not legally be identified. But that problem could be eliminated tomorrow by simply removing campaign contribution limits to candidates.

Something is preventing the American political system from identifying and addressing the discontents of the American people. But there is no reason to believe that money per se is the reason for the current deadlock in American public life. Nothing at all prevents candidates from proposing policies that would benefit, and be supported by, ordinary people. If it does not happen, and it plainly does not, we must look elsewhere for the reason.

Technology

The other common explanation for the breakdown in American public life is technology, in particular the rise of social media. The anonymous, pervasive power of the Internet is said to encourage outrage and to discourage calm, rational thought.

Anyone who has been caught up in the frenzy of social media can attest that there is some truth to this.

In addition, the Internet as a whole allows the construction of bubbles around our views of the world. It is possible, for example, to watch only Fox News and follow certain conservative websites and never to come into contact with arguments and views with which one disagrees.

---

[4] Bruce Ledewitz, *The Threat of Independent Political Spending to Democratic Life—and a Plan to Stop It*, 64 CLEV. ST. L. REV. 133 (2016).

And, obviously, the same thing is true for liberals.

In fact—though liberals would deny this—because most of the media is still dominated by the Left—as is clear from the difference in tone in coverage of President Trump as compared to the coverage of President Obama—it is even easier for liberals to avoid engagement with conservative thought than it is for conservatives to do the opposite. I have politically informed friends who have never had a serious conversation with a person who voted for President Trump and do not think there is anything strange in this.

However, social media only exacerbates our divisions, rather than giving rise to them. For one thing, our polarization predates not only social media, but the widespread use of the Internet. The best illustration of this is the unanimous opposition of congressional Republicans to President Clinton's first budget, in 1993, which was just one aspect of the toxic atmosphere in Washington throughout his presidency. Fox News was not founded until 1996. All the pieces of the breakdown in American public life were in place before 2000.

Nor was this just a DC phenomenon. The rise of conservative talk radio with all of its hyper-partisanship arose just before Clinton's first term. By 1990, Rush Limbaugh already had 5 million listeners. Those listeners probably exhibited many of the symptoms of breakdown we now see as dominating society as a whole.

Nor is the protective anonymity of the Internet in general, and social media in particular, the reason for our breakdown. I was reminded of this fact when John Micek, the editor of my column at the *Pennsylvania Capital-Star*, reported on his experience with anonymity covering Dr. Rachel Levine, the Pennsylvania Secretary of Health, during the pandemic.[5] Micek wrote that he expected some pushback because of Levine's transgender status. But he did not expect to spend three days scrubbing the *Capital-Star*'s Facebook feed because of "vile bigotry." In response, Micek arranged that comments would have to be posted under a person's real name. He had heard that this was a way to moderate commentary.

But that turned out to be a fiction, Micek wrote: "Every single comment I removed from our Facebook feed was someone posting—I assume—under his or her real name. And as the story gained national traction and this tiny, cruel minority followed the links back to our page, the hate, all filed under real names, continued to multiply."

If people are willing to exhibit their bigotry even under their own names, we can be fairly certain our problems are not caused by technological anonymity.

---

[5] John L. Micek, *Levine's Policies Are Fair Game for Criticism. Attacking Her Identity Is Vile Bigotry*, PENNSYLVANIA CAPITAL-STAR (May 15, 2020), https://www.penncapital-star.com/civil-rights-social-justice/levines-policies-are-fair-game-for-criticism-attacking-her-identity-is-vile-bigotry/.

We can also see that social media only contributes to our problems, rather than causing them, by looking at partisan reactions to videos. We can call what happens today the Covington effect. In January 2019, a video surfaced showing a group of Covington Catholic High School students wearing Trump MAGA hats at a pro-life rally, apparently taunting a Native American man. The social media reaction was immediate and devastating. The boy in the center of the controversy was vilified nationally as a bigot.

But, almost as quickly as the first reaction happened, other videos and background information came to light showing at the very least a more nuanced version of what had actually happened. The actions of the boys were no longer self-evidently racist.

The new information led to a wave of apologies and reinterpretations, including a widely read essay by Julie Zimmerman in the *Atlantic* entitled, "I Failed the Covington Catholic Test."[6] Today, everyone is a little more careful about immediate reactions to videos.

In fact, what is most telling about the video showing the death of George Floyd is that there is no alternative narrative or counter-video. Floyd's death was just as horrible as it first appeared.

The point about the instantaneous partisan reactions to videos, however, is that the Internet is just spreading our hyper-partisanship and competing narratives. It is not causing them.

Of course, instantly sharing videos is also a part of the rise of social media. But unlike the ability to comment on social media, which is relatively new, videos are just speedier versions of the news reports we have seen for many years. There is nothing really new about them. So, if we now react with instant venom upon seeing them, the change is in us rather than in the technology.

There is another story told about technology that attributes our breakdown to the new market forces that the Internet has created. This account is given in related ways by Ezra Klein in *Why We're Polarized* and Lawrence Lessig in *America, Compromised*.

According to Klein, once the political parties became more ideologically cohesive in the 1960s, political polarization created incentives for media and politicians that increased polarization. The Internet provided the richest arena for this new competition.

Lessig, although not dropping his theme of the power of big money to corrupt American politics, pointed out that the consensus viewpoint and influence of a figure like Walter Cronkite in the 1960s was a result of the dominance of the

---

[6] Julie Irwin Zimmerman, *I Failed the Covington Catholic Test: Next Time There's a Viral Story, I'll Wait for More Facts to Emerge*, ATLANTIC (Jan. 21, 2019), https://www.theatlantic.com/ideas/archive/2019/01/julie-irwin-zimmerman-i-failed-covington-catholic-test/580897/.

three major broadcast networks. Once that media oligopoly was broken technologically with the rise of cable networks, the Internet, and social media, niche audiences allowed competing viewpoints to emerge.

While Cronkite reigned, the problem of competing narratives could not arise. In Lessig's view, this was not altogether a good thing. It did provide a common national narrative, but it also suppressed legitimate voices from being heard.

Neither Klein's nor Lessig's account is convincing as an explanation for our situation, however.

It is easy to caricature Klein as saying that we are polarized because we are polarized. Even beyond that problem, however, Klein cannot explain why the process of polarization did not stop when it became unreasonable. Why is no one today saying that the reactions we have to each other are fantasies woven primarily out of our own fears rather than reasonable interpretations of the facts? Why is there no audience to hear such a plain truth?

Lessig does not explain why the ideological competition did not begin earlier. It may be that if Walter Cronkite appeared today, he would not be able to gain a national audience, as Lessig maintains. But the question is, why didn't ABC compete with the NBC/CBS consensus of the 1960s by offering a different ideological view? One-third of the audience could have been up for grabs. ABC could have been Fox.

The reason that did not happen is that something in us has changed since then. In the 1960s, both journalists and the viewing audience expected accounts of events to verge toward a consistent truthful presentation. It would have struck people as lunacy to have consistent, different viewpoints on basically factual matters.

That change between then and now—now being when we accept dueling narratives—is what must be explained.

The Internet certainly was going to change things. But it was opening up possibilities, not determining what the future would look like. We could have fractured into numerous and complementary groupings. Instead, we became basically two warring centers. What we need to ask is why that happened.

Racism

A consistent theme in accounts on the Left about the breakdown in public life is race. For Steven Levitsky and Daniel Ziblatt in *How Democracies Die*, the two major political parties could treat governance by the other side with equanimity, and therefore keep political competition from deteriorating into warfare, because of a shameful, unstated agreement between the parties not to challenge the racial oppression against blacks so prevalent in the nation and particularly prevalent in the South. That unspoken two-party agreement was shattered by the fight over the Mississippi Freedom Democrats delegate slate at the 1964 Democratic Party Convention, which led to the end of the solid South, paving the way for Richard Nixon's Southern strategy.

For Ezra Klein in *Why We're Polarized*, racial identity has become the linchpin of all our other identity commitments. The major reason for our polarization is racial resentment by many white voters over the loss of white status.

I certainly do not deny the importance of race both in American history and in American politics. It is simply the case, for example, that Social Security is untouchable politically because it is perceived as a "white" program whereas food stamps and Medicaid are under constant assault because they are perceived as programs that aid minorities. This is so even though no program assists minority communities more than Social Security.

So, to say that race is in some way at the heart of our divisions is impossible to deny.

But there are two problems with the simplistic accounts offered by these authors. First, while the American breakdown is getting worse, racial relations are getting better. In a poll released during the week after the George Floyd killing, 76 percent of Americans, including 71 percent of whites, called racism and discrimination "a big problem" in the United States. That was a 26 percentage-point change since 2015. And 78 percent of Americans said the demonstrators' anger was either fully or somewhat justified.[7]

In that same poll, on the crucial issue of race discrimination in policing, 57 percent of Americans said that the police are more likely to treat black people unfairly than white people.

The improvement in race relations is particularly evident when one listens to President Trump. He may sound like George Wallace on issues of law and order, but he claims constantly to have been the best president in history for black Americans. Whether this claim is defensible, President Trump not only believes it, it is important to him.

Second, the history of our breakdown does not track race per se. President Obama certainly inspired a great deal of racist resistance, but President Clinton was resisted for reasons other than race.

Finally, as important as race is, it has little to do with many of the aspects of the breakdown in American public life. For example, there is no direct connection between race and dueling narratives on issues like climate change. Nor is the disintegration of social structures in much of white America, and the resulting despair, premised on race relations. Many of the areas in which suicides, drug

---

[7] Giovanni Russonello, *Why Most Americans Support the Protests*, NEW YORK TIMES (June 5, 2020), https://www.nytimes.com/2020/06/05/us/politics/polling-george-floyd-protests-racism.html.

overdoses, and alcoholism—the deaths caused by despair—are most prevalent are basically white, demographically.

Race is important in all areas of American life. But it is not the driver of the breakdown in American public life.

The Other Side

It is a tautology to say that we are divided because each party has an intensely negative view of the other side. That is practically a definition of being divided.

On the Democratic Party side, this theme of blaming the other side is expressed in the title of Charles Sykes's 2017 book, *How the Right Lost Its Mind*. There is only one villain in the story. The Republican Party has lost faith in democracy and now is actually a threat to the American constitutional tradition.

Of course, it helps that Sykes is a veteran of the conservative movement. So, one could say that a reasonable and healthy Right will emerge from the wreckage if President Trump is defeated in the 2020 election. That seems to be the position of other members of the anti-Trump conservative movement as well, including the columnist George F. Will.

Most Democrats would go further than that and indict the Republican Party generally, and over a longer period, for the breakdown of American public life. Nevertheless, they would endorse Sykes's message.

On the Republican side, Democrats are viewed as having moved rapidly to the left and as having become increasingly militant. So, Joe Biden is viewed as having won the Democratic Party presidential nomination because he either adopted many items from the Bernie Sanders platform or at least dropped his opposition to them.

This move left extends not only to economic issues but also abortion, which, it is claimed, has gone from a necessary evil—to be protected as safe, legal, and rare—to an absolute good.

In terms of militancy, the refusal of Democrats to allow a live-and-let-live perspective on same-sex marriage—accepting religious exemptions, for example—means that there is no way to simply accept Democratic Party victories. As the Flight 93 rhetoric demonstrates, many Republicans consider themselves literally doomed if the Democratic Party takes over the government.

Republicans view Democrats as just as unprincipled as Democrats consider Republicans. So, for example, many Republicans reacted bitterly when liberals applauded the demonstrations over the killing of George Floyd after having just denounced demonstrations against the pandemic shutdown as a public health threat. In the words of Michael Brendan Dougherty of *National Review*, "Want to hold an Orthodox Jewish prayer service in Brooklyn? Mayor Bill de Blasio will bring the police crashing down on you. But his own daughter is out there at the much larger George Floyd protests."[8]

It is pointless to contest these conflicting narratives. To point out their one-sidedness just leads to the accusation of promoting a false equivalency.

So, I will leave this section with a question. Assuming one party has lost its mind, why did that happen? And why do millions of ordinary Americans continue to support a political coalition that has lost its mind?

It is not only unhelpful to assert that my opponents are unreasonable, it also fails to get at the real problem. Why are my opponents unreasonable now, when they did not used to be so?

Weakened Institutions

The important contribution of the book *How Democracies Die* is that it focuses on the process by which democratic government can cease to operate. The authors demonstrate how the institutional guardrails of American political life have gradually weakened. Politicians now do things that they would not have done before.

A good example of this trend is the filibuster in the Senate. Originally, the filibuster functioned as a rarely-invoked protection of the interests of the Senate minority against genuinely perceived threats. Most of the time, the majority was free to legislate the program the voters had presumably endorsed.

But as politics became warfare, the filibuster became just another partisan tool to prevent effective rule by political opponents. When politicians cease to practice "mutual toleration and institutional forbearance," say the authors, democracy dies.

Levitsky and Ziblatt blame the Republicans both for starting us down this road and for provoking each new step. Whether that is a fair indictment is not important here. They acknowledge that, at a certain point, each side comes to believe that it is just responding to unfair actions by the other side.

Democrats would certainly have filibustered the 2017 tax cut if the Republican leadership had not invoked an obscure Senate rule to prevent it. Filibustering a tax cut is a perfect illustration of the kind of easily reversed policy that the minority is not supposed to filibuster. The minority is supposed to be content to vote against something like a tax cut and then to take the matter to the country in the next election. America has lost that kind of political discipline.

---

[8] Michael Brendan Dougherty, *Michael Brendan Dougherty: Mass Protests and Lockdowns Can't Coexist*, PITTSBURGH POST-GAZETTE (June 6, 2020), https://www.post-gazette.com/opinion/Op-Ed/2020/06/06/Michael-Brendan-Dougherty-Mass-protests-lockdowns-cannot-coexist/stories/202006060007.

Using this kind of institutional lens, one can see the institutional rot all over American public life. The best example is the declining commitment to democracy itself. A healthy democratic life requires not only toleration of rule by political opponents, but also confidence that voters will over time choose the right path. As noted in Chapter 1, this faith in democracy is lacking today.

Some Republicans clearly no longer believe that voters will choose properly. That is why they impose unnecessary restrictions on voters, like voter ID, and oppose easy voting procedures like voting by mail. President Trump practically gave this game away when he predicted in April 2020 that, with mail-in voting, "You'd never have a Republican elected in this country again."

But some Democrats no longer trust voters either. They don't have confidence in the capacity of voters to reject nonsense. That is why there were such stringent calls for Facebook to censor President Trump. That is also why there is such concern about election interference by Russia. Truly, if some substantial proportion of voters are going to believe, as Edgar Maddison Welch apparently did,[9] that Hillary Clinton runs a pedophile ring, then you should not have democracy. You need a different system if voters are that crazy.

This concern about the potential of elections to produce a fair, just, and free society is precisely the theme of Yascha Mounk's 2018 book, *The People vs. Democracy*. Mounk reflects the broad concern about illiberal democracy, in which elections just confirm autocratic rule.

The waning faith in democracy, at least among American elites, is why *New York Times* columnist David Brooks felt it necessary to announce in December 2017 that "over the next few months I'm going to use this column, from time to time, to go back to first principles, to go over the canon of liberal democracy—the thinkers who explained our system and why it is great."[10]

The suggestion that Americans have to be reminded how great democracy is should dismay us. Presumably, if you are at that point, an op-ed about democracy is too little, too late.

There is a fear today that the institutional guardrails of constitutional democracy have been weakened and need to be strengthened. This is the theme of the book *How to Save a Constitutional Democracy*, by Tom Ginsburg and Aziz Huq.

While these concerns are entirely justified, this decline in institutional health is a symptom of the breakdown of American public life rather than an explanation. The question we need to understand is why and how this process began in the first place and why no one tries very hard, let alone very effectively, to stop it. Only then can we address the steps that might arrest the decline.

---

[9] Amanda Robb, *Anatomy of a Fake News Scandal*, ROLLING STONE (Nov. 16, 2017), https://www.rollingstone.com/politics/politics-news/anatomy-of-a-fake-news-scandal-125877/.

[10] David Brooks, *The Glory of Democracy*, NEW YORK TIMES (Dec. 14, 2017), https://www.nytimes.com/2017/12/14/opinion/democracy-thomas-mann.html.

Human Nature

Some thinkers identify the roots of the decline of public life in aspects of human biology, psychology, and sociology. One way or another, human beings may not be cut out for healthy democratic life.

One aspect of this theme is that human beings are tribal, which is the message in Amy Chua's book *Political Tribes*, and was also the theme of her earlier book, *World on Fire*. Because of our tribal nature, it is supposedly not surprising that a political figure like Donald Trump would gain success from promoting ethnic divisions. Ezra Klein makes a similar point in *Why We're Polarized* that maintaining our group identities is a basic human need.

So, tribalization is said to explain, in part, why Americans are so divided. This tendency to group belonging also may explain the power that identity politics displays in American political life.

As for the cognitive side, in particular the problem of dueling narratives, Steven Sloman and Philip Fernbach argue in *The Knowledge Illusion* that one reason it is so hard for humans to change false beliefs is that our knowledge is mostly communal. So, to get me to change my mind about things, you have to also get the members of my group to change their minds about things.

In addition, we now know that our thinking errs in predictable ways. That is the message of much behavioral psychology these days, as reported by Michael Lewis in *The Undoing Project*, which describes the friendship and intellectual partnership of Daniel Kahneman and Amos Twersky. Ben Yagoda wrote of these two in the *Atlantic*: "The whole idea of cognitive biases and faulty heuristics—the shortcuts and rules of thumb by which we make judgments and predictions—was more or less invented in the 1970s by Amos Tversky and Daniel Kahneman."[11] It is to Kahneman and Twersky that we owe our understanding of things like confirmation bias.

These insights into the way people identify, act, and think are obviously significant. And they provide guidance for policy going forward. Lewis told the story in *Moneyball* of how these insights could even improve performance in running a baseball team. Chua, for her part, wants American foreign policy to respect ethnic differences.

The problem for our purposes is that all of these insights prove too much. Since these tendencies are always present in human interactions, they do not help us understand why, at a particular time, things went so wrong in American public life.

---

[11] Ben Yagoda, *The Cognitive Biases Tricking Your Brain*, ATLANTIC (Sept. 2018), https://www.theatlantic.com/magazine/archive/2018/09/cognitive-bias/565775/.

We have not always been as divided as we are now. We have not always disagreed about the facts to the extent that we do now. We have not always affirmed only one side of a political story to the degree that we do now. These changes are what we need to understand. What happened during the late 20th century, and continuing to today, that changed the nature of American public life?

These accounts, helpful as they are in many ways in designing policies for the future, do not provide an explanation of how things came to be as bad as they are.

Historical Cycles

I have been suggesting up to this point that there is a reason, or reasons, why things changed in American public life, presumably to make a proposal to do something about it. But this might just be a prejudice on my part. What if there is no reason for our current breakdown? What if, to paraphrase Sally Field in the movie *Forest Gump*, it is just our time?

This kind of fatalism was promoted by two opinion pieces, one from the Right and one from the Left, in the *New York Times* on February 9, 2020. In one, you could read, "Our civilization has entered into decadence." In the other, "History doesn't always move forward."

The longer piece was written by the columnist Ross Douthat,[12] hyping his book, *The Decadent Society*. Douthat convincingly demonstrates that American society, and the West generally, are exhausted, which is what Douthat means by decadence. He uses Jacques Barzun as the model for his conception: "decadence refers to *economic stagnation, institutional decay* and *cultural and intellectual exhaustion at a high level of material prosperity and technological development.*"

For Douthat this stagnation, occurring at a high level of material accomplishment, "is often a consequence of previous development: The decadent society is, by definition, a victim of its own success."

The other account in that day's *New York Times* was by columnist Jamelle Bouie,[13] attacking the Republican Party for its acquittal of President Trump in the impeachment trial. The subtitle of the piece was, "Reaction and Retrenchment Often Triumph." According to Bouie, things just go that way sometimes in American history:

> If the story of the American republic is the story of democratic decline as much as it is of democratic expansion—if backlash shapes our history as much as

[12] Ross Douthat, *The Age of Decadence*, NEW YORK TIMES (Feb. 7, 2020), https://www.nytimes.com/2020/02/07/opinion/sunday/western-society-decadence.html.

[13] Jamelle Bouie, *The Republican Party Has Embraced Its Worst Self*, NEW YORK TIMES (Feb. 7, 2020), https://www.nytimes.com/2020/02/07/opinion/sunday/senate-impeachment-acquittal.html.

progress does—then the current moment is easy to understand. We are living through a period of democratic erosion, in which social and political reaction limits the reach and scope of past democratic victories. In this way of looking at the present, we're living through a period of institutional deterioration, during which American government ceases to function in the face of polarization, zero-sum conflict and constitutional hardball.

For both Douthat and Bouie, periods of decline, like periods of advance, just happen. The implication would seem to be, though I cannot believe that Bouie really means this, that there is nothing much to be done. These authors seem to reject the idea that concerted human action might change a historical moment like ours.

It is not as if we lack for potential explanations for a cycle of decline or stagnation. It could be, for example, that the West in general, and America in particular, are declining because they are aging societies. You would not necessarily expect an aging society to be a source of breakthroughs.

That explanation would also apply to the new emphasis on safety that characterizes our politics—the emphasis on health care, for example, and the worry about reopening the economy after the pandemic shutdown. This demographic account would seem consonant with Douthat's view that we are exhausted.

It could also be, in Bouie's terms, that this moment is the last gasp of the demographically doomed conservative white establishment, which, relatively soon, will be swept away into the dustbin of history by the new minority-majority composition of American society.

Instead of accounts like these, we get no explanation from these authors about why we are in this cycle. History just happens. Sometimes good and sometimes bad. This appears to me to be a surrender of analysis rather than an insight. The real decadence, in this instance, belongs to the authors rather than to the age.

Enlightenment

As Harold Berman complained in 1992,[14] there is a tendency in American intellectual life to call any European thought from the 17th or 18th century "the Enlightenment," and then to consider the American Constitution as a product of "the Enlightenment" so broadly conceived as to be meaningless.

---

[14] Harold J. Berman, *The Impact of the Enlightenment on American Constitutional Law*, 4 YALE J.L. & HUMAN (1992).

Nevertheless, and with due regard to this warning, it is still fair to consider the American Constitution to be a product of the Enlightenment. Charles Montesquieu's defense of separation of powers and checks and balances and John Locke's arguments about natural rights and representative government provided the Constitution's primary building blocks.

Perhaps, then, it is also appropriate to consider the breakdown of American public life as a kind of judgment on the Enlightenment. One writer who could be thought of in this way is Justin Smith in his book, *Irrationality*. Smith's basic idea is that imposing reason as the supreme organizing principle of society, and suppressing unreason, as the Enlightenment tended to do, provokes an outpouring of irrationality. Society cannot be made into a machine.

This sounds like a defense of freedom against an excess of coercive authority, which the book is. But Smith is unwilling to carry his argument to its logical end. He should defend all sorts of irrationality as long the irrationality is peacefully expressed. Instead, Smith now thinks that the free speech tradition that would have allowed the Nazis to march in Skokie, Illinois, in 1977 is a mistake:

> When I was a kid, I assumed it was good to allow Nazi parades in Skokie or wherever, in part because I believed this was an effective form of containment. I see now that I took for granted that these parades would never build to anything truly threatening, and I think it's impossible to think that anymore. The parades have moved online, but with that minor difference accounted for, they are much, much larger than they were a few decades ago.[15]

So, Smith appoints himself the coercive authority suppressing unreason—just the thing his book warns against.

Smith may be thought of as a critic from the Left. The view of the Enlightenment and its aftermath as promoting coercion has been a staple of criticism from the Right for years, especially the Religious Right. You can substitute suppression of religion in these criticisms for suppression of irrationality in Smith, and you have a parallel critique.

The best recent example is Harvard Law professor Adrian Vermeule, who agrees with critics that the heir of the Enlightenment, modern liberalism, imposes "a spreading social, cultural, and ideological conformism" despite its claim to champion "toleration, diversity, and free inquiry."[16] This spreading conformism now has the name "cancel culture."

---

[15] Sean Illing, *The Myth of Irrational Thinking*, Vox (Apr. 25, 2019), https://www.vox.com/future-perfect/2019/4/25/18291925/human-rationality-science-justin-smith.

[16] Ryszard Legutko, *The Demon in Democracy: Totalitarian Temptations in Free Societies*, First Things (Jan. 2017), https://www.firstthings.com/article/2017/01/liturgy-of-liberalism.

Another example of this criticism of the contradictions in modern liberalism is Patrick Deneen in *Why Liberalism Failed*. There is a widespread feeling in America and in the West that, as Vladimir Putin puts it, "the liberal idea" has "outlived its purpose."

Putin was emphasizing immigration and the rise of populist, nationalist movements. That is related to another aspect of this critique, in Deneen, for example, that the Enlightenment has left us privatized, isolated, and alone.[17] R. R. Reno, in *Return of the Strong Gods*, argues that all strong and sacred attachments have been more or less intentionally weakened, especially since WWII. The populist, nationalist explosion of recent years is the inevitable result.

In *Alienated America*, Timothy Carney extends sociologist Robert Putnam's emphasis on social isolation in *Bowling Alone* in 2000 to explain the divisions in America and the rise of Donald Trump. Ben Sasse, Republican senator from Nebraska, makes a similar point in *Them*: Americans are lonely and that leads to anger and hatred. And, from a kind of pop public health perspective, this is the view of Dr. Vivek Murthy, former surgeon general of the United States, in *Together: The Healing Power of Human Connection in a Sometimes Lonely World*.

Obviously, I am depicting a mood rather than a cohesive analysis. But I think it is fair to sum all this up, as David Brooks does in *The Second Mountain*, as the human need for a life of purpose and meaning that this society no longer supports or even explains. In its modern manifestation, the Enlightenment has done away with anything larger than oneself. This is clearly to put the crisis of American public life into a spiritual context.

Capitalism

The critique of the Enlightenment as spiritually deadening tends to emanate from the Right. This conservative view now encompasses, surprisingly, a critique of capitalism as a part of that criticism. Reno, for example, argues that capitalism undermines both democracy and moral life.

Reno even explains the Left's renewed interest in socialism as part of the yearning for a life of meaning. In voting for socialism, "some voters haltingly recognize that our freedom must be directed toward enduring ends if it is to serve something higher than itself."[18]

---

[17] I owe the clarity of this interpretation of Deneen to Christine Emba's review. *See* Christine Emba, *Liberalism is Loneliness*, WASHINGTON POST (Apr. 6, 2018), https://www.washingtonpost.com/opinions/liberalism-is-loneliness/2018/04/06/02a01aec-39ce-11e8-8fd2-49fe3c675a89_story.html.

[18] R. R. Reno, *The Spirit of Democratic Capitalism*, FIRST THINGS (Oct. 2017) https://www.firstthings.com/article/2017/10/the-spirit-of-democratic-capitalism.

In the hands of Republican politicians like Senator Josh Hawley, of Missouri, one has to be skeptical of anti-capitalist tropes and criticisms of the "cosmopolitan economy." The policies of the Republican leadership, including Hawley, remain robustly pro-capitalist. But in the more religious realms of the Right, especially Roman Catholic thinkers, the criticisms of the free market are sincerely felt.

On the Left, the criticisms of capitalism are mostly about inequality, as discussed above. Reno's view to the contrary notwithstanding, the supporters of Bernie Sanders are mostly about redistribution of income and an improvement in government services.

But there is also a more general feeling of a spiritual problem in capitalist life. A column about the 2020 meeting of the economic elite of the World Economic Forum in Davos, Switzerland, was titled, "In Davos, a Search for Meaning with Capitalism in Crisis."[19] And in the *Atlantic*, a headline ran, "The Spiritual Crisis of the Modern Economy," with the subheading, "The Main Source of Meaning in American Life Is a Meritocratic Competition That Makes Those Who Struggle Feel Inferior."[20]

Again, we see a yearning for meaning larger than oneself.

Criticisms of the Enlightenment and of capitalism might help us understand division and alienation in America. But do they have anything to do with the rise of dueling narratives? They do, because these criticisms emanate from a broader critique of the growth of secularism.

Secular Society

Two writers who have written on a spiritual level about the crisis of America and the West are Ross Douthat and Michael Ignatieff, though in different contexts. Before he wrote *The Decadent Society*, Douthat wrote in a *New York Times* column in June 2019[21] that there are now serious concerns within the Right and the Left that traditional, liberal politics, which Douthat calls "liberal proceduralism," might generate genuine evils: regimes of euthanasia, for critics on the Right, and environmental catastrophe, for critics on the Left. Among activists on both sides,

---

[19] Ishan Tharoor, *Ishan Tharoor: In Davos, a Search for Meaning with Capitalism in Crisis*, PITTSBURGH POST-GAZETTE (Jan. 21, 2020), https://www.post-gazette.com/opinion/Op-Ed/2020/01/21/Ishaan-Tharoor-In-Davos-a-search-for-meaning-with-capitalism-in-crisis/stories/202001210015.

[20] Victor Tan Chen, *The Spiritual Crisis of the Modern Economy*, ATLANTIC (Dec. 21, 2016), https://www.theatlantic.com/business/archive/2016/12/spiritual-crisis-modern-economy/511067/.

[21] Ross Douthat, *The Politics of Dystopia*, NEW YORK TIMES (June 8, 2019), https://www.nytimes.com/2019/06/08/opinion/euthanasia-netherlands-noa-pothoven.html.

there is a feeling that some form of post-liberal politics might be needed, in contrast to the usual American encomiums for the Constitution.

Douthat was plainly writing a warning. Ignatieff wrote a similar kind of warning in the *New York Review of Books* in 2018, entitled "Making Room for God":

> A cardinal fact about liberal society is that it disappoints. It offers no radiant tomorrows, no redemption, no salvation. The most that the social democratic variants of liberalism have promised is a welfare state that seeks the slow reduction of unmerited suffering, the gradual diminution of injustice, and the increase of prosperity and individual flourishing. These public goals are what Western liberalism at its best has had to offer since Franklin Roosevelt, but they leave many people yearning for deeper collective belonging and stronger ties to tradition and community. This dissatisfaction leaves a void, which is constantly being filled by nonliberal doctrines.[22]

In both these accounts, the current crisis has to do with a yearning for something more than consumer life that is affecting society as a whole, even when those affected cannot articulate what is wrong. In the absence of this something more, political forms of chaos and authoritarianism arise.

The situation these writers set forth is not how our system would have been described in earlier times. In Douthat's terms, constitutional democracy used to be able to engage substantive, fundamental ideas of human rights—as in the instance of Justice William Douglas's invocation of "the basic civil rights of man" in 1942, in *Skinner v. Oklahoma*,[23] which found forced sterilization to be unconstitutional. If liberalism has become mere proceduralism, that is something relatively new.

Similarly, who decided that secular political life has nothing to do with the good, but only with transfer payments, as Ignatieff asserts? The framers of the Constitution were hoping, and maybe expecting, a "radiant tomorrow." The current narrowed political frame is something new as well.

Something has happened to truncate the hopes and dreams of many, and maybe most, Americans. The desire for something more, something beautiful and good, has been frustrated, when this longing was somehow not frustrated before. That is the change that has led to the pathologies of the moment. How and why did it happen?

---

[22] Michael Ignatieff, *Making Room for God*, NEW YORK REVIEW OF BOOKS (June 28, 2018), https://www.nybooks.com/articles/2018/06/28/making-room-for-god-liberalism-religion/.

[23] *Skinner v. State of Oklahoma ex rel Williamson*, 315 U.S. 789 (1942).

Ignatieff is right that the issue in the breakdown of American public life is, finally, secular society itself. The change that explains the breakdown in American public life is the Death of God. The Death of God is not just about the absence of objective morality and a life of purpose. This death also included the death of truth and explains our dueling narratives. Americans are now divided even about what is, in fact, the case.

These claims need to be justified, of course, which I will do in the next chapter. I also have to be clear that I do not mean that the Death of God is reversible. We have to adapt to it. First, however, we have to actually see the event in order to appreciate its consequences.

3

The Arrival of the Death of God

How Could the Determining Factor in the Breakdown be the Death of God?

American public life broke down because of the Death of God. That is the reason Americans today are divided, distrustful, angry, and fearful, why we cannot agree on what is happening, even at the most basic level, why we lack trust in each other, in our institutions, and in the future and why many of us are in despair. That is also why Part I of this book is subtitled, "The Death of God Comes Home to Roost."

But how could this possibly be the case? Think of the objections. For one thing, it is not even clear that God is dead. Although numbers vary by how the question is asked, millions of Americans, 87 percent by a Gallup poll in 2017,[1] say they believe in God. Furthermore, if God did die, wouldn't that mean that He was not real to begin with? So, there is no reason to think that this event would have the drastic effects that we are seeing today in America. That would be like saying that the end of belief in Santa Claus caused an economic recession. In addition, there was no drastic change in America in recent years regarding belief in God, so why would there be any dramatic changes in public life? Anyway, there are many reasons for the breakdown in American public life, even if lack of belief in God may have had something to do with it.

This chapter is about the claim that the Death of God is the determining factor in the breakdown in American public life. It will rebut the above objections. But first, let me telegraph the basics of the argument.

For one thing, the story of the Death of God is not about individual faith. Certainly, there are many sincere individual believers. Nor is it about claims and practices of group faith. The Death of God is about the influence of a cultural formation.

Simply put, does this *culture* any longer believe in the God whose power founded the West?

The answer to that question is clearly, no. If you want to be certain, ask yourself whether any serious effort was made to ask God to spare America the worst

---

[1] Zach Hrynowski, *How Many Americans Believe in God?*, GALLUP (Nov. 8, 2019), https://news.gallup.com/poll/268205/americans-believe-god.aspx.

The Universe Is on Our Side. Bruce Ledewitz, Oxford University Press. © Oxford University Press 2022.
DOI: 10.1093/oso/9780197563939.003.0004

effects of the coronavirus. It goes without saying that President Trump did not ask God to do that on the proclaimed National Day of Prayer on March 15, 2020. The president would not ask God for that because he is not a genuine believer. However, neither did any other public official, or any religious leader in any important national forum, at the beginning of this trial, beg God just to spare us.

Furthermore, when the traditional problem of theodicy did arise in public—the question, that is, of why God allowed this virus to kill so many people—and Reverend Ralph Drollinger, who led Bible study for the Trump Cabinet, appeared to blame environmentalists and gay people for igniting God's wrath,[2] it is fair to say that no one supported him. Certainly, the president did not. President Trump apparently did not feel that even his base would entertain thoughts like that.

A state figure like Louisiana governor John Bell Edwards might later ask God in a gingerly way to halt the virus, but no serious figure in American public life dared to talk of divine punishment.

After the Lisbon earthquake of 1755 killed an estimated 50,000 people, Europe seriously engaged the question of God's relationship to this terrible natural event. In contrast, some 270 years later, we treat the virus as a natural event, without supernatural causation. .

But even more importantly, sporadic prayers to the contrary notwithstanding, we assume there will be no supernatural end to the virus either. .

This reality of natural action seems so obvious that we forget that a monumental change has taken place. Our culture's current view of reality clashes with the Biblical understanding of God that is still formally maintained by many people.

We can see the tension between a modern view of the world and a Biblical understanding of God in Pope Francis's formal *Urbi et Orbi* address about the virus on March 27.[3] Pope Francis repeated the New Testament story from the Gospel of Mark about Jesus calming the storm when the disciples feared death. But the Pope was very careful to omit verse 41 from his rendition—"They were terrified and asked each other, 'Who is this? Even the wind and the waves obey him!'" The power of God, the Pope implied, is not that He will prevent the virus, "but this is God's strength: turning to the good everything that happens to us, even the bad things."[4] In the garden of Gethsemane, Jesus prayed that the cup pass from him; but we, apparently, are not any longer to pray that way.

---

[2] Brooke Sopelsa, *Trump Cabinet's Bible Teacher Says Gays Cause "God's Wrath" in COVID-19 Blog Post*, ABC NEWS (Mar. 25, 2020), https://www.nbcnews.com/feature/nbc-out/trump-s-bible-teacher-says-gays-among-those-blame-covid-n1168981.

[3] Pope Francis, *Pope Francis' Urbi et Orbi Address on Coronavirus and Jesus Calming the Storm*, AMERICA: THE JESUIT REVIEW (Mar. 27, 2020), https://www.americamagazine.org/faith/2020/03/27/read-pope-francis-urbi-et-orbi-address-coronavirus-and-jesus-calming-storm.

[4] *Id.*

C. S. Lewis famously called Christianity one grand miracle. Not anymore.

Later, on May 14, the Pope did join with other religious leaders in asking God to end the pandemic,[5] but by May 14, in Europe at least, the virus was already ebbing and supernatural intervention would not be so miraculous or its absence so dramatically obvious.

The view of God that Pope Francis presented in March is much more plausible to a modern ear than is a God who intervenes to end a raging pandemic. But that view is not really an appeal to the omnipotent creator of the universe. Pope Francis still prays to God to spare the world, but he is not going to ask publicly for a miracle. The God who might actually act supernaturally has died.

Well, then, so what? Many would respond that there never was any such God. Waking up to the truth about things could only have good effects. We don't need God to live meaningful and good lives. Why do I need God when I have the love of friends and family and the beauty of the world?

Lynne Kelly, an Australian science writer, put this idea very well: "Some believers accuse skeptics of having nothing left but a dull, cold, scientific world. I am left with only art, music, literature, theatre, the magnificence of nature, mathematics, the human spirit, sex, the cosmos, friendship, history, science, imagination, dreams, oceans, mountains, love, and the wonder of birth. That'll do for me."[6]

This is the crux of our failure to understand the breakdown in American public life. People really did believe that the Death of God would have no consequences. They did not comprehend how dependent everything was on the foundation of God. They did not realize that moral knowledge would disappear. They did not know that truth requires a certain kind of universe. They did not realize how crucial purpose and enduring meaning are to human beings. It turns out Lynne Kelly was wrong, even though she sounds entirely right. That is why the breakdown in American public life seems so overwhelming and mysterious. We fail to acknowledge its obvious cause.

It is true that there was no dramatic change in Western and American spiritual consciousness in recent years. Rather, faith in God just continued to ebb over time. Eventually, the concept of God was no longer adequate to support our civilization. The West lived well for hundreds of years on the momentum of Christendom. But, as in the case of a beach that slowly erodes, one day you wake up to find that the sea has reached your house.

---

[5] Cindy Wooden, *Pope Joins Interreligious Prayer, Begging God to End Pandemic*, CATHOLIC NEWS SERVICE (May 14, 2020), https://cruxnow.com/vatican/2020/05/pope-joins-interreligious-prayer-begging-god-to-end-pandemic/.

[6] LYNNE KELLY, THE SKEPTIC'S GUIDE TO THE PARANORMAL viii (2004).

Or, to paraphrase the philosopher Bernard Williams, we will perhaps become more conscious of having to do without God than any previous generation in human history.[7]

As for other factors in the breakdown in American public life, as the previous chapter showed, they are present. But they are not determinative. The Death of God is determinative.

Certainly, we have had warnings about the Death of God. Now we can see that it finally came to fruition and that the consequences really have come about. The Death of God was a myth, to be sure, but it was one of those myths that turned out to be true.

One final point before the more detailed presentation in this chapter. The death of the omnipotent Creator of the Universe is irrevocable. We may come to understand divinity or ultimacy in some new way, or we may learn to do without these things in a much healthier way than at present. Part II of this book presents both of those possibilities. But there is no going back.

Usually, when someone darkly discusses the Death of God, the point is some reconciliation. There won't be any such rescue this time.

Nietzsche, Heidegger, and the Death of God

As is well known, Friedrich Nietzsche announced the Death of God through the figure of the madman in *The Gay Science* in 1882.

THE MADMAN—Have you not heard of that madman who lit a lantern in the bright morning hours, ran to the marketplace, and cried incessantly: "I seek God! I seek God!"—As many of those who did not believe in God were standing around just then, he provoked much laughter. Has he got lost? asked one. Did he lose his way like a child? asked another. Or is he hiding? Is he afraid of us? Has he gone on a voyage? emigrated?—Thus, they yelled and laughed.

The madman jumped into their midst and pierced them with his eyes.

"Whither is God?" he cried; "I will tell you. *We have killed him*—you and I. All of us are his murderers. But how did we do this? How could we drink up the sea? Who gave us the sponge to wipe away the entire horizon? What were

---

[7] This is the actual Williams quote: "Greek ethical thought rested on an objective teleology of human nature, believing that there were facts about man and his place in the world which determined, in a way discoverable to reason, that he was meant to lead a co-operative and ordered life. Some version of this belief has been held by most ethical outlooks subsequently; we are perhaps more conscious now of having to do without it than anyone has been since some fifth-century sophists first doubted it." BERNARD WILLIAMS, THE SENSE OF THE PAST: ESSAYS IN THE HISTORY OF PHILOSOPHY 44–45 (2006). Williams would not have spoken this way about God because he felt Greek ethical thought did not actually need God.

we doing when we unchained this earth from its sun? Whither is it moving now? Whither are we moving? Away from all suns? Are we not plunging continually? Backward, sideward, forward, in all directions? Is there still any up or down? Are we not straying, as through an infinite nothing? Do we not feel the breath of empty space? Has it not become colder? Is not night continually closing in on us? Do we not need to light lanterns in the morning? Do we hear nothing as yet of the noise of the gravediggers who are burying God? Do we smell nothing as yet of the divine decomposition? Gods, too, decompose. God is dead. God remains dead. And we have killed him.

"How shall we comfort ourselves, the murderers of all murderers? What was holiest and mightiest of all that the world has yet owned has bled to death under our knives: who will wipe this blood off us? What water is there for us to clean ourselves? What festivals of atonement, what sacred games shall we have to invent? Is not the greatness of this deed too great for us? Must we ourselves not become gods simply to appear worthy of it? There has never been a greater deed; and whoever is born after us—for the sake of this deed he will belong to a higher history than all history hitherto."

Here the madman fell silent and looked again at his listeners; and they, too, were silent and stared at him in astonishment. At last he threw his lantern on the ground, and it broke into pieces and went out. "I have come too early," he said then; "My time is not yet. This tremendous event is still on its way, still wandering; it has not yet reached the ears of men. Lightning and thunder require time; the light of the stars requires time; deeds, though done, still require time to be seen and heard. This deed is still more distant from them than most distant stars—*and yet they have done it themselves.*

It has been related further that on the same day the madman forced his way into several churches and there struck up his *requiem aeternam deo.* Led out and called to account, he is said always to have replied nothing but: "What after all are these churches now if they are not the tombs and sepulchers of God?"[8]

In this striking scene, Nietzsche is not proposing an argument that God does not exist. As Martin Heidegger explains, the pronouncement "God is dead" should not be thought of as an expression by Nietzsche the atheist.[9] God means for Nietzsche "the suprasensory world in general." This is the Platonic world of the form that for Plato was the real world. The world of ideals. Heidegger teaches

    [8] FRIEDRICH NIETZSCHE, THE GAY SCIENCE 181–82 (Walter Kaufman trans., Vintage Books ed. 1974) (1882).
    [9] MARTIN HEIDEGGER, *The Word of Nietzsche: "God Is Dead," in* THE QUESTION CONCERNING TECHNOLOGY 57 (William Lovitt trans., 1977).

that the suprasensory world, which includes concepts like goodness, truth, and beauty, for us now "is without effective power. It bestows no life." That is the Death of God.

We might say that the Western metaphysical tradition can no longer found a civilization or, more to the point, sustain one that already exists—ours.

Notice how monumental this change is for the madman. Nothing will ever be the same. There are no longer standards by which to measure things—no longer "up" or "down." And the madman knows that whatever occurs, the future will be "colder."

Notice also that the bystanders are laughing at the idea that God is dead. They do not "believe" in God, but they do not consider that this is an important matter one way or the other. They certainly do not seem invested in whether God is dead or not.

It is no accident that these bystanders occupy the "marketplace" and that they are just standing around. They have no life but commerce—that is, things—but even in that life of things, they have no deep commitments. They are not serious people.

Finally notice that "there has never been a greater deed" than murdering God and that man may now have to become a god in order to be worthy of it. So, humanity now continually acts like God, such as in our willingness to change the Earth's climate, for example.

We today are absolutely Nietzsche's bystanders. If you spend any time listening to today's stand-up comedians, you have heard, as I have, the bit in which the performer asks the audience whether anyone present believes in God. Once a victim is found, the mocking and profane commentary is launched—"then you actually believe that zombie movies are true." The tone is exactly the same as at the beginning of Nietzsche's scene.

Like the bystanders, belief in God is not even an option for us. The idea is almost an insult. Our catechism is stated by the character Seon-ju in Han Kang's novel, *Human Acts*:

> I could never believe in the existence of a being who watches over us with consummate love.
> I couldn't even make it through the Lord's Prayer without the words drying up in my throat.
> Forgive us our trespasses, as we forgive those who trespass against us.
> I forgive no one, and no one forgives me.[10]

---

[10] HAN KANG, HUMAN ACTS 149–50 (Deborah Smith ed., 2015).

Nor, aside from belief in God, is there any feeling of any other kind of piety from Nietzsche's bystanders. They are, in the term of Max Weber that we will return to, disenchanted. By and large, we today echo that attitude as well.

This is important because of the various calls to try to recapture the feeling of some sort of enlarged horizon in the secular age. In his important book, *A Secular Age*, Charles Taylor calls this the "intermediate position." Taylor denies that there is any room between the wasteland of secularism and a more or less full-blown return to traditional theism that he calls conversion.[11]

But other thinkers have been more hopeful than Taylor for an enriched secular life, which in this context is one without God. Morris Berman wrote of *The Reenchantment of the World*, which is the title of his classic 1981 treatment of this theme. Brian Swimme says at the end of his documentary, *Journey of the Universe*, that "wonder" at the natural world will be a source of renewal for humanity. David Brooks wrote of the need for an "enchanted secularism," which, he affirms, is the "only secularism that can really arouse moral motivation and impel action." I myself set forth what I called *Hallowed Secularism*, in a book by that title, out of a similar hope.

From the perspective of the breakdown in American public life, it is fair to say that nothing along this line has penetrated the culture. Not only are we not enchanted, we are quite the opposite. Just like Nietzsche's bystanders.

"I have come too early"

The statement by the madman most relevant to the theme of this book is that he has come too early. The scene proceeds with the madman first asserting that he seeks God. The bystanders, who expect a kind of conventional piety, are ready to make fun of a normal religious seeker.

But they mistake the madman. He already knows that God will not be found, because God is dead. The power of genuine spiritual insight that the madman manifests—the existential stakes of the status of the divine that he displays—astonishes the bystanders. In their conventionality, they have not been confronted with any kind of burning question. They literally don't know what to say.

It is their silence that leads the madman to the conclusion that he has come too early. When the madman says that the event has not yet reached the ears of men, he obviously does not mean that no one has said that God is dead. The madman himself had just said this.

---

[11] I discuss Taylor's position at more length in Bruce Ledewitz, Charles Taylor and the Future of Secularism (2009), https://expositions.journals.villanova.edu/article/view/133/105.

Rather, his point is that the bystanders, who reflect society in general, are not yet ready to appreciate the Death of God. They are not ready to see that something momentous has happened.

Today, the time might finally be right to announce again the Death of God. This might be the time for the madman to return.

If one asserts today that up has become down, many today will agree that something like this has happened, that we should consider the cause of it and what it might mean for us.

In this sense, the breakdown of American public life is an indicator of the Death of God. Nietzsche was speaking to the West in general and so America may fairly be used as one possible forum for the announcement of the Death of God.

I don't mean that I am Nietzsche's madman. For one thing, as Part II of this book shows, there is more possibility today in the announcement of the Death of God than there was in 1882. For another, the madman did actually make his announcement and therefore, there is already some sense today of what the Death of God might mean. It does not come as a complete surprise.

Nevertheless, it is true that something that began as an announcement in 1882 has continued to unfold. Now it confronts us with precisely the power that the madman expected.

The Unfolding of the Death of God

Within thirty years of Nietzsche's announcement of the Death of God, Max Weber explained its implications for social life in three critical insights: that the governance structure of the modern Western world is rational/legal, in *Economy and Society*; that capitalism arose out of Protestant religious piety, which associated economic gain with virtue, in *The Protestant Ethic and the Spirit of Capitalism*; and, more generally, that modern life had become an "iron cage" of rationalized bureaucracy in a disenchanted world. In "Science as a Vocation," a lecture he gave in 1918, Weber said, "The fate of our times is characterized by rationalization and intellectualization and, above all, by the disenchantment of the world,' " quoting a phrase from Friedrich Schiller. Weber added that in this modern world, "the ultimate and most sublime values . . . retreated from public life."

Weber did not mean that no one would ever speak again of ideals like justice and truth. Rather, echoing Nietzsche and anticipating Heidegger, Weber meant that scientific rationality had displaced prior, ultimate assessments of values, but had not provided a substitute. The result is unlimited and incessant contesting of unmoored value claims. As Nicholas Gane writes, "The transition to modernity is thus a paradoxical one, for it brings new 'rational' means for controlling and systematizing life while at the same time inaugurating an endless struggle between (and within) opposing value-spheres."[12] Values could no longer found or sustain a civilization. Politics is, therefore, only an unending struggle between irreconcilable differences.

Thus, with the Death of God, we have lost confidence in any claim of value as truth, for we know that such claims can be endlessly contested.

This knowledge leads to a peculiar modern idiom that wants to speak of truth but cannot. So, when Mary Karr, the memoirist and pious Catholic, was discussing whether writing is a form of spiritual discipline in the *On Being* radio series in 2016, she felt obliged to say, "I think that's really true, in an age when even to use the word 'truth' or even to say the word 'truth,' it always comes now with finger squiggles around it, comes with quotes around it, as though, 'How dare one presume to know the truth?' "[13] Karr had been made to feel self-conscious about her commitment to truth. That is Weber's modernity.

Like Nietzsche, Weber did not expect religion to disappear. Nevertheless, Weber did articulate what became known as the secularization thesis: that in modernity there would be a decline in religious belief and practice, that religion would be privatized, and that autonomous spheres of rationality would emerge that were independent of religion.

In his biography of F. Scott Fitzgerald, *Paradise Lost*, David Brown refers to "the death of Victorian idealism that followed the Great War." That change illustrated secularization in a more twisted way than Weber had anticipated. The scientific, rational, and industrialized killings of the Western Front put God completely out of play for much of Western civilization. The scientific achievement of the atomic bomb presumably finished religion off. Anything beautiful surely could not have survived the bomb.

Instead, and surprisingly, there was a resurgence of religious life in America after WWII. In the realm of ethics, Steven Porter, Aaron Preston, and Gregg Ten Elshof, three former students who completed *The Disappearance of Moral Knowledge* after Dallas Willard's death, explained this resurgence as necessitated by the emergence of "genocidal regimes in Europe and the ugliness of racism in the United States." There was a feeling that this "demanded a form of opposition that could be characterized as something more than a morally neutral pitting of preference against preference."[14]

---

[12]   NICHOLAS GANE, MAX WEBER AND POSTMODERN THEORY: RATIONALIZATION VERSUS RE-ENCHANTMENT 29 (2002).

[13]   *Mary Karr: Astonished by the Human Comedy*, ON BEING WITH KRISTA TIPPETT (Oct. 13, 2016), https://onbeing.org/programs/mary-karr-astonished-by-the-human-comedy-jan2018/#audio.

[14]   DALLAS WILLARD, THE DISAPPEARANCE OF MORAL KNOWLEDGE xxiv (Steven L. Porter, Aaron Preston, & Gregg A. Ten Elshof eds., 2018).

In law, this same postwar phenomenon was going on, in which forms of natural law, popularized in part by Lon Fuller, contested legal positivism.

And the same resurgence of objective norms paved the way for a resurgence of popular religion.

Later, with the re-emergence of religion in public life worldwide in the 1980s, doubts began to be voiced about the secularization thesis, most notably by Jose Casanova in *Public Religions in the Modern World*, which introduced the notion of the "deprivatization" of religion. As late as 2009, John Micklethwait and Adrian Wooldridge could write that the global renewal of faith showed that *God Is Back*. We will return to the situation for religion worldwide in the next chapter.

In America, these efforts to put normative life on new objective foundations did not prove lasting. The post-WWII boom in religious practice was short-lived. God remained dead. By 2000, in America, which had been touted as an exception to the secularization of Europe, religious practice began a steep decline in membership and attendance at any sort of organized religious activity plummeted.

Shortly after the new century began, the New Atheist wave[15] would crash over the American landscape. After that, there could be no doubt that we indeed live in *A Secular Age*, as Charles Taylor described it in 2007.

The End of Faith

Christopher Hitchens is doubtless remembered as the leading New Atheist voice. His contribution to the New Atheist wave, *God Is Not Great*, in 2007, caught the public's ear in a way no other author did. It did not hurt him with his Anglo-American audience that his book was really aimed at narrow-minded and violent religious institutions—in particular, in his view, Islam. Hitchens's book was as much opposed to human beings who could be thought of as using religion as it was aimed at belief in God.

It is not remembered as much today that the ground had already been prepared for Hitchens by another New Atheist, Sam Harris, in 2004, in his own best-seller titled *The End of Faith*. Harris was really the leading edge of New Atheist thought.

Harris sounded all the themes that other New Atheist writers would display. There is the simple mockery: "Our situation is this: most of the people in this world believe that the Creator of the universe has written a book" (13). There is

---

[15] I do not deal with the New Atheist movement comprehensively. There is nothing here about Daniel Dennett, for example, one of the movement's seminal figures. I am using the movement thematically as a lens through which to see the effects of the Death of God.

the pointing out that all religions promote intolerance: "The central tenet of every religious tradition is that all the others are mere repositories of error, or, at best, dangerously incomplete" (13). There is the insistence that moderate believers are also part of the problem because religion itself is dangerous: "The very ideal of religious tolerance—born of the belief that every human being should be free to believe whatever he wants about God—is one of the principal forces driving us toward the abyss" (15). There is the claim that every religion commands violence and cruelty that moderate believers just ignore: "It is only by ignoring such barbarisms that the Good Book can be reconciled with life in the modern world" (18). There is the assertion that Islam in particular promotes violence: "Subtract the Muslim belief in martyrdom and jihad, and the actions of suicide bombers become completely unintelligible" (33). There is the claim that the religious promise of life after death corrupts our lives: "A single proposition—*you will not die*—once believed, determines a response to life that would otherwise be unthinkable" (38). There is the view of history that faith guarantees the future to reassure the faithful: "Where faith really pays its dividends, however, is in the conviction that the future will be better than the past, or at least not worse" (69).

But the foundational idea in Harris's book is that all religious believers believe what they do without evidence:

> Tell a devout Christian that his wife is cheating on him, or that frozen yogurt can make a man invisible, and he is likely to require as much evidence as anyone else, and to be persuaded only to the extent that you give it. Tell him that the book he keeps by his bed was written by an invisible deity who will punish him with fire for eternity if he fails to accept its every incredible claim about the universe, and he seems to require no evidence whatsoever. (19)

Phrases like these about evidence and rationality abound in the book, which begins with chapter 1, "Reason in Exile": faith is not "compatible with reason" (19); every religion preaches religious truths for which there is "no evidence" (23); religion is the best example of accepting ideology due to "an insufficient taste for evidence" and "an uncritical faith" (25); religion promotes "a suicidal level of enthusiasm for these subjects *without* evidence" (27); or "no evidence" (31).

The heart of the book is this formulation, responding to the theologian Paul Tillich's assertion that faith is more than belief: "Religious faith is simply *unjustified* belief in matters of ultimate concern" (65).

So, the title of the book *The End of Faith* should have been *The End of Unjustified Belief*.

Unfortunately, Harris spends little time discussing what it is that justifies a belief. This is a problem because Harris himself is no mere materialist relying on public verification principles as the only evidence for truth. He introduces early in the book a section called "The World Beyond Reason," which is comprised of "'spiritual' or 'mystical'"—note the quotation marks he uses for these terms— "experiences of meaningfulness, selflessness, and heightened emotion that surpass our narrow identities as 'selves' and escape our current understanding of the mind and brain" (39–40). These experiences are not simply emotional or psychological: they "uncover genuine facts about the world" (40). Harris considers mysticism to be rational and empirical, even calling the "Wisdom of the East" "nondualistic, empirical mysticism" (214–215). Harris suggests that the Western religious emphasis on faith may have prevented the emergence of this tradition here.

Critics claim these statements represent Harris's own "unjustified beliefs." As a new afterword in a later edition of the book makes clear, Harris has been accused of writing a book that is not about atheism, but is "a stalking horse for Buddhism, New-Age mysticism, or some other form of irrationality" (234).

The spiritual events that Harris describes are precisely the sort of experience out of which our religious traditions spring. Harris knows this but instead of starting with the proposition that "we cannot live by reason alone" (43) and proceeding to find common ground between himself and the religious traditions, he immediately retreats to particular religious beliefs about texts: "Nothing about these experiences justifies arrogant and exclusionary claims about the unique sanctity of any text" (40).

Harris goes beyond simplistic notions of sense verification as a measure of truth. But he does not offer clarity about how this relates to justification of our beliefs. This failure leaves us adrift in terms of whether we can believe anything.

The section of the book that deals with justification is a short treatment of "What Should We Believe?" (73–77). Harris acknowledges that most of what we believe about the world is told to us by others and that this is an entirely appropriate way for people to make their way in the world. In fact, the more educated we are, the more our beliefs are "secondhand."

So, we need to rely on the authority of someone or something. The question then becomes, which forms of authority are valid? What follows in the book, however, is just a kind of common-sense analysis of three reports—the evening news report of a fire, a biological claim about DNA, and the Pope's claim that Jesus was born of a virgin. The evening news report is reasonably verifiable. The DNA claim is simply the latest advance in genetics based on fifty years of experiments. In contrast, Harris says that the Pope's claims are susceptible to no possible form of evidence. Even visionary experiences can never answer questions of historical fact. The Biblical accounts cannot justify this belief because standards of evidence at the time of the composition of the Gospels did not rigorously require factual truth for such claims.

This is Harris's conclusion: "There are good arguments and bad ones, precise observations and imprecise ones; and each of us has to be the final judge of whether it is reasonable to adopt a given belief about the world" (74).

This solipsism is so strange and absurd that you have to feel sorry for Harris. Sure, legally, everyone gets to decide—you don't go to jail for bad beliefs. Nor we should we bully each other over differing beliefs.

But, no, "each of us" is not the final judge. How about nature, truth, and history as the final judges, if there is no God? Harris has no political theory to offer—there is no suggestion of listening to your fellow citizens as final judges. But Harris does not even offer an obvious correction: if we believe stupid things, bad things will happen.

Harris did not mean to be this nihilistic. He did not mean to write a skeptical book about the inadequacy of all authority. He did not mean to justify climate change denial. He certainly did not mean to contribute to the phenomenon of the death of truth.

But this is precisely what Harris did. By using the title *The End of Faith* when he really meant the end of unjustified belief, he undermined all trust. He used the title he did because he was not prepared to consider that the religious traditions actually practice justification. Many religious believers consider their beliefs eminently justified. Indeed, I remember encountering N. T. Wright's astounding and convincing argument for the accuracy of the bodily resurrection of Jesus in *The Resurrection of the Son of God* with a great deal of grudging respect.

Harris and the New Atheists did not cause the Death of God. But they helped turn the consequences of that death in a very unfortunate direction. Harris's implied insistence on verification and not authority, despite his evident intention to the contrary, helped lead that negative movement.

Clearly, God's word is not justification. But, after Harris, there is no longer any objective, binding justification in the universe. There is nothing in which to have faith. There is only my own decision. And who would have faith in that?

The Implications of the Death of God

The New Atheists were so busy attacking God and religion that they mostly did not address what might happen next. Not only was there no reason to trust, there was no basis for humans to live lives of ultimate significance. What would this do to people?

The New Atheist writer who came closest to worrying about this, probably because he best understood the implications of the Death of God for human morale, was Phillip Kitcher in *Living with Darwin*. Kitcher explained that "Christian resistance to Darwin rests on the genuine insight that life without God, in the sense of a Darwinian account of the natural world, really does mean life without God in a far more literal and unnerving sense. Even those who understand, and contribute to, the enlightenment case can find the resultant picture of the world, and our place in it, unbearable."[16]

What makes this scientific account of existence unbearable for human beings is that it is no longer obvious "how lives can matter" in a universe dominated by accident and chance, in which human significance is an illusion.

Harris makes a similar point that, in the presence of death, "the present significance of anything—your relationships, your plans for the future, your hobbies, your possessions—will appear to have been totally illusory."

As Neil deGrasse Tyson put it in Episode 3 of the 2014 *Cosmos* series: "We hunger for significance. For signs that our personal existence is of special meaning to the universe. To that end, we are all too eager to deceive ourselves and others. To discern a sacred image in a grilled cheese sandwich." But that hunger for significance must now go unfulfilled.

Our hunger for significance is undermined by sensationalist epistemology and materialist ontology, especially, for example, in the writing of Richard Dawkins. In *The Magic of Reality: How We Know What's Really True*, his 2011 book for young adults, Dawkins tried to show that this scientific way of knowing, and the natural universe to be known, had much more poetry and beauty than any bag of supernatural tricks. But, Dawkins's attempt notwithstanding, this combination of epistemology and ontology reduces humans, and everything else in nature, to matter in motion, in the 18th century French philosopher Denis Diderot's famous formulation.

This is the very epistemology and ontology that Harris tried to contest in order to promote a higher kind of empiricism and make room for robust introspection as a form of knowledge. But this part of Harris's message did not make a lasting impression.

This restricted view of epistemology and ontology means that there is no possible higher purpose to human life. This is odd in a way because the New Atheists were determined to tell the truth about God and religion. So, it would appear that in another formulation by Tyson in the *Cosmos* series, "It matters what's true." Yet how could any truth ultimately have significance in the context of matter in motion?

Kitcher was right that meaninglessness of human life was the implication of the message of the New Atheists. This also drained politics of meaning.

Admittedly, there was not much of a political side to the New Atheist thrust. In general, they were not a political movement. The exception was Mark Lilla in

---

[16] PHILIP KITCHER, LIVING WITH DARWIN 156 (2007).

The Stillborn God in 2007. This is a strange story because of what happened next, in 2016.

Lilla adapted his book in a *New York Times Magazine* article titled "The Politics of God," contrasting liberal, Western politics with the politics of other traditions:

> We have made a choice that is at once simpler and harder: we have chosen to limit our politics to protecting individuals from the worst harms they can inflict on one another, to securing fundamental liberties and providing for their basic welfare, while leaving their spiritual destinies in their own hands. We have wagered that it is wiser to beware the forces unleashed by the Bible's messianic promise than to try exploiting them for the public good. We have chosen to keep our politics unilluminated by divine revelation. All we have is our own lucidity, which we must train on a world where faith still inflames the minds of men.[17]

But, then, having ruled out any form of universalism, Lilla turned around, after the 2016 election, and criticized identity politics in the Democratic Party as having "distorted liberalism's message and prevented it from becoming a unifying force capable of governing."[18]

This was bizarre since, given Lilla's earlier message, liberalism could not be a unifying force. We were not supposed to be unified. We were to be individuals pursuing happiness in our own way in order to keep any form of common commitment from turning into dangerous political enthusiasm.

It would have been appropriate for Lilla to acknowledge that the Death of God narrative could lead to problems of its own—like leaving the field to identity groupings—but Lilla did not acknowledge that he had said anything about such things. He took no responsibility for the identity politics that today renders genuine human solidarity nearly impossible and thus, ironically, frustrates the building of an inclusive anti-racist coalition.

Finally, while all of the New Atheists attributed reliability to science, their undermining of trust in the universe, and undermining of trust in our fellow human beings, ultimately left science itself on insecure foundations. To paraphrase Harris, each of us has to be the final judge of whether to trust the pronouncements of science. That is where we are now, and it is a disaster.

The New Atheists had differing reactions to the difficulty of living in the universe that they described. Kitcher thought his fellow thinkers were callous in their indifference to the human longing for unity and meaning—that their

---

[17] Mark Lilla, *The End of Identity Liberalism*, NEW YORK TIMES (Nov. 18, 2016), https://www.nytimes.com/2016/11/20/opinion/sunday/the-end-of-identity-liberalism.html.
[18] *Id.*

atheism would disappoint. Harris thought there was a worthwhile higher form of human life, though surely he realized it would be unattainable for most people. Hitchens was just not worried about it.

It was Dawkins in *The Magic of Reality* who explained that the Death of God should free humanity for an even more exhilarating intellectual adventure. The universe was so much larger than anyone's God. Dawkins anticipated a brilliant future. But that is not what happened.

The Death of God and the Breakdown

We are now in a position to complete the link of the breakdown in American public life to the Death of God, completing the movement of Chapters 1 and 2.

In Alexander McCall Smith's 2019 detective novel *The Department of Sensitive Crimes*, the main character, Ulf Varg, considers the meaning of life:

> Life was a matter of regret—how could it be anything else? We knew that we would lose the things we loved; we knew that sooner or later we would lose everything, and beyond that was a darkness, a state of non-being that we found hard to imagine, let alone accept.[19]

This regret is not about the absence of an afterlife. It is that nothing in life can be said to be lasting. My life does not—and given the nature of reality, could not—matter.

Abraham in the Bible does not go to Heaven. He just dies. But Abraham is satisfied, knowing that because he lived, his descendants would be a blessing for all humankind.

Varg lives under the Death of God. Abraham did not.

How does this feeling of regret affect public life? We have the feeling we have been cheated of something we should have had. Varg's tone of melancholy is the feeling of having lost something promised. We have nothing positive to anticipate. This is either infuriating or devastating, leading either to anger or despair. Of course, it could be both.

On June 13, 2020, in its printed edition, the *New York Times* published a bleak description of the current moment in American life.[20] The article was entitled "Left, Right or Center, Voters See a Bleak Future." Voters on all sides looked at the combination of the continuing threat of the virus, the economic downturn, and

---

[19] ALEXANDER MCCALL SMITH, THE DEPARTMENT OF SENSITIVE CRIMES 291–92 (2019).

[20] Lisa Lerer & Dave Umhoefer, *On the Future, Americans Can Agree: It Doesn't Look Good*, NEW YORK TIMES (June 12, 2020), https://www.nytimes.com/2020/06/12/us/politics/election-coronavirus-protests-unemployment.html?searchResultPosition=1.

the protests over the killing of George Floyd and concluded that America was diminished, if not finished.

Though the Americans quoted in the article manifested similar worries, the hyper-partisanship was still expressly present. The article was filled with both anxiety and division.

This atmosphere of extraordinary anxiety could only partly be explained by the actual situation of the country in mid-June. The article appeared before the resurgence of the virus began. At the same moment that the article described gloom, promising vaccine trials were going on and deaths from the virus were still in decline. The economy appeared to be recovering. As the article noted, some supporters of the president believed that the extraordinary economic growth of recent years would return, at least eventually. And the growing national consensus against racism, demonstrated by the degree of national support for the protests, was clearly progress on the racial front, not racial disaster.

It was the lens that was clouded, not the picture. That lens is the current state of American consciousness. That is the spiritual crisis. America was doing OK, maybe even pretty well, especially given the circumstances. But Americans were not.

Supernaturalism reared its head at the end of the article. K. K. Bell, a black Trump opponent, said, "Revelations talks about the end of time, and this may be it." Brendan Hermanson, who said he will vote for President Trump if he votes at all in 2020, and who previously voted for Barack Obama, echoed, "We need divine intervention."

These religious references actually demonstrate the phenomenon of the Death of God. For, as Harris wrote in *The End of Faith*, genuine faith believes that the future will be better than the past. The anxious fear, the fatalism, and the hopelessness voiced in the article are evidence of a lost faith. The religious vocabulary that was used is just a mode of expressing ultimate despair. It did not reflect religious commitment.

We have now come to the foundation of the breakdown in American public life. The breakdown is not about the difficulty of any of our national problems, difficult though their solutions may be. The breakdown is not about our divisions, though we are certainly divided.

Our breakdown is about a lack of trust. The article refers to two instances of lack of trust. One is a lack of faith in the future. The other, shown in the political divisions, is a lack of trust in each other and in ourselves. We don't trust that solutions will be found because we no longer have confidence in our leaders, our thinkers, or anyone else.

We know something is wrong, but we cannot even agree even about what is happening because I don't trust you and your experts and you don't trust me and mine.

Social media helps spread all this anxiety. But the Americans in the story are not talking about, or even through, social media.

The relation of the Death of God to all this has to do with the nature of the universe. When God was real to the culture, even though perhaps not grasped in a sophisticated theological mode, the ultimate cultural commitment was that the universe was trustworthy. It had some purpose behind it. We humans had some role to play in its development. There was something to anticipate.

All that is now over. With the Death of God, the universe is cold, indifferent, maybe even hostile. Dawkins may be able to flourish under such circumstances, but the rest of us find it crushing. Not only is there no moral story any longer, there is no story at all—no narrative we can tell to make sense of our existence.

This condition not only causes problems in and of itself; the newspaper story also noted the rise of depression among Americans and we already know about our anger. The condition of distrust in the universe also manifests in an inability to cope with other problems as they inevitably arise. The story contrasted our current state with how Americans felt during earlier, much more serious crises, such as the Depression, or the Cold War, or Vietnam. We were much better able to cope at that time, even though material conditions were worse.

The virus, after all, will eventually yield to a vaccine. Its economic effects, though very serious, likely temporary.

The Death of God is responsible for our situation. Now, having linked the breakdown generally to the Death of God, we are ready in the next chapter to examine the particular ways that the end of faith manifests in American public life today.

4

Faithless American Public Life

Truth Is Fine

In the same way that the phrase "God Is Dead" describes human understanding and not whether God actually exists—the theologian Dietrich Bonhoeffer suggested that God is teaching us to do without Him—the phrase "The Death of Truth" has to do only with our understanding of reality. The phrase is not really about truth.

So, *The Death of Truth* by Michiko Kakutani is about postmodernism, lying politicians, cultural forces, and how our disagreements over simple matters are making effective politics impossible. There is little in the book about the actual power of truth.

We may be "psychologically walled off" from each other,[1] but we are not actually walled off. We continue to affect each other. Similarly, we may resist truth with all our might, but truth continues its drip-by-drip influence. We may no longer believe in objectivity, but objective forces continue to operate.

Even as news and science about climate change are suppressed, ignored, and resisted, for example, climate change continues its inexorable movement with undeniable effects. It becomes harder and harder to claim that nothing is occurring. People with agendas switch from simple denial to talking about natural cycles making it warmer and the prohibitive cost of carbon reduction. And when big bills start to come due, as in the water treatment systems in South Florida, where rising sea levels threaten to contaminate freshwater aquifers, even those efforts will collapse. Climate change denial is like any Ponzi scheme. Reality will not be denied forever.

And this is not just a matter of the power of facts, but also of values. Truth continues to operate in that realm as well. Thomas Jefferson knew that slavery was wrong and that, because of its evil, slavery must lead his country to catastrophe. This is part of the inscription in the Jefferson Memorial in Washington, DC:

---

[1] Michiko Kakutani, The Death of Truth 114 (2018).

The Universe Is on Our Side. Bruce Ledewitz, Oxford University Press. © Oxford University Press 2022.
DOI: 10.1093/oso/9780197563939.003.0005

I tremble for my country when I reflect that God is just, that his justice cannot sleep forever. Commerce between master and slave is despotism. Nothing is more certainly written in the book of fate than that these people are to be free.

That memorial was dedicated in 1943, when segregation and violent racial oppression were still commonplace in American life. Nevertheless, the truth expressed by Jefferson could not be suppressed.

The same power of truth was manifested in the protests after the killing of George Floyd. For all our bubbles, America came together to confront racism. President Trump denounced the evil of slavery. Calls for law and order aimed at the demonstrations petered out as the nation decided that, finally, the historic legacy of the cancer of racism had to be addressed.

That is the power of truth. And despite all our problems, nothing has happened that sets that power aside. So, as we look at the effects of our lack of faith, we have to be clear that this is a problem of our making. It is not a problem built into the universe.

What follows in this chapter is not a refutation of the power of truth. It could not be, if, as I am suggesting, the universe works in a certain way regarding truth. I will return to these themes in Part II of this book.

But, clearly, the prevailing view in our culture is that what I have just asserted is false. In the material that follows, I am presenting the destructive opinions we have formed on matters of truth and faith. I wanted to note upfront, however, that our lack of faith is neither justified nor reasonable.

Lack of Faith Generally

What Sam Harris actually meant by "faith" is "unjustified belief." His concern in *The End of Faith* was that religious faith represented just such an unjustified belief and should, therefore, be rejected.

Another word that could be substituted for "faith" and "belief" here is "trust." Sam Harris essentially said to us in 2004, as Governor Tarkin said to Princess Leia in *Star Wars*, "You're far too trusting." You, religious practitioners, believe that everything will turn out for the best. You believe that you live in a universe that has your best interests at heart. You believe that your life has ultimate meaning. According to Sam Harris, not only do we have no evidence for these beliefs, there is no conceivable evidence that could support these beliefs.

Sam Harris should be a happy man today. Certainly, we're a lot less trusting than we used to be. Our current slogan about these matters would be the headline for Joseph Carter's op-ed in the *New York Times* in 2017, "The Universe

Doesn't Care About Your Purpose."[2] The title could have been, "The Universe Doesn't Care About You or Your Purpose."

I interviewed Joseph Carter for the *Bends Toward Justice Podcast*. He is a lovely man. He knows that human beings need a sense of purpose to live flourishing lives. But he feels he is being realistic in asserting that this need is not embedded in the universe. We learn through our senses. Matter and forces comprise all reality. So, purpose, which is not an aspect of matter or forces, is just not present as a cosmic category.

It is ironic that some months before the *New York Times* published Carter's opinion piece, the newspaper was running ads about how important the truth is: "The truth is worth defending."[3] This was an effort by the *New York Times* to counter the Death of Truth, and the attacks on the mainstream media as false news, attacks that the paper associated with President Trump.

It apparently did not occur to the editors of the *New York Times* what "the truth is worth defending" means. It means that truth matters ultimately. It means that human beings should dedicate their lives to the pursuit of the truth. It means that is a proper way for human beings to live. It means that journalists pursue the truth.

Or, to put it simply, it means that the universe cares about truth. So, in publishing Carter's opinion piece, the newspaper was discounting the very nature of the truth it purported to be serving.

Did the *New York Times* really believe what it said about truth in the ads? When we no longer trust in one overarching viewpoint on reality—what is called the God's-eye-view—we are like Mary Karr in the previous chapter. We generally hesitate to speak of the truth. We are convinced that there are just perspectives on things. This is actually called perspectivalism in postmodern thought.

According to perspectivalism, not only does the truth not matter ultimately, there isn't any such thing as truth anyway. It seems to me that this, rather than the ads, really reflects the view of the *New York Times* and most people.

The New Atheists did not convince us of these things. They just came along at the right moment, when the old reliabilities had already faded away without our noticing. If the New Atheists had come earlier, no one would have paid much attention to them. Of course, had they come later, they would have been seen as old hat.

Harris does not agree with this denigration of truth. He denies that morality is subjective. Harris believes that science can determine human values—which was

---

[2] Joseph Carter, *The Universe Doesn't Care About Your "Purpose,"* THE NEW YORK TIMES (July 31, 2017), https://www.nytimes.com/2017/07/31/opinion/the-universe-doesnt-care-about-your-purpose.html.

[3] NEW YORK TIMES, TRUTH TEXT POSTER, https://store.nytimes.com/products/truth-text-poster.

the subtitle of his 2010 book, *The Moral Landscape*—in the same way science can determine other facts.

But Harris is not persuasive. Nor do any of the New Atheists or new humanists succeed in showing how we can be good without God. The reader can consult Christian Smith's book, *Atheist Overreach*, to see why this is so in convincing detail. Here, let me just say that the problem with Harris's position is twofold. First, Harris can only demonstrate that if we care about alleviating suffering, then science can be helpful in showing us how to do that. That is certainly the case, but it prompts the normative question: Why should we care about alleviating suffering in the first place?

The second objection is more fundamental. If the universe does not endorse certain values, in some sense, then those values are not real. Harris does not have the right kind of ontology—that is, what is real in reality—that can explain normative endorsement by the universe. This is why Harris ended up in the solipsism noted in Chapter 3, that "each of us has to be the final judge" of what to believe. Thus, as James Davison Hunter and Paul Nedelisky argue in *Science and the Good*, the effort to ground values in science becomes a form of moral nihilism with only instrumental goals possible.

Harris, for example, breezily endorses abortion. He completely dismisses the human rights of the unborn because he says they lack sentient qualities. He maintains this position, even though sentience would be forthcoming if the human beings in question were not killed. This is so callous that Harris forfeits any claim to moral authority or even coherence. Most people are uncomfortable with abortion.[4] Harris is not. Remember, science was once used to enthusiastically endorse eugenics.

The reader might suppose that even with our skepticism, we could reach a reliable consensus on facts. But, as the philosopher Hilary Putnam argued in *The Collapse of the Fact/Value Dichotomy*, if all values are subjective, so are all facts, because establishing facts depends on values such as reasonableness, consistency, and simplicity. For Putnam, attempts to disentangle facts from values always fail.

In his op-ed, Carter puts his finger on the crucial issue. Are we alone in an uncaring universe? As a culture, we now believe we are. This is an important source of our pain, as well as the anger and aggressiveness that result from that pain. Stephen Buhner calls this, in *The Lost Language of Plants*, "the wound that comes from believing we are alone amid dead uncaring nature."[5]

---

[4] While polls show most Americans want abortion to remain legal, only 21% want to relax restrictions to permit abortion at any time during pregnancy. https://www.npr.org/2019/06/07/730183531/poll-majority-want-to-keep-abortion-legal-but-they-also-want-restrictions.

[5] STEPHEN BUHNER, THE LOST LANGUAGE OF PLANTS: THE ECOLOGICAL IMPORTANCE OF PLANT MEDICINES TO LIFE ON EARTH 22 (2002).

We now even lack the fundamental purposes of our own that Carter took for granted. In *To Mend the World*, the Jewish theologian Emil Fackenheim warned against despair of the world, "lest we help make it a meaningless place in which God is dead or irrelevant and everything is permitted." Though his book, *The End of History and the Last Man*, in 1992, is remembered as a paean to liberal values and constitutional government, Francis Fukuyama actually predicted the spiritual meaninglessness likely to befall late capitalist societies, in which atheist consumers have nothing serious to live for. Carter did not know he was making a prediction that the universe does not care about our purposes because we do not have any fundamental purpose.

Is it any wonder that our public life is broken?

Lack of Faith in Experts

The last section is about our lack of faith in everything. But our lack of faith also has numerous, particular aspects.

It is often said by liberals that their opponents don't "believe" in science and that is the reason for such phenomena as climate change denial.

This is not the case, however. Climate change denial—or better, skepticism— is not really based on the limits of the scientific method. Rather, the issue is much simpler. Many deniers believe that scientists are lying for partisan, monetary, or other reasons.[6] Their position is skepticism about motives, not ignorance of facts.

Support for skepticism was an important aspect of the message of the New Atheists, especially Sam Harris. Harris specifically criticized the acceptance of the authority of the Church in matters of faith. According to Harris, we should either be finding evidence and proof ourselves or, and this will be the case for most of us, finding reliable sources of information. But in the absence of a reliable universe, reliable sources cannot be found.

Why is it crazy to fear a scientific cabal that seeks power by hyping climate change scenarios? Plenty of people on the Left are convinced that Big Pharm supports dangerous vaccines. Plenty of people on the Left are convinced that Big Ag supports dangerous genetically modified food. And plenty of people on the Left are convinced that the government suppressed data showing an increase in virus cases and reinterpreted deaths as not related to Covid-19 in order to justify an early reopening of the economy.

When conservatives see climate change being used to support policies like the Green New Deal, much of which has little to do with fighting climate change, why should they not be suspicious?

---

[6] See https://www.heritage.org/environment/commentary/follow-the-climate-change-money.

Since the Enlightenment, thinkers have challenged authority as a way of undermining religion. This is why a magazine like *Skeptic*, which is dedicated to fighting irrational beliefs of all kinds, is so named. In a *Bends Toward Justice* podcast, I asked the founder, Michael Shermer, if he had any regrets about the name of the magazine, given the recent growth of denials of scientific consensus in various areas. Shermer responded that you have to be skeptical about skepticism too. In other words, unreasoning skepticism, in which no claims that one disagrees with are accepted, is not really skepticism but is a new form of dogmatism.

Shermer is giving wise counsel, but his message just emphasizes Harris's inability to enunciate grounds for justified reliance on the wisdom of others. All Harris can say in the end is that each person decides for herself. This is precisely the problem. Each person in our current situation distrusts the counsel of any political opponent.

We should not call any of this a problem of truth. It is not a lack of belief in science per se, either. It is a lack of trust in our fellow human beings. As noted above, we were, in effect, told that we were too trusting. We are not too trusting anymore.

Lack of Faith in the Future

We saw in the previous chapter that Americans are pessimistic. In Chapter 1, William Gibson called this "the end of the future." This should come as a surprise, given that things have generally been going pretty well.

There is a loosely organized movement of optimists in America. One of the best-known is Steven Pinker, whose hopefulness is particularly highlighted in his 2018 book, *Enlightenment Now*. The group is occasionally labeled the New Optimists. They came to notice with a raft of pronouncements that, counter to the prevailing narratives, 2016 was the best year in human history.[7] The recent origin of this perspective can be traced to Pinker's 2011 book on the decline of violence in human history, *The Better Angels of Our Nature*.

Shermer is also a member of this group, especially in his 2015 book, *The Moral Arc*, where he argues that science—empiricism, rationality, testing, and so forth—makes us better people. Shermer is not as anti-religion as are other enthusiasts for science, but clearly, for him, science is a healthier way of life.

These optimistic pronouncements tend to be about the entire world, not just about particular nations. And they clearly omit important concerns, such as

---

[7] Nicholas Kristof was only the most prominent of these voices. Nicholas Kristof, *Why 2017 May Be the Best Year Ever*, NEW YORK TIMES (Jan. 21, 2017), https://www.nytimes.com/2017/01/21/opinion/sunday/why-2017-may-be-the-best-year-ever.html.

rising economic inequality or rising nationalism. They ignore these things because these optimists are relentlessly materialistic and utilitarian. Fewer people are living in poverty, for example, and that fact is unaffected by how many new billionaires there are.

You could argue that Americans are an exception to these positive trends and that we are justified in our pessimism. Our public life is broken, we are unable to work together, and there is no reason to think that this will change.

On the other hand, it could be that American pessimism is causal, rather than a response to the way things are. Certainly, our pessimism is exaggerated.

Take, for example, the rise of China at America's expense. In June 2020, George Will published a column in which he made gentle fun of American angst over the rise of China.[8] Will pointed out that for all its recent economic growth, China was at that time 72nd in the world in gross domestic product per capita.

Will also noted how well America had recently been doing economically and in other ways, the downturn from the virus notwithstanding.

You could say the same about American concerns about the rise of authoritarianism worldwide. None of the flaws in that mode of government have been erased. Putin in Russia, Erdogan in Turkey, Modi in India, Duterte in the Philippines, Bolsonaro in Brazil, and you could name other strongmen, have not brought progress for their countries. Their popular support has tended to wane over time.

There is less confidence in the tradition of liberal government around the world—elections, a free press, an independent judiciary, human rights, free markets—but this is a symptom of our malaise, not a cause of it. We Americans and other Westerners have lost confidence in liberal government and that is why others have as well. On every measurable level, the performance of countries under liberal government has been pretty good. You would not trade that performance for Russia's performance.

Our attitude is summed up by Farhad Manjoo: "The Worst Is Yet to Come."[9] But that attitude is not justified.

Manjoo is a good illustration of lack of faith because, he says, he used to be an optimist. The virus and the American response to it convinced him otherwise. And there is a general feeling that the virus proved the "preppers" correct.[10] These

[8] George Will, *Joe Biden Needs a China Narrative That Refutes Today's Political Angst*, WASHINGTON POST (June 12, 2020), https://www.washingtonpost.com/opinions/global-opinions/joe-biden-needs-a-china-narrative-that-refutes-todays-political-angst/2020/06/11/0295e5b8-ac0e-11ea-94d2-d7bc43b26bf9story.html.

[9] Farhad Manjoo, *The Worst Is Yet to Come*, NEW YORK TIMES (May 20, 2020), https://www.nytimes.com/2020/05/20/opinion/coronavirus-worst-case.html.

[10] Nellie Bowles, *I Used to Make Fun of Silicon Valley Preppers. Then I Became One*, NEW YORK TIMES (Apr. 24, 2020), https://www.nytimes.com/2020/04/24/technology/coronavirus-preppers.html.

are the people described in Mark O'Connell's book, *Notes from an Apocalypse*, who have expected the worst and prepared for the coming apocalypse.

But as bad as the virus turned out to be, with almost half a million deaths worldwide by June 2020, it was not an apocalypse.

In this gloomy atmosphere, even a consciousness as healthy as that of Bill McKibben, the admirable leader in the worldwide movement to fight climate change, wrote a pessimistic book, *Falter*, with the subtitle, *Has the Human Game Begun to Play Itself Out?*

Of course, McKibben is looking at a situation in which 20-foot rises in world-wide sea level and civilization-killing heat may now be inevitable in a little more than one hundred years. That is pretty sobering and there does not seem to be the political will to take the dramatic steps that might head off catastrophe. That not only suggests that the human game might be ending but also that an author is obligated to adopt a tone of existential crisis in hopes of shocking people.

But this section is not about realistic threats and efforts to deal with them. It is about unrealistic gloom. It would actually be helpful if Americans were gloomy about climate change. Then, maybe we could take steps to avoid it.

Instead, Americans are experiencing the kind of generalized dread of the future that makes it difficult to take any helpful steps at all. As a society, we are paralyzed.

Lack of Faith in Objectivity

The proclaimed impossibility of objectivity is an important aspect of Kakutani's indictment of postmodernism: all truths are partial and are a function of one's perspective.

Kakutani does not blame postmodernism for all the "free-floating nihilism" in America. But she does suggest that the thinking of figures like Jacque Derrida, Jean Baudrillard, and Jean-François Lyotard have penetrated the culture and pre-pared the ground for arguments by conservatives that emphasize the ideological foundations of purported objective scientific findings in the realms of climate change and other, similarly unpleasant, realities.

Kakutani is not the first to make this argument. Albert Camus, quoted in the Introduction, was saying much the same thing much earlier. And it is amusing to watch someone like Bruno Latour try to explain how his critiques of scientific objectivity in the 1980s did not lead to climate change denial.[11]

---

[11] Ken Rice, *Bruno Latour*, . . . AND THEN THERE'S PHYSICS BLOG (Oct. 15, 2017), https://andthentheresphysics.wordpress.com/2017/10/15/bruno-latour/.

Nevertheless, it is important to note two things. First, the basic idea that all our truths are partial is true—even that truth is only partially true. This insight is always a needed correction to our certitudes.

Second, postmodernism only became possible because of the Death of God. For the real issue is not whether our understanding is partial. That was so even for St. Paul, who could only see through a glass darkly.[12] The question postmodernism raises, in the shadow of the Death of God, is whether our understanding can be considered closer to what is the case—or further away. Postmodernism denies that we can know even that.

The other aspect of postmodernism that Kakutani criticizes is the idea that "anything can mean anything." In this regard, she quotes Stanley Fish: "The death of objectivity 'relieves me of the obligation to be right.' It 'demands only that I be interesting.'"[13]

The view that there is no text here became a much-contested issue in American academic legal circles in the 1980s. Fish was one of the leading protagonists in this epistemological debate. One thing you can say about that debate is that Stanley Fish tried very hard to get his audience and readers to understand what he was trying to say. So, you could observe that Fish's message was completely self-contradictory. He thought there was a text there—his.

The American thinker who took the limits of language the furthest was Richard Rorty in *Philosophy and the Mirror of Nature*, and other works, in which Rorty challenged the conception of knowledge as a mirror of nature and argued instead that knowledge is a matter of conversation and social practice. Everything becomes for Rorty a matter of what he called "cultural politics."

And so, in the current breakdown, everything is now in fact "cultural politics."

Hilary Putnam, who maintained an ongoing debate with Rorty over these matters, tried to chart a middle course between the God's-eye-view of traditional theism and the forces of despair—nihilism, materialism, and relativism—on the other. Putnam thought that Rorty was really a disappointed believer in metaphysical realism—that is, in a kind of traditional religion. If Rorty could not have the certainty of traditional theism, then he would insist that we have nothing.[14] Today, our public life is like Rorty—we will have the traditional God or nothing.

Whether Putnam's attempt was successful intellectually is not our focus here. It was certainly not successful culturally. Culturally, the Death of God has robbed us of objectivity.

Nowhere has this lack of faith in objectivity affected us more negatively than in the practice of journalism. Here, two trends coincide. First, it is clear that

---

[12] 1 *Corinthians* 13:12.
[13] KAKUTANI, *supra* note 1.
[14] HILARY PUTNAM, WORDS AND LIFE 300 (James Conant ed., 1994).

a lot of Americans do not want to hear an objective account of things. If the media outlet that viewers rely on has an obvious ax to grind with regard to national politics, and viewers stick with its accounts, then it may be said that the audience does not want an objective account. We may not even believe such an account is possible.

We believe that the media associated with the other side at best exaggerates and at worst constantly lies. But we must know on some level that the media on our side exaggerate and lie as well. Surely people noticed, for example, that when case infections went up in July 2020, the mainstream media kept ignoring the stubborn refusal of deaths, or even serious illness, to keep pace. The experts like Dr. Graham Snyder at UPMC in Pittsburgh, who said the virus had become less dangerous, were ignored or marginalized. The local newspaper even launched its own investigation of Dr. Snyder's scientific claims, which seemed to me to be a first for the *Pittsburgh Post-Gazette*, so people would not relax their guard.[15]

Surely, people also noticed that red states received criticism for reopening too early when their virus infections spiked, but that the same spike in cases in California went mostly without media notice.

These are examples of biased mainstream media reporting. Certainly, Fox is biased as well. And other conservative news sources are far more partisan than Fox. But that is the point. Viewers overall do not want to hear neutral news. That is our lack of faith in objectivity.

The second trend undermining objectivity in the media is the advent of movement journalism. The most dramatic example of that trend is the 1619 Project at the *New York Times*, marking the 400th anniversary of the arrival of slaves in Virginia.[16] The project aims at framing American history as "understanding 1619 as our true founding, and placing the consequences of slavery and the contributions of black Americans at the very center of the story we tell ourselves about who we are."

The *New York Times* did not say it was abandoning journalistic objectivity. The editors claimed to be finally telling the American story "truthfully."

But Andrew Sullivan, reflecting on both the text of the 1619 Project and leaks surrounding it, views the project differently, even though he admires a great deal about it: "The *New York Times*, by its executive editor's own admission, is increasingly engaged in a project of reporting everything through the prism of white

---

[15] Sara Simon, *UPMC'S Claim of "Less Severe" Coronavirus Strain in Pa. Is Not Supported by Science, Some Say*, PITTSBURGH POST-GAZETTE (July 14, 2020), https://www.post-gazette.com/news/health/2020/07/14/UPMC-s-claim-less-severe-coronavirus-strain-in-Pa-is-not-supported-by-science/stories/202007140102.

[16] Jake Silverstein, *Why We Published the 1619 Project*, NEW YORK TIMES (Dec. 20, 2019), https://www.nytimes.com/interactive/2019/08/14/magazine/1619-america-slavery.html.

supremacy and critical race theory, in order to 'teach' its readers to think in these crudely reductionist and racial terms."[17]

With the protests that followed the killing of George Floyd, this tendency in journalism spread beyond the *New York Times* to much of the mainstream media and beyond. Now, many reporters would presumably say that their central obligation is not to objective truth, which is an unattainable and unworthy goal that only serves to perpetuate illegitimate power relations, but to expose these unjust relations.

At this point, journalism is no longer dedicated to the idea of an objective reality that we all can encounter as a common-ground starting point on the way to then deciding what policies to pursue. Now, journalism is a part of the struggle.

Some of this commitment is a healthy correction to the previous failure of journalism to tell the truth about race in America. But this change is not being presented or understood as a correction toward a fuller objectivity. It is now objectivity itself that has disappeared from view.

Lack of Faith in Law

When we speak of faith *in* any human activity, we are taking both an outside and an inside perspective. The outside perspective asks whether we, the public, have faith in this human activity. The inside perspective asks whether the participants in the activity have faith in it.

Sometimes an expression of a lack of faith can represent both perspectives. This was the case with the remarkably nihilistic poem published by Yale Law Professor Arthur Leff in 1979, as the conclusion of an article entitled *Unspeakable Ethics, Unnatural Law*:[18]

> As things now stand, everything is up for grabs.
> Nevertheless:
> Napalming babies is bad.
> Starving the poor is wicked.
> Buying and selling each other is depraved.
> Those who stood up to and died resisting Hitler, Stalin, Amin,
> and Pol Pot—and General Custer too—have earned salvation.
> Those who acquiesced deserve to be damned.
> There is in the world such a thing as evil.

---

[17] Andrew Sullivan, *The New York Times Has Abandoned Liberalism for Activism*, NEW YORK INTELLIGENCER (Sept. 13, 2019), https://nymag.com/intelligencer/2019/09/andrew-sullivan-ny-times-abandons-liberalism-for-activism.html.

[18] Arthur Leff, *Unspeakable Ethics, Unnatural Law*, 1979 DUKE L.J. 1229 (1979).

[All together now:] Sez who?
God help us.

The poem is a statement of a lack of faith expressly premised on the Death of God. It affirms that we, the public, cannot have faith in law that makes claims about truth and justice. And, by this very act, this participant in the activity of law, Arthur Leff, demonstrates his lack of faith in the institution as well.

It is easy to see the lack of faith by the public in law. The promise of the American constitutional system of judicial review and the rule of law is that America would be "a government of laws and not of men," as Chief Justice John Marshall proclaimed in the founding case of *Marbury v. Madison* in 1803.

But our view today is quite the opposite. That is why in the November 2018 exchange between President Trump and Chief Justice John Roberts over whether we have "Trump Judges and Obama Judges"—Roberts claimed that we don't divide that way—most people agreed with President Trump.[19]

The public now sees even judges in terms of "sides." Liberals see conservative judges as furthering the political agenda of the Republican coalition, and vice versa, rather than as seeking in good faith to reflect constitutional values.

That is why Republicans in the Senate have been busy as beavers stacking up Republican judicial nominees in the federal courts and why control of the Supreme Court was viewed as so important that it spawned a justification— called, "But Gorsuch!"—for voting for President Trump despite his flaws. The idea is that conservatives got that fifth vote on the Supreme Court, even if they had to support Trump to do it.

That is also the reason that some Democrats are intent on "packing" the Supreme Court to overcome the current conservative majority by adding to the number of justices. That number is currently nine and has been set at nine Justices for 150 years, but could be changed at any time by a new federal statute.

For the public, including politicians, these divisions go beyond disagreements over what the law is and how that should be determined. Judges are now expected to be loyal to the coalition that put them on the court, which is a change from the way judges used to be regarded. So, Senate Majority Leader Mitch McConnell could say to the 2018 Federalist Society National Lawyers Convention: "The closest thing we can do to have a permanent impact is to confirm judges and transform the judiciary. [A]nd we are going to keep on doing it for as long as we can." He received a standing ovation.

---

[19] Bruce Ledewtiz, *The Obama Judge and the Foundations of the Rule of Law*, JURIST (Dec. 2, 2018), https://www.jurist.org/commentary/2018/12/the-obama-judge-and-the-foundations-of-the-rule-of-law/.

Similarly, if a Democratic Supreme Court nominee decided to vote to over-turn *Roe v. Wade*, you can be sure the resulting rage would be overwhelming.

This expected commitment is not just differing judicial philosophies. Judges are expected not to ever change their minds about these commitments once on the bench.

The lack of faith internally is somewhat different. Although this is changing under the pressure of our hyper-partisanship, judges still do not think of them-selves as part of anyone's team. Several notable decisions in 2020, including Justice Neal Gorsuch's opinion expanding sex discrimination protection to same-sex and transgender claims in *Bostock v. Clayton County*,[20] did not break along partisan lines.

It is sufficiently rare to be noteworthy when a candidate for judicial office speaks in terms of sides, as Judge Justin Walker did when he was sworn in as a federal district judge by Justice Kavanaugh: "In Brett Kavanaugh's America we will not surrender while you wage war on our work, or our cause, or our hope, or our dream."[21]

The lack of faith internally for judges, as for law professors like Arthur Leff, is a lack of faith in rationality generally understood—that is, reasoned judgment reaching objective conclusions about fundamental values and human purpose.

This is not a function of political or judicial orientation. I made that point in a 2015 *Akron Law Review* article that pointed out that in a five-day span in 1992, every justice on the Supreme Court joined an opinion in one of two cases asserting that values are only human constructs, not something to be discovered in reality.[22]

On the conservative side, the origin of the movement known as originalism—the view that terms in the Constitution should be interpreted in accordance with their original public meaning—itself originated in a values skepticism that the framers of the Constitution would not have shared. This is the reason that the great conservative thinker Harry Jaffa criticized the movement in the 1990s.

That is why Justice Antonin Scalia, who wrote one of the opinions in 1992 that endorsed the absolute subjectivity of values, wrote in his seminal statement of his judicial philosophy, *A Matter of Interpretation*, that cruelty in the Eighth Amendment ban on "cruel and unusual punishments" is "not a moral principle of 'cruelty' that philosophers can play with in the future, but rather the existing society's assessment of what is cruel."

---

[20] *Bostock v. Clayton County, Georgia*, 140 S.Ct. 1731 (2020).
[21] Elizabeth Williamson & Rebecca Ruiz, *McConnell Protégé Takes Center Stage in Fight to Remake Judiciary*, New York Times (May 5, 2020), https://www.nytimes.com/2020/05/05/us/politics/justin-walker-mcconnell-judicial-nomination.html.
[22] Bruce Ledewitz, *The Five Days in June When Values Died in American Law*, 49 Akron L. Rev. 115 (2015).

The idea that a punishment might be objectively cruel, whatever a group of human beings might think, is simply impossible. The universe is thought not to work that way.

This is also why originalists today commonly assert that under the other interpretive school, the Living Constitution, terms can mean anything at all. They echo in this way the postmodernism that Kakutani criticized.

As I say, this skepticism is not a position endorsed by only one side. Liberal justices just express their value skepticism differently. Fundamental rights, for example, are not defended as objectively true but simply as expressions of individual self-determination. So, in the *Casey* case, which reaffirmed *Roe v. Wade* in 1986, the plurality wrote that "at the heart of liberty is the right to define one's own concept of existence, of meaning, of the universe, and of the mystery of human life."

The skepticism about objectivity extends to the idea of human purpose. Justice Scalia led the movement, now largely successful, to bar legislative history from judicial consideration. Now, when a statute is interpreted in the federal courts, judges no longer inquire about the "purpose" of the statute. The legal thinker Lon Fuller noted in his famous 1958 debate with the champion of legal positivism, H. L. A. Hart,[23] that positivism eschews the idea of human purpose. There is just what some individual does or says.

The flight from value objectivity explains the almost universal rejection of the call by Harvard law professor Adrian Vermeule, in the *Atlantic* in March 2020, for a "more moral framework of constitutional interpretation," which he called "common good constitutionalism." No one, it seems, but Professor Vermeule has confidence that a genuine common good could be found and employed by judges. That is our lack of faith.

As I said at the beginning of this section, our skepticism does not change the universe. When something is felt to be morally wrong, judges and law professors respond, despite their ideology. One instance of this is that conservative justices on the Supreme Court protect religious believers and institutions even when doing so is in tension with their vaunted originalism. This has led to decisions like *Trinity Lutheran Church*[24] in 2017, opening government programs to participation by church groups. In 2020, in *Espinoza v. Montana Dept. of Revenue*,[25] the Court even included the requirement of tax credits for religious schools that amounted to public support for religious activities. No one knows how far these decisions will go, but they certainly flout originalism.

---

[23] H. L. A. Hart, *Positivism and the Separation of Law and Morals*, 71 HARV. L. REV. 593 (1958); Lon L. Fuller, *Positivism and Fidelity to Law—A Reply to Professor Hart*, 71 HARV. L. REV. 630 (1958).
[24] *Trinity Lutheran Church of Columbia, Inc., v. Comer*, 137 S.Ct. 2012 (2017).
[25] *Espinoza v. Montana Department of Revenue*, 140 S.Ct. 2246 (2020).

Lack of Faith in the Disciplines

Law is the preeminent public discipline and so the breakdown in public life that manifests in lack of faith is most evident there. But a similar story could be told about the rest of the disciplines.

Looking at economics, for example, the public still retains some confidence in the objectivity of the Federal Reserve, because economics deals with material facts rather than with values. That is why the independence of the Federal Reserves is more closely protected in Washington than is the independence of the Supreme Court.

Furthermore, there is an academic discipline of economics, which, to a far greater degree than is the case in academic law, purports to maintain standards of objectivity in analysis.

Nevertheless, the public face of economics, for which the academic side must bear some responsibility, is entirely politicized. So, during the 2012 presidential campaign, former chief executive at General Electric, Jack Welch, claimed that the jobs report number was cooked in order to aid President Obama's re-election hopes.[26] If we had actually been closer to election day when the May 2020 unemployment rate was announced, Democrats would probably have said the same thing, since even the Department of Labor had to release a second unemployment report attempting to capture the experience of some temporarily laid-off workers during the pandemic shutdown.

The major politicization of economics comes in the matter of the national debt. On the one hand, the so-called supply-side theory keeps insisting that tax cuts pay for themselves despite convincing evidence that they usually do not. If it had not been for this false claim, the 2017 tax cut, which only passed narrowly, would not have been enacted.

On the Democratic side, there is a new attachment to Modern Monetary Theory, which as far as the public is concerned suggests that the United States can print money to cover deficits in perpetuity and nothing bad will happen. Why we have to have taxes at all is never explained.

Still, economics retains more faith than does any other social science.

In the humanities, the situation is far worse than in either law or economics. In history's internal perspective, according to Jo Guldi and David Armitage, since the 1970s, most researchers have limited their investigations to the last fifty years and to very limited and technical issues.[27] Guldi and Armitage attribute this to

---

[26] Margaret Sullivan, *Jobs . . . Jack Welch . . . and Cooking the Books*, New York Times (Oct. 8, 2012), https://publiceditor.blogs.nytimes.com/2012/10/08/jobs-jack-welch-and-cooking-the-books/.

[27] David Armitage & Jo Guldi, *Bonfire of the Humanities*, Pocket, https://getpocket.com/explore/item/bonfire-of-the-humanities?utm_source=pocket-newtab-- (originally appeared on Aeon, November 30, 2014).

the influence of Lyotard's "suspicion toward grand narratives." This tendency removed history from its traditional role of informing the public sphere since there was felt to be no underlying story of truth or values in human affairs to tell.

So, in history, the lack of faith is an internal perspective first.

The lack of faith by the public in history—the external perspective—was demonstrated by Attorney General Barr's comment when asked how history would judge him after his dismissal of charges against former national security advisor General Michael Flynn. Barr responded, "Well, history is written by the winners, so it largely depends on who's writing the history."[28]

Barr did go on to claim that he was doing the right thing, but his willingness to indulge his nihilism in public shows that he believed the public would accept this ultimate failure of truth.

This was not Barr's first brush with public nihilism. In a May 2019 interview with CBS News,[29] Barr was asked about the effect on his reputation of his defenses of President Trump. He could have said he was only pursuing the truth. Instead, Barr responded, "Everyone dies. I don't believe in the Homeric idea that, you know, immortality comes by, you know, having *odes* sung about you over the centuries."

If public figures are willing to say things like this on public occasions, they clearly do not expect a negative public response to their nihilism.

Ross Douthat made a similar observation about English departments, which he described as having a "crisis of faith."[30] Regarding essays in a special issue of the *Chronicle Review* entitled "Endgame," Douthat wrote that "the custodians of humanism are 'befuddled and without purpose.'" A "belief in truth and beauty" might not be enough to keep such departments open in the face of economic and job pressures, he added, but they certainly won't stay open without some sense that there are objective standards of transcendent truth that some literary works embody. By all means, he argued, open the canon beyond the limits of the European male past. But don't abolish the notion of enduring value.

And, as for what can be called social theory, there is now nothing to rival the theoretical schools of the past. Socialism may be getting a renewed life politically in America, but Marxism remains thoroughly discredited. The critical schools are mostly about deconstruction and so cannot build a new world. And even critical race theory, so now in vogue, is basically partial and sectarian—not a position from which to build a new civilization.

---

[28] Jonah Goldberg, *Is William Barr Right That History Is Written by Winners? Not Anymore*, LOS ANGELES TIMES (May 12, 2020), https://www.latimes.com/opinion/story/2020-05-12/william-barr-history-written-by-winners.

[29] Interview by CBS News with William Barr, Attorney General of the United States (May 31, 2019), https://www.cbsnews.com/feature/william-barr-interview-with-cbs-news/.

[30] Ross Douthat, *The Academic Apocalypse*, NEW YORK TIMES (Jan. 11, 2020), https://www.nytimes.com/2020/01/11/opinion/sunday/academics-humanities-literature-canon.html.

There remain, then, only the natural sciences, which, of all the disciplines, retain objective and materialist foundations. Here, something of the old internal commitment to objectivity and truth remains. Yet there is still a crisis.

Perhaps a temporary aspect of the crisis in science is the reckoning with racism forced on all the disciplines in the aftermath of the George Floyd killing. Theoretical physicist Lawrence Krauss worried in a commentary in the *Wall Street Journal* that cancel culture was infecting scientific inquiry.[31] If so, this would be both an internal and external crisis of faith. But, hopefully, it is just a correction and the objectivity of science will remain.

The more fundamental internal crisis of physics has to do with its inability to discover and understand the nature of reality. As Adam Becker explains in *What Is Real*, the question that physics cannot determine is whether quantum theory is an actual description of nature or is simply an effective mathematical mode of expression. Science may be losing its faith in the discoverable intelligibility of nature.

The fundamental external lack of faith in science is even more damaging. After repeated instances of misleading corporate-sponsored research, from cigarettes to the environment, the public mood is one of skepticism with regard to the simplest, most well-established, and most objective of scientific claims in politically-contested fields. It is amazing that there can still be doubt about whether the Earth's climate is warming and whether human activity is causing it.

Worse, the consensus of experts in public health during the pandemic did seem thoroughly politicized. Conservatives were gleeful in their criticism that while most public health experts condemned demonstrations against the shutdown as dangerous in light of potential infections, many of these same experts then pivoted almost instantly to endorse the demonstrations against police brutality following the George Floyd's death. Of course, it did not help the credibility of health science that the earlier demonstrations did not in fact lead to greater numbers of infections.

David Michaels calls the result of public distrust in scientific findings *The Triumph of Doubt*. He is referring primarily to the success of greedy corporations and corrupt scientists to sow doubt in the public in the interest of profit. But the title contains a second meaning—doubt itself triumphs in America.

This lack of faith by the public in scientific claims is primarily a lack of trust in the honesty of human beings. The doubts may be expressed epistemologically—the question may be asked, for example, how can a model predict the future?—but the real doubt is, how can I believe you when you are such a liar? This kind of doubt is an acid that eats away at everything.

---

[31] Lawrence Krauss, *The Ideological Corruption of Science*, WALL STREET JOURNAL (July 12, 2020), https://www.wsj.com/articles/the-ideological-corruption-of-science-11594572501.

Lack of Faith in Religion and Morality

In 2017, Peter Harrison published an essay entitled, "Why Religion Is Not Going Away and Science Will Not Destroy It."[32] He argued that the secularization thesis, which Harrison interpreted to mean that with the rise of science, religion will decline and eventually disappear, had failed in two respects. First, not only has religion not declined, it is ascendant "in countries as varied as Iran, India, Israel, Algeria and Turkey." Second, not only has science not led the movement toward secularization, it has been its victim, "with science becoming a collateral casualty of resistance to secularism." Thus, the theory of evolution was removed from the high school curriculum in Turkey, according to Harrison, not so much as a reaction against Darwinian theory as a protest against "secular materialism."

Harrison was pointing to a real phenomenon. But is it really religious faith that is resurgent?

From the external perspective, religion is no longer a unifying national enterprise in America. William Barr's speech at Notre Dame in October 2019 emphasized the unifying role that religion can play in the culture.[33] Secularism itself is reliant for its moral foundation, Barr said, on the "vapor trails of Christianity." Religious liberty is in everyone's interest.

But Barr also embraced the partisan view of religion in the culture by accusing secularists of waging war on religion. It is not that he was wrong—many secularists view religion as benighted ignorance, including, of course, the New Atheists. But, if there is a war, Barr would do us all a favor by seeking a ceasefire, rather than continuing the fighting. Barr was not attempting to restore faith in religion by the public generally. He was taking partisan advantage.

From the internal perspective, the resurgence of religion in certain American contexts, like Orthodox Judaism and evangelical Protestantism, and worldwide, as Harrison describes, might mean that for the practitioners of religion, faith abides.

But this is not the case. Even Harrison had to qualify the kind of religion that is growing in influence in the world—he called it "nationalist." I made a similar point some years ago in *American Religious Democracy*, in which I argued that religious believers had just as much right to the public square as anyone else and were now exercising that right. But this was, and is, a political fact of life, not a religious one.

---

[32] Peter Harrison, *Why Religion Is Not Going Away and Science Will Not Destroy It*, Aeon (Sept. 7, 2017), https://aeon.co/ideas/why-religion-is-not-going-away-and-science-will-not-destroy-it.

[33] Bruce Ledewitz, *This Is the Notre Dame Speech That Bill Bar Should Have Given—and Didn't*, Pennsylvania Capital-Star (Jan. 3, 2020), https://www.penncapital-star.com/commentary/this-is-the-notre-dame-speech-that-bill-barr-should-have-given-and-didnt-bruce-ledewitz/.

Are our religions entering a new creative period in which the divine is encountered in new and meaningful ways? I see no sign of that. Instead, religious resurgence comprises mere nostalgia for old certainties.

The Death of God is so powerful an event that the German philosopher Peter Sloterdijk simply called his reflection on theology *After God*. Certainly, something has changed from the high point of secular confidence. But Sloterdijk rejects any simplistic three-part movement of the pre-secular, followed by the secular, followed by the post-secular. Instead, "what could transpire now, what deserves to come to an end, is the period in which a certain rationalist skepticism was able to emerge as a dogmatic power."[34]

As Part II of this book will show, I share this hope with Sloterdijk. And, as the above shows, the secular skepticism Sloterdijk refers to in the modern period has led to a loss of faith in everything.

Nevertheless, it is also the case that even from the internal perspective of many religious believers, there has been a loss of faith. This loss can be measured by the angst prevalent among American religious practitioners—by their fear of the future and hatred of their political opponents.

A genuine religious resurgence may emerge in the future. It is not here now.

All of this has to be qualified. When I read the pious, loving words founded in Christ that would transform public life in James K. A. Smith's *Awaiting the King*, I had to acknowledge that with God as understood by Smith, all things are possible. Unfortunately, his is a book for believers, not for the rest of us. Even more unfortunately, it does not seem to be a book for most American Christians. But as soon as it is, I will have to rewrite Part I of this book.

As for morality, the situation is the same as in every other field. Here, we have Dallas Willard's book *The Disappearance of Moral Knowledge* as a reliable guide. Willard's point is twofold, in our terms. From the internal perspective, many of the purveyors of moral knowledge gave up out of a lack of faith in the enterprise of gaining moral knowledge. Under the weight of modern epistemology and ontology, it was presumed by many, for a long time, that there could not be any such thing as moral knowledge.

From the external perspective, even the philosophical attempts that were made to resuscitate moral realism, epistemologically and ontologically, failed "as a social reality," both because of "society's unwillingness to hear what philosophers had been saying" and because of deep flaws in the approaches that those thinkers pursued.

The result was, as elsewhere, the loss of faith in morality.

---

[34] PETER SLOTERDIJK, AFTER GOD 206 (2020).

The Effect on Politics of Our Lack of Faith

Can political willfulness sustain us? This is how Tony Judt described our political situation: "Even if we concede that there is no higher purpose to life, we need to ascribe meaning to our actions in a way that transcends them."[35] In other words, politics does not work without transcendent meaning, which is no longer available to us. Thus, we must "ascribe" meaning where it does not arise organically.

Judt's observation is not that far from Sloterdijk's characterization of William James in James's essay, "The Will to Believe." Sloterdijk characterized James's position as the "voluntarist re-interpretation of belief."

The difference, though, is this. James meant what he said. He spoke of "our right to adopt a believing attitude in religious matters." James thought that this is what people actually do and have to do. For Judt, on the other hand, coming later, this prescription is merely a vague hope.

This is why healthy politics is impossible in America right now. Either we do not believe in anything, in which case our politics becomes style, or we choose to believe in small, seemingly attainable, real things, like nation or race or money or power. Capacious dreams like human solidarity, economic equality, environmental sustainability, human rights, and a peaceful world just seem too much like a dream to sustain enthusiastic and generous political life.

We are then left with winning at all costs. When that is frustrated, since there is nothing broad and whole to define us, we explode with anger.

In June 2020, when mad rumors spread of Antifa terrorists invading rural American communities and people reacted by arming themselves, and in one instance by threatening an innocent mixed-race family, Nicholas Kristof asked in the *New York Times*, where is this hysteria coming from?[36]

> In rural Indonesia, I once reported on a mob that was beheading people believed to be sorcerers, then carrying their heads on pikes. But I never imagined that the United States could plunge into such delirium.

But there is no mystery. A quote attributed to G. K. Chesterton explained it all years ago: "When a man stops believing in God he doesn't then believe in nothing, he believes anything." This is where the Death of God has left us.

Admittedly, not everything is gloom. When, before Super Tuesday, Pete Buttigieg and Amy Klobuchar saw they were not going to win the Democratic Party nomination for president, but that their continuation in the race meant

---

[35] Tony Judt, Ill Fares the Land 179–80 (2010).
[36] Nicholas Kristof, *When Antifa Hysteria Sweeps America*, New York Times (June 17, 2020), https://www.nytimes.com/2020/06/17/opinion/antifa-protests.html.

splitting the moderate vote, they withdrew and endorsed Joe Biden. Biden then went on to win the nomination. Without reference to the propriety of their goal—Bernie might have been a great candidate for president—they acted responsibly in pursuing it. They did what Republican candidates could not bring themselves to do in 2016 with regard to Donald Trump.

So, there is still hope. But we don't want to be like Tony Judt, just hoping. We want to have a program of some kind.

Before getting to that point, however, in Part II, there is one more consequence of the Death of God that must be set forth. Not only is this the time of the end of faith, it is the era of evasion.

5

The Age of Evasion

Our public life is broken—we are angry, divided, and distrustful. We lack faith in everything. All this is bad enough. But there is something even deeper that is wrong with American public life after the Death of God. We now live in the age of evasion.

In the previous chapter, I suggested that either we believe in nothing, in which case our politics become a matter of style, or we believe in small things that are unworthy of a total commitment, like national or racial or political identity.

In this chapter, I want to look at the issue of style. The dominant style of American public life is to evade resolution or engagement with serious questions and issues. There are many reasons for this, as for everything else in this book. Nevertheless, the major reason is the Death of God.

The sections that follow, starting with the unreality of American public life, are overlapping. The categories are impressionistic. The main point, though, is this: America does not confront difficult matters.

Unreal American Public Life

American public life is a simulacrum. I don't mean in the sense of simulacra used by the French sociologist Jean Baudrillard, in which models create a kind of "hyperreal" that never existed, like a reality TV show.

I mean almost the opposite—a tired, scripted performance that is completely predictable while using breathless rhetoric, like a State of the Union Address.

A simulacrum is an imitation of an activity rather than the thing itself. American public life is not really public life, but an imitation of public life. We engage in symbol manipulation and not, for the most part, problem-solving. Or even problem-engaging.

Of course, politics is always partly show. The 19th century had its torchlight parades. But America has now entered a realm of extreme showmanship.

The height of absurdity of the Left was the "Rally to Restore Sanity and/or Fear," held in Washington, DC, on October 30, 2010. The rally was obviously a spoof on Glenn Beck's earlier "Restoring Honor" rally, though Jon Stewart, who organized the later rally along with Stephen Colbert, denied this.

The Universe Is on Our Side. Bruce Ledewitz, Oxford University Press. © Oxford University Press 2022.
DOI: 10.1093/oso/9780197563939.003.0006

Around 215,000 people attended this nonsensical event. Meanwhile, real politics were going on at home that same weekend. I remember thinking afterward that if all of these people had gone door to door in their local voting districts instead of partying in Washington, maybe the GOP would not have retaken the House in the 2010 midterm elections.

Since 2010, the tenor of American politics has become grimmer, so something as daft as this rally could no longer take place.

But politics have not become more real. Now, the unreality on the Left is comprised of things like virtue signaling, in which symbolic action is more significant than real action.

So, for example, in June 2020, PNC Financial Services Group, a bank headquartered in Pittsburgh, pledged $1 billion to fight structural racism in America, after a few other banks had made similar pledges. PNC CEO William Demchak said, "Each of us has a role to play in combating racism and discrimination and PNC is committed to driving real change in areas in which we can make the greatest impact."[1]

But PNC didn't need special spending to fight racism. Hiring a person of color to replace Demchak, who is white, would have been a great blow against structural racism. And many of the bank's tellers, who are underpaid, are people of color. The bank could have just raised teller salaries. That would have been a real action for equality.

Granted, symbols can be important. There is no reason why the U.S. military should honor the men who fought against our country by retaining the names of military bases that honor Confederate generals. Nor is there any reason why a state that is a member of the Union should honor with a statue someone who tried to destroy that Union.

Our symbolism, however, tends to be fake. On the eve of Juneteenth 2020, House Speaker Nancy Pelosi removed the portraits of four Speakers of the House who had served the Confederacy, from the speaker's lobby, the corridor outside the House chamber where the portraits of her predecessors are displayed.

This did not make sense. It is not like removing a statue honoring a Confederate general. These men were not being honored personally. Their portraits were there because they had been Speakers of the House, which in fact they had been. Removing their portraits was like removing their names from a list of Speakers of the House of Representatives. If anything, their portraits in the lobby were an important critique of American history. Removing them was letting the House off the hook.

---

[1] Patrick Varine, *PNC Commits $1 Billion to Programs, Efforts to Stem Systemic Racism*, TRIBLIVE (June 18, 2020), https://triblive.com/local/regional/pnc-commits-1-billion-to-programs-efforts-to-stem-systemic-racism/.

Of course, when it was electing three of these men as Speaker, the House did not know that they would later wage war against their country. But, what about Charles Crisp, of Georgia, who served as Speaker of the House from 1891 to 1895, thirty years after he fought in the Confederate Army as a young man? The House elected him Speaker anyway. How can a later Speaker reverse that decision, even symbolically? Surely Crisp, at least, was a different matter.

Unreality on the Right takes different forms but is at least as unconnected with reality as is the Left. So, the basically isolated instances of violence and looting that took place after the death of George Floyd were treated as if 1968 had returned and America was in flames.

Obviously, any unlawful conduct is wrong, especially any violence, and I am not defending it. I am only noting that the protests were mostly peaceful and the unlawfulness mostly contained and sporadic. And it all faded away, as such things do.

The overreaction on the Right was especially noteworthy because one celebrated instance of simple premeditated murder during the protests—the assassination of Federal security officer David Patrick Underwood on May 29, 2020, as he and his partner, who was also shot, guarded the Federal Building in Oakland—turned out to have been perpetrated by an alleged right-wing anti-government extremist. But this went almost unnoted on the Right.

The basic peacefulness of the protests, and the involvement of non-protestors in acts of violence, did not keep the Trump campaign from posting warnings on Facebook about "Dangerous MOBS" and did not keep Fox News from warning rural white America about mythical roving Antifa terrorists.

Unreality in American public life goes beyond symbol manipulation and exaggeration. Policies are also affected.

In the last chapter, I noted that Americans have more faith in economics than in other social sciences, partly because economics deals with real things.

But I also noted that in recent years, economics in public life has drifted into fantasy land. Politicians keep repeating the claim that tax cuts will pay for themselves. This is a lot worse than false claims about Antifa, which are at least just temporary madness.

Tax cuts don't pay for themselves and everybody in the government probably knows it by now.

The other side of economic unreality in America has to do with stock prices and the national debt. By June 8, 2020, stocks, and the S&P 500 in particular, had recovered most of the losses that had been suffered with the advent of the virus and the shutdown, and returns on investment had turned positive for the year.

Even given the usual disconnect between the real economy and the stock market, this result was surprising because future corporate profits were going to be constrained, both by added health and safety costs in the reopening and by reduced consumer spending because of health concerns and related issues. Everybody knew this.

Most observers attributed this stock market rise not to any misunderstanding about the actual situation, but to the fact that, with enormously expansive fiscal and monetary policies flooding the country with cash, and with the Federal Reserve pledging to keep interest rates around zero for the foreseeable future, there was all this money with no place to go but the stock market. Hence, we had inflated stock values.

This means America was experiencing an intentionally inflated stock price bubble.

If you assume that you can just print money without any negative real-world consequences, as the popular version of Modern Monetary Theory suggests, then why not inflate the stock market when the country is facing a serious, unprecedented, and interrelated financial and health crisis?

But that is a crazy assumption. In June 2020, the budget deficit hit $864 billion. And there was not a single Washington politician who had any plan, no matter how far-fetched, to try to deal with it. This is unreality.

The question that occurs, though, is why do the American people accept the lies and exaggerations? Why don't we reward prudent and careful leaders? Lying to us is a very rational action by politicians given that we don't mind voting for good news even if the good news is false and even if we strongly suspect that the good news is false.

Neil Postman offered an explanation for this in his 1985 book *Amusing Ourselves to Death*, which has been called a 21st century book published in the 20th century. Postman thought that the advent of television had transformed public life into show. To say that further advances in electronic media have vindicated him would be an understatement.

But there is more to it than that. We treat public life as entertainment because we are bored. In *The Fundamental Concepts of Metaphysics*, Martin Heidegger treats boredom—Langeweile—and our efforts to avoid boredom, as a fundamental category of human experience. Waking up to our boredom can be a step toward authentic living. Obviously, the full implications of Heidegger's insight are beyond the scope of this book. My point here is that with the meaninglessness of life brought about by the Death of God, boredom with existence is a dominant mood in the culture. The deterioration of public life follows.

We should not think of electronic media as causing this deterioration, but as saving us from having to face the reason for it.

"Nothing Finishes, Everything Festers"

New York Times columnist Frank Bruni was wrong in the short run, and right in the long run, when he wrote about America on February 23, 2020: "Nothing finishes, everything festers."[2]

The title of Bruni's column was "Why Democrats Are Bound for Disaster." Bruni was expecting a brokered 2020 Democratic National Convention in which the eventual presidential nominee would have no legitimacy. That was his broader point: "There's no legitimacy in America anymore."

Bruni failed to anticipate the extraordinary turn of events that I mentioned in the previous chapter. First, black Democratic Party voters rallied to Joe Biden in the South Carolina presidential primary a week after Bruni's column, and then, on March 2, just in time for Super Tuesday, Pete Buttigieg and Amy Klobuchar endorsed Biden. This enabled Biden to dominate Super Tuesday and effectively gain the Democratic Party nomination for president. In our terms, their actions were real, rather than fake.

Who can blame Bruni for failing to anticipate a moment of health in American public life? Bruni was not wrong in his comments in general that in America, "the rules are all blurry. The processes are all suspect. . . . More and more defeats are prone to dispute . . . exploiting and accelerating a crisis of faith in traditions and institutions. . . . Cries of cheating and fraudulence fly in every direction."

Think of the matters that America has not been able to decide, let alone do anything about. I mean by "decide," to render a final judgment about a matter, and then, as Bruni also put it, "move on." A decision about something would include deciding what, if anything, we should then do about the matter.

Probably the best example of this is that America has been unable to decide about climate change. This is a kind of national insanity. After all, the world is either getting hotter or it is not. Humans are either causing that or we are not. The consequences of such warming are either catastrophic or they are not.

Instead, we hear things like "climate changes all the time." This kind of comment is designed, consciously or unconsciously, to avoid deciding whether humans are causing this change, whether this change is serious, and whether we should do anything about it. It is more evasion than it is climate change denial.

Climate change is not a difficult issue. A mature and responsible electorate would insist that the matter be decided one way or the other. But, of course, a responsible class of political leaders would not need such insistence.

Deciding about climate change would determine only whether America should do something. Such a decision would not tell us what should be done.

---

[2] Frank Bruni, *Why Democrats Are Bound for Disaster*, NEW YORK TIMES (Feb. 21, 2020), https://www.nytimes.com/2020/02/21/opinion/sunday/brokered-convention-democrats-2020.html.

Such a decision would certainly not entail actions akin to the broad government initiatives proposed in 2019 by Representative Alexandria Ocasio-Cortez of New York and Senator Edward J. Markey of Massachusetts in the Green New Deal.

Nor could America decide how serious the virus was, whether masks and social distancing were necessary before a vaccine was produced, or whether shutdowns were really effective. Was the goal to keep people from contracting the virus or to keep hospitals from being overwhelmed? We never decided.

Later, when the death count declined, even though confirmed cases of the virus continued to spike, we could not decide whether the virus had become less of a threat.

And then, in July, when the death count did go up, but never remotely matched national numbers from April, we could not decide whether this was progress or disaster.

We never decided the proper trade-off between a functioning economy and a certain level of virus cases and deaths. We either pretended that only the economy mattered or only public health mattered.

We could not decide whether Russia attempted to interfere with the 2016 election in favor of candidate Donald Trump, even though Russia plainly did this. We could not decide whether Donald Trump colluded in the hacking of the Democratic National Committee and the Clinton campaign—even though that hacking occurred before Trump became the likely Republican nominee and he plainly had nothing to do with it.

We could not even decide whether the president asked Ukraine to investigate Joe Biden and his son as a favor in return for aid, when the White House released the transcript in which he did so.

And we have never decided how much national debt is safe to carry.

These are just a few recent instances of evasion. We have never even decided whether the risks of nuclear power are worth running, given climate change.

Paul Krugman writes about ideas that should have been dismissed from public discourse as having been discredited by contrary evidence on numerous occasions. Krugman calls these "zombie ideas" in his book *Arguing with Zombies*.

Krugman is partisan, but not wrong, in his list of ideas that never go away, including supply-side tax cuts, predictions of inflation that never come true, policy, denials of climate change, and so forth.

Krugman's list could be expanded by including some of the Left's zombie ideas, such as the power of big money to swing nominations, elections and the enactment of policy. This interrelated set of ideas gives the Left an excuse to ignore its repeated political failures.

One could add ideas on the fringe of the Left, such as the anti-vaccine movement, ideas more mainstream, such as the supposed danger of genetically modified foods, and ideas accepted but probably false, such as that gun control measures short of confiscation would significantly affect the American homicide rate.

I don't just mean that these ideas are false. I mean, as Krugman says, that they hang around sucking the oxygen from the room.

Bruni is right: nothing finishes, everything festers. We replay the same events and return to the same grudges.

The question is, why?

The answer, in part, has to do with a lack of faith, as Bruni points out. You cannot decide anything without a shared commitment to the legitimacy of standards and processes. Decisions, in Bruni's sense, require trust. And trust is what is lacking.

Clearly, any hope of moving forward in America requires some kind of clarity and decisiveness. The absence of these qualities means that we don't finish, we just fester.

The Questions That Are Not Asked

The previous section described America's failure to deal with important issues. This is a serious problem.

But there is a more fundamental evasion. In America, many serious questions are not only not decided, they are not asked.

The most important such omission is: When does human life begin? This question is obviously relevant to abortion, the single most divisive issue in American politics.

The treatment of this crucial question in *Roe v. Wade*,[3] the case that upheld a constitutional right to abortion in 1973, was so perfunctory as to be intellectually embarrassing. In the case, Texas first argued that a fetus is protected by the Due Process Clause of the Fourteenth Amendment as a "person" entitled to "life." But instead of answering that question, Justice Harry Blackmun's majority opinion for a 7–2 Court just held that the framers of the 14th Amendment did not understand the word "person" to apply to the unborn and that this reflected the general public understanding in the 19th century.

This is an example of the worst kind of originalism, practiced by a justice who did not generally embrace that mode of constitutional interpretation, in order to avoid a moral issue that should have been faced.

[3] *Roe v. Wade*, 410 U.S. 113 (1973).

Texas then argued that even if the Constitution did not recognize the unborn as a "person" with constitutional protection, nevertheless, the unborn child is a human being and therefore the State has a right and a duty to protect it.

Again, Justice Blackmun sidestepped the question:

> We need not resolve the difficult question of when life begins. When those trained in the respective disciplines of medicine, philosophy, and theology are unable to arrive at any consensus, the judiciary, at this point in the development of man's knowledge, is not in a position to speculate as to the answer. . . . we do not agree that, by adopting one theory of life, Texas may override the rights of the pregnant woman that are at stake.

In other words, in the face of the right to privacy, the Court would insist that if there was controversy over the beginning of life, the matter was undecidable. The Court made no attempt to decide when life begins.

This is not a criticism of the outcome in *Roe*. The Court could have concluded that an unborn child is obviously a human being, but that the decision to carry a child to term is too intimate for the government to override the wishes of a pregnant woman. There were hints of such an analysis in later abortion cases.

Nor would this decision have been a departure from tradition. Parents in America, after all, are not even legally obligated to give up a kidney to save their child's life. But that kind of decision in *Roe* would at least have addressed the difficult moral issue.

This was more or less the view of the great feminist thinker Catharine MacKinnon, who wrote in 1991 that "the fetus is a form of human life," but that, given sex inequality, live birth had to "mark the personhood line."[4]

The sidestepping of difficult questions in American constitutional law goes beyond *Roe*. In *Lawrence v. Texas*,[5] which struck down the criminalization of sexual contact between persons of the same gender, Justice Anthony Kennedy could have held for the majority that such criminalization reflected a flawed morality. But that would have required an express moral judgment by the justices. Instead, the Court held, echoing a previous dissent by Justice John Paul Stevens, that "the fact that the governing majority in a State has traditionally viewed a particular practice as immoral is not a sufficient reason for upholding a law prohibiting the practice." In the future, morality would be irrelevant to law. I guess justice would be irrelevant, too.

A similar failure to make a judgment about homosexuality is why the *Obergefell* decision,[6] which ruled that same-sex marriage is constitutionally

---

[4] Catharine MacKinnon, *Reflections on Sex Equality Under Law*, 100 YALE L.J. 1281, 1316 (1991).

[5] *Lawrence v. Texas*, 539 U.S. 558 (2003).

[6] *Obergefell v. Hodges*, 576 U.S. 644 (2015).

protected, was premised entirely on a pre-existing constitutional right—the right to marry—which the government had no convincing reason to restrict, even though marriage had always been in large part about procreation. The failure to make a moral judgment about homosexuality per se, however, meant that other discriminations against gay people remained constitutional.

On the other side of the judicial aisle, Justice Antonin Scalia greatly restricted the reach of the Free Exercise Clause in *Smith v. Employment Division* in 1990, on the ground that the Court could render absolutely no judgments on the reasonableness or centrality of any religious belief. Thus, no religious beliefs would be protected in the face of prohibitions by generally applicable laws. There was never to be a judicial discussion of the quality of religious belief.

Outside of law, the same kind of avoidance of the most significant questions also operates. So, for example, Joseph Carter in the previous chapter announced to me that he is a materialist. In this, Carter undoubtedly spoke for many Americans.

But materialism has many flaws as an explanation of reality. This is a point that we will return to in Part II, but it is not something unknown. The 2010 book *The Waning of Materialism* brought together twenty-three thinkers to set forth some of the problems. Materialism has never been able to explain human consciousness, for example. For that matter, materialism cannot even give a satisfactory account of what matter is.

I don't mean that the criticisms of materialism are determinative. But they are serious. Yet, our culture simply adopts materialism. We don't ask whether materialism is true.

There are a host of important matters that this culture takes for granted now, even though these positions are not particularly persuasive and certainly are not beyond question. We assume, without thinking about it, that values are subjective. We assume that there are no essences or foundations for things.

As in Leff's poem, these things are just asserted and the burden of disproving them, like the burden of persuasion in the above legal cases, is placed on the critic. We don't ask questions directly and simply.

These evasions extend even to philosophy. As the political thinker Todd May pointed out in his 2005 introduction to the thought of Gilles Deleuze, philosophy used to ask, "How should one live?" then later asked, "How should one act?" but has finally reached the point of asking, in the absence of a guiding cosmological order, "How might one live?" The previous questions are no longer asked.

The same is the case with questions like: Is life worth living? What is the nature of evil? The reader can no doubt come up with numerous other fundamental questions that this culture no longer asks.

There is even the sense that politics should be cleansed of serious questions for fear of igniting deep and violent strife. This was Mark Lilla's point in *The Stillborn God*.

Roberto Unger noted this anti-political tendency. This was his observation in the opening of his 1996 book *What Should Legal Analysis Become?*: "The conflict over the basic terms of social life . . . ha[s] fled from the ancient arenas of politics and philosophy" and now takes place in technical terms in the specialized professions, like law.

Ross Douthat, echoing Unger's criticism, wrote a column on June 21, 2020, entitled, "The Tempting of Neil Gorsuch,"[7] in which Douthat criticized the general tendency in America to resolve political questions in courts, rather than debate them in legislatures. He called this tendency "Juristocracy." Douthat felt that the American people had become perfectly adapted to it.

In fact, it was considered the great accomplishment of the political theorist John Rawls in *A Theory of Justice* in 1971 that he supposedly resolved these basic political conflicts without ever having to reason about them. Rawls relied on social contract theory to predict the terms of social life that would be selected in a hypothetical original position. In other words, these matters were decided without having to discuss their merits—in Unger's terms, decided as a technical matter in a specialized arena.

These are all questions that are not asked.

Nothing Important Is Debated

In a culture in which important questions are not asked, it follows that when important matters do come up, they are not debated.

This happens in a few different ways. On the one hand, Steven Pinker likes to invoke "shared values" to decide matters, such as the desire that as many people as possible live long, happy, healthy lives.[8] Sometimes he calls these ideas universally accepted.

The problem is that even if such values are universally accepted, their interpretation and their trade-offs are not.

For that matter, they are not universally accepted. There are many people in the world who still deny the right of education to women or the right of gay

---

[7] Ross Douthat, *The Tempting of Neil Gorsuch*, NEW YORK TIMES (June 20, 2020), https://www.nytimes.com/2020/06/20/opinion/sunday/neil-gorsuch-supreme-court.html.

[8] Colleen Walsh, *Wielding Data Against Doom and Gloom*, THE HARVARD GAZETTE (Feb. 27, 2018), https://news.harvard.edu/gazette/story/2018/02/harvards-pinker-makes-case-for-human-progress-in-new-book/.

people to be who they are. These views are wrong, but one has to make the actual case that they are wrong.

Nor would shared values be enough to resolve issues anyway. There must be motivation to pursue these values when they conflict with self-interest. Ignoring that is part of what Christian Smith criticizes as "atheist overreach."

Another form of the absence of debate in American public life is the new censorship, called "cancel culture," practiced mostly on the Left. In this context, debate does not take place because the other side is treated as unacceptably evil, their positions harmful to people, and debate itself skewed in favor of power. This is the tendency to, as *Rolling Stone* writer Matt Taibbi puts it, "eschew debate, moving straight to shaming, threats and intimidation."[9]

This is the tendency that cost James Bennet his job as opinion editor at the *New York Times* because he published an op-ed by Senator Tom Cotton of Arkansas that argued that President Trump should call out the military to quell violence and looting in the protests after the death of George Floyd. The justification by the *New York Times*, that the op-ed should have been put in context, was laughable. Possible lack of context is why opinion pieces are called opinion pieces. The *New York Times* would once have assumed that its readers were not children.

Five weeks later, Bari Weiss, a writer and editor for the opinion department of the *New York Times*, resigned from the paper, citing "bullying by colleagues" and an "illiberal environment."[10]

Nor did we actually have the vaunted, "national conversation about race" after the George Floyd killing. Instead, there were a series of virtue signals. Taibbi pointed to an instance in which a data scientist was fired from a research firm for retweeting a study that suggested that nonviolent protest was more effective than violent protests in effecting change.

Or, there was the contextless, clueless white person picking a black person she doesn't know to have a "conversation" about race, so ably lampooned by the black writer Damon Young.[11]

Even when this culture actually engages a serious matter, like race, we do it in an unserious way.

A third way in which we do not debate matters is the insistence, most notably in the popular thinker, Cass Sunstein, that grand narratives just get in the way. Sunstein criticized both Paul Ehrlich and Julian Simon, who in the 1980s

[9] Matt Taibbi, *The American Press Is Destroying Itself*, REPORTING BY MATT TAIBBI (June 12, 2020), https://taibbi.substack.com/p/the-news-media-is-destroying-itself.

[10] Edmund Lee, *Bari Weiss Resigns From New York Opinion Post*, NEW YORK TIMES (July 14, 2020), https://www.nytimes.com/2020/07/14/business/media/bari-weiss-resignation-new-york-times.html.

[11] Damon Young, *Yeah, Let's Not Talk About Race, Unless You Pay Me*, NEW YORK TIMES (July 10, 2020), https://www.nytimes.com/2020/07/10/opinion/george-floyd-racism.html.

entered into a famous bet over whether population growth would cause scarcities in certain commodities in a decade's time. Sunstein wrote about both men that "too much of the time, they were driven by grand, abstract narratives about history's supposed arc. In dealing with the changing environment, as elsewhere, such narratives tend to be an obstacle to both understanding and progress."

Of course, we should debate important matters armed with the facts. But Sunstein's warning can easily translate into the idea that grand themes should not be debated at all. In this way, important matters would never be discussed.

In a similar fashion, we hear about contingency in history and the absence of moral absolutes. All of this sort of language is aimed at cabining moral and political discourse.

The Failure to Dream

Ironically, though Tom Berry liked to say that we live in a dream world, it is a dream world without dreams. We find it difficult to imagine that the world could be much different from the way it is today. In the book *Capitalist Realism*, Mark Fisher refers to the quote, which he attributes to both Fredric Jameson and Slavoj Zizek, that "it is easier to imagine an end to the world than an end to capitalism." In other words, we feel that our basic socio/economic/political arrangements are impervious to change.

Roberto Unger also writes about this failure, which he attributes to a failure of imagination in institutional design.

So, when erstwhile socialist Bernie Sanders talks about new policies, he is really just invoking the example of social welfare services of European countries, such as free education and health care. Sanders is not talking about radically new or different economic arrangements.

And when young people talk about not having the luxury to dream, as in an opinion piece by Katherine Hu in the *New York Times* on March 24, 2020,[12] the "radical change" that seems out of reach is pretty tame: universal health care, forgiveness of student loans, and more affordable housing. And that is what Hu feels she cannot dream of attaining.

It is not that people do not want to think about larger issues and possibilities. Amna Akbar, a law professor at Ohio State University, argues that the in the George Floyd protests, the Left was remaking the world.[13] Clearly that is his hope.

---

[12]   Katherine Hu, "*I Just Don't Think We Have the Luxury to Have Dreams Anymore*," NEW YORK TIMES (Mar. 24, 2020), https://www.nytimes.com/2020/03/24/opinion/coronavirus-recession-gen-z.html.

[13]   Amna A. Akbar, *The Left Is Remaking the World*, NEW YORK TIMES (July 11, 2020), https://www.nytimes.com/2020/07/11/opinion/sunday/defund-police-cancel-rent.html.

But it seems to me that the popular vision on the Left is limited to quite ordinary identity politics and redistributive proposals. The popular vision on the Right is limited to nostalgia for a lost world. Something prevents more imaginative possibilities from surfacing.

The Rhetoric of Perhaps

Jeff Toobin, a staff writer for the *New York Times*, and a legal analyst for CNN, reviewed Gilbert King's book, *Beneath a Ruthless Sun*, in 2018. King was telling the story of the false charge of rape that led to a nineteen-year-old white teenager being committed to fourteen years in a mental hospital awaiting trial, before his release. It is also the terrible story of the brutal sheriff of Lake County, Willis McCall.

Here is Toobin's opening to the review: " 'The arc of the moral universe is long,' Martin Luther King Jr. famously asserted, 'but it bends toward justice.' Well, perhaps. An alternative view is that progress on civil rights in the United States has been episodic and inconsistent, with victory often followed by backlash."[14]

Perhaps? As we will see in Part II, everything depends on King's claim—the nature of the universe, our place in it, everything. Given these stakes, doesn't Toobin owe his readers a forthright statement? If the truth is that sometimes the universe does, and sometimes it doesn't, bend toward justice and that there is no pattern, not even an elongated one, then King was wrong. There is no "perhaps" about it.

Now, contrast Toobin's feeble response to Dr. King with the rejection, albeit carefully couched, by Rich Cohen in *Vanity Fair* in 2017. Cohen writes that, as a member of Generation X, "I'm careful not to always say what I know—that the long arc of history does not in fact bend toward justice."[15]

Toobin is evading. Cohen is not. Cohen is willing to commit in public. Toobin cannot bring himself to do so.

We are much more like Toobin.

I call this "the rhetoric of Perhaps" because it is a style adopted for public consumption. I have no sense of what Toobin's commitments really are. But Toobin knew his audience would accept this rhetorical stance.

You can hear the same stance in the statement by Jasper Johns in 2006 that became the title of a 2017 exhibition of his work at the Royal Academy of Arts in

---

[14] Jeffery Toobin, *How a Racist Sheriff Railroaded a Disabled Teenager and Got Off*, NEW YORK TIMES (May 3, 2018), https://www.nytimes.com/2018/05/03/books/review/gilbert-king-beneath-ruthless-sun.html.

[15] Rich Cohen, *Why Generation X Might Be Our Last, Best Hope*, VANITY FAIR (Aug. 11, 2017), https://www.vanityfair.com/style/2017/08/why-generation-x-might-be-our-last-best-hope.

London—"Jasper Johns: 'Something Resembling Truth' ": "One hopes for something resembling truth, some sense of life, even of grace, to flicker, at least, in the work."[16]

You can hear the weight of the Perhaps in Maggie Doherty's review of Jia Tolentino's 2019 book of essays, *Trick Mirror*: "This kind of fatalism, dispiriting but perhaps fair, runs through the book."[17] The Perhaps is something that we really don't want, but feel incapable of contesting.

The Perhaps is why we say that "perhaps" our form of liberal democracy is "too fragile" to protect us from unfettered capitalism, economic inequality, and surging populism.[18]

It is not clear whether this rhetoric represents a fear of the truth, a fear of telling the truth, or a fear of disagreeing about the truth. One thing, though, is clear from the rhetoric of Perhaps—we believe we have the luxury of not committing our lives to the resolution of the truth.

The Inability to Choose

To be neither one thing nor another was for Jesus a condition for condemnation in the book of Revelation: "So because you are lukewarm—neither hot nor cold—I am about to vomit you out of My mouth!"[19]

In addition to the above categories of evasion, we are also unable to choose. So, there is now a category of cultural Judaism, for example, for those unable to choose between religion and non-religion.

We have the separate realms of science and religion, so we don't have to choose between them, as if there were somehow more than a single world.

We pretend that we can be neither male nor female in terms of gender, as if millions of years of evolution did not give us pretty hard divisions in those categories. I was recently given a name tag that stated, in addition to my name, my "preferred pronouns." But I'm pretty sure I never had a choice about my pronouns.

We have even reinterpreted what the concept of transgender means. As Joy Ladin makes clear in *Soul of a Stranger*, she always felt that she was female. But now we pretend that transgender means that we need not be male or female.

---

[16] *Jasper Johns: "Something Resembling Truth,"* THE ROYAL ACADEMY OF THE ARTS, https://www.royalacademy.org.uk/exhibition/jasper-johns..

[17] Maggie Doherty, *Jia Tolentino on the "Unlivable Hell" of the Web and Other Millennial Conundrums*, NEW YORK TIMES (Aug. 4, 2019), https://www.nytimes.com/2019/08/04/books/review/jia-tolentino-trick-mirror.html.

[18] David A. Bell, *The Many Lives of Liberalism*, NEW YORK REVIEW (Jan. 17, 2019), https://www.nybooks.com/articles/2019/01/17/many-lives-of-liberalism/.

[19] Revelation 3:16.

Of course, and ironically, in the New Testament, Paul does say that in Christ there is neither male nor female, but he means that there is no distinction between men and women in the Kingdom of God. We are still literally men and women in the Kingdom.

There is a genuine philosophical category of the Between, in thinkers like Martin Heidegger and William Desmond, but it is not used to avoid decision. For us, something like the Between is applied offhandedly, in order to avoid decision.

Granted, in the basics of politics, we seem to absolutely choose. We are Democrats or Republicans. We are members of one base or the other. Yet, this choice actually just avoids decision, or even thinking. Once we make this decision, we become intellectually passive, simply rooting for our side, like a sports team. Once committed, we tend not to criticize in a serious way and certainly rarely favor the other side.

Similarly, those who do not choose a side in politics tend to avoid politics altogether. They also do not decide.

What is missing, and here I am anticipating the way decision manifests in Chapter 9, is a center that actively judges and goes its own way. Such a center would be independent of the surface commitments and identifications of politics but would nevertheless be intensely committed. A few such people have surfaced, in the Never Trump movement, for example, and in some left-wing critics as well, but that just shows it is an unusual phenomenon.

The Privilege of Fatalism

When Doherty, above, referred to the fatalism in *Trick Mirror*, she was not just invoking the Perhaps. She was also endorsing fatalism, albeit meekly.

Ross Douthat's book *The Decadent Society* also endorses fatalism. According to Douthat, there is nothing to be done about our condition except to wait for rescue, possibly from a religious renaissance in Africa.

I know I am adopting an odd usage, but you have to be pretty confident to endorse this kind of fatalistic comportment. If people really were afraid that all was lost, wouldn't they try to do something about it?

And if people thought all might be lost but could not figure out what to do about it, wouldn't they at least be panic-stricken? None of the new fatalists are panic-stricken.

None of them expect to be put in a prison camp next week. None of them are stacking up Molotov cocktails for use when the fascists come for them—or when the progressives come.

The protestors in the street from the Right and the Left, protesting first the continuation of the shutdowns and then protesting racism, were much healthier.

The only message that fatalism gives is that we are justified in doing nothing.

Deep Unseriousness

To return to the theme with which I began this chapter, American life is unserious. But below the obvious unseriousness—the scripted vocabulary and events—there lies an even deeper unseriousness.

One of the themes of modern life is that we are beset by longing that we cannot satisfy. But this longing is a pose and a double irony. There are many people in this society who are experiencing despair. And, given the meaninglessness in which we live, their despair is entirely justified. This is the background of the opioid epidemic.

But people in that condition do not describe themselves as filled with longing or with any other precious terminology.

In contrast, the people invoking the pose of longing may indeed on some level be experiencing despair. But they are masking it in their descriptions. This is the double irony of evasion.

This is the situation that the writer Lauren Groff unselfconsciously calls "longing for longing."[20] Groff complains—actually, she sort of apologizes for complaining—that the most recent works of the writer Jeffrey Eugenides "no longer seem to embody spiritual yearning, but rather hold it at arm's length for gently pointed ridicule." Groff admits that "nobody could blame him if he eventually found faith or spiritual hunger a childish thing to be put away," but she goes on to admit, as "one deeply secular reader," to experiencing "an unappeasable longing for longing," especially in this "fractured and worrisome time." She wants her writers to stretch "toward the ineffable mysteries of human existence."

I'm sorry, but Groff sounds to me like a tourist complaining that the meal was cold. She wants to be reassured by a secondhand experience of the ineffable, in literature, rather than attempting to do something in her own life to move in that direction.

In another instance, for its tenth anniversary, the Immanent Frame, a well-known collaboration of the Social Science Research Council which publishes "interdisciplinary perspectives on religion, secularism, and the public sphere,"[21] invited noted thinkers to answer the question, "Is This All There Is?" on any terms the writer chose.

---

[20] Lauren Groff, *Jeffery Eugenides, Great American Novelist, Turns to the Story*, NEW YORK TIMES (Oct. 12, 2017), https://www.nytimes.com/2017/10/12/books/review/jeffrey-eugenides-fresh-complaint-stories.html.

[21] Charles Taylor, *About*, IMMANENT FRAME, https://tif.ssrc.org/about/.

A number of the contributors, though committed to natural explanations for everything, described longing for something more. At one time, this felt "poignant" to me,[22] but I have become suspicious of such activity as actually quite disconnected from any genuine spiritual seeking.

We are in the situation of Sophie Baker, a character played by Emma Stone in Woody Allen's 2014 film *Magic in the Moonlight*, who says, referencing Nietzsche, that "we need our illusions to live." These are the illusions of fables, fairy tales, and myths. This is the magic of the title of the movie.

But, of course, you cannot have it both ways. It is not really magic if you know that it is an illusion. This is also known to the characters in the movie. That is the movie's deeper unseriousness.

Why Do We Evade?

The columnist Joe Nocera wrote an op-ed in June 2020 criticizing the firing of Estée Lauder board member, Ronald Lauder, after employees in the company demanded that he be removed because he had poured money—$1.6 million at the time—into pro-Trump organizations.[23] The company agreed to remove him.

Nocera understood that the president was really beyond the pale for some younger workers. He even sympathized with this feeling.

But Nocera had a broader view on the matter, having to do with the "culture of millennials." His theory, premised on a suggestion from Charlotte Alter's book, *The Ones We've Been Waiting For*, is that because the parents of millennials were overprotective, they were overly strict, imposing draconian punishments for even minor rule infractions. So, according to Alter, millennials developed a merciless morality. They have no tolerance for people who think in the slightest differently from them.

In this chapter, I have agreed that we don't debate anything—that we just move from one condemnation to another depending on which side we're on.

But I don't agree with Nocera about the reason we are like this. I don't see that this tendency has anything to do with age or parenting style. The reasons we are like this lie in our beliefs about the nature of reality.

First, we cannot act reasonably because there is nothing to be reasonable about. You debate matters when there is the possibility of learning something. But under the reign of the Death of God, there is nothing to learn. There is no knowledge about important matters to be gained.

---

[22] Bruce Ledewitz, *The Resurrection of Trust in American Law and Public Discourse*, 56 Duq. L.Rev. 21 (2018).

[23] Joe Nocera, *Ronald Lauder Shouldn't Be Fired for Backing Trump*, Yahoo News (June 12, 2020), https://www.yahoo.com/news/ronald-lauder-shouldn-t-fired-090031707.html.

If you want to know why millennials are like this, you can ask whether their parents engaged in thoughtful exchange and debate. Mostly, they did not.

We also do not engage large questions, because we feel that resolving them will prove impossible. We don't expect progress. Again, we feel that way because we are living under the Death of God.

Finally, we are afraid of what genuine discussion would unearth. If you suspect that the universe is an abyss of unreasoning forces, that the self is an illusion and that the sense of significance that you feel in life is a spandrel—that is, a by-product of evolutionary advance that somehow appeared along with a bigger, better problem-solving brain—you do not want to probe into any important matters.

It is hard to live with these feelings. But at least if you evade anything important, you will be like the fool in the saying "Better to be quiet and be thought a fool than to speak and remove all doubt." We are afraid of what the truth would show.

We have now come to the end of the coming home to roost of the Death of God. I repeat, as I have said previously, there is no going back. The God who died will not return, at least not in any time frame that makes a difference to us.

So, if our condition is to improve, we will have to pursue a new and different path. We don't any longer have the old story. We need a new one. That new story is the subject of Part II—"Restoring Faith in American Public Life."

PART II
RESTORING FAITH
IN AMERICAN PUBLIC LIFE

6

Is the Universe on Our Side?

We Cannot Go on This Way

I hope it is clear to the reader that the breakdown in American public life cannot continue without risking catastrophe. If we continue this way we risk the end of our constitutional democracy. That is the message of the book, *How Democracies Die*. Steven Levitsky and Daniel Ziblatt give examples from history of countries in which the norms of democratic life gradually eroded and eventually disappeared. They do not list any examples in which those norms spontaneously regenerated.

The authors show that since the 1990s, respect for democratic norms and practices has declined in America. They are plainly worried that something drastic may happen in the near future.

How would it happen here? There are already many Americans who have lost faith in our constitutional system. Ross Douthat refers to them as the "post-liberals"—*the new radicals* on the Left and *the new reactionaries* on the Right.[1] Both sides are questioning the post-WWII consensus behind the constitutional/capitalist/democratic Western order.

This dissatisfaction means that there might not be a popular revolt in America against a postponement of elections or temporary military rule. Such action might be accepted.

Of course, any such interruption would be called "defensive." If you believe that your opponents might overthrow the government, then you are halfway toward acting pre-emptively yourself.

Am I serious? Do I expect our experiment in constitutional democracy to end in dictatorship? Levitsky and Ziblatt don't expect Donald Trump to do anything like that and neither do I. But I read a lot of nervous commentary asking whether Trump would accept an election defeat—as if he would have a choice. And what about the next president or the one after that?

Just what message was I supposed to take from watching those rifles at the anti-shutdown protests in May 2020? Was that not meant to be a threat? If a

---

[1] Ross Douthat, *Among the Post-Liberals*, New York Times (Oct. 8, 2016), https://www.nytimes.com/2016/10/09/opinion/sunday/among-the-post-liberals.html.

The Universe Is on Our Side. Bruce Ledewitz, Oxford University Press. © Oxford University Press 2022.
DOI: 10.1093/oso/9780197563939.003.0007

requirement of wearing a mask is tyranny that justifies the threat of armed re-action, what actions by a government controlled by the Democratic Party would not be considered tyranny worthy of armed revolt?

Similarly, I hear a lot of commentary about how undemocratic our system is, both because of its structural aspects—the Electoral College and the makeup of the Senate—and the supposed power of dark money. So, why not just take direct action in the streets?

Yes, it can happen here and if we do not change things, it seems to me eventu-ally it will happen here. I'm sure this has occurred to many other people.

So, why is there no panic about the future of constitutional democracy?

But There Is Nothing to Be Done

What is the point of panic if there is nothing to be done? Most of the books about the current state of American public life share two attributes. First, the fault for our terrible situation is on one side. Either the Right has lost its mind—they don't even believe in facts—or the Left has lost its mind—they will not even allow their opponents to speak. Second, these books spend almost all their pages describing the breakdown and almost no space about how to change things. Or, if they con-tain some suggestions, like some form of constitutional amendment, the changes are unlikely to occur.

These books are rarely serious about changing things, beyond a vague hope of finally winning and vanquishing the other side. In that sense, these books are just political disaster porn. They are fun to read for vindication.

It might seem that there would especially be nothing to do if the source of the breakdown is, as Part I argued, the Death of God. About that phenomenon, what could possibly be done?

Religious believers who still feel the presence of God certainly have no ob-vious task, beyond pondering in their hearts, like Mary, the meaning of the huge cultural shift toward secularism.

Meanwhile, secularists, whether those like me, who used to believe in God but no longer do, or the increasing number who have never had any experience of life with God, may not even have a vocabulary to describe what has happened, let alone a program going forward.

No direct action about the Death of God is possible.

So, if something is to be done, we have to think about things in a new way.

Part I of this book is meant to point us in a spiritual direction and to provide ample motivation for change. This is not one of those books that is content to watch the disaster unfold.

To think about change, we must first decide what we are trying to accomplish. If we could begin to cure the breakdown in American public life, what would we see that is different from the way things are now?

Recovering Normal Public Life

It is a pleasure to contemplate movement toward a more normal public life in America. A friend of mine read an early draft of Part I of the book and asked me whether it had to be so dark. Addressing positive change in America makes me realize how much thinking about the breakdown is like carrying around a Horcrux in the Harry Potter books. We need to move beyond focusing on what is wrong.

We are not talking in this chapter about flourishing public life. I take up that subject in Chapter 9. For now, we would benefit just from a reduction in the toxicity that we experience today—a return to normalcy.

The main attribute of normal political life is that it is not personally threatening. I can contemplate temporary rule by the other side without angst. I will not agree with the policies that my opponents enact. I may lose benefits. Terrible international alliances may be entered into, or faithful allies abandoned. But I will not feel personally at risk.

Because I will not feel threatened by rule by the other side, I will also not have to resort to extraordinary measures to forestall it.

And, as a part of all that, I will not feel the need to live and die by the Twitter, social media, and cable news cycles. Nor will I be interested in following hysterical voices in the media. Or online. I will not need such voices to vindicate myself.

In other words, the importance of politics and policy would recede. We would still be invested in the public life of our country. But we would be following science, the humanities, the arts, even sports—national life apart from the political sphere.

How do we move in that direction?

The Need for Something Significant

It would help us tremendously if we had something else to do other than politics. Someone else to be other than a member of a political coalition. Somehow a category of thinking that would occupy us apart from the vicissitudes of every daily crisis. Somewhere else to be, other than the political realm. We need to break the overwhelming magnetism of these forms of public life.

But it is important to note that the problem is not that public life became too important. What actually happened is that our lives, both individually and collectively, became insignificant because of the Death of God. Public life just poured in as an alternative to our empty existence.

So, the answer to our need is not more stimulation. We don't need Neil Postman's amusement. In fact, entertainment is the last thing we need.

We need to experience significance. We need to feel that we are living in depth. That way, our actual lives will be sufficient to sustain our interest and commitment. We won't need to look so much at our phones.

I don't mean that we fool ourselves in that regard. The only way to experience significance and to feel that one is living in depth is to engage a matter of significance and thus live in depth.

The way to do that is to ask a question. Asking a question is the program of beginning to restore faith in American public life.

What? That is my answer to America's crisis, with everything that is going on? Asking a question sounds like the strangest suggestion there could be.

How Does Asking a Question Restore Faith?

I said in Chapter 4 that Americans have lost faith in everything. I gave examples of our lack of faith in a variety of human activities, including a lack of trust in our fellow human beings. Will asking a question restore that faith?

The answer is, not necessarily. That depends on the answers, or provisional answers, that we come up with. The next chapter, in fact, is about a negative answer that does not restore faith in any form of public life.

What questioning does do, however, is restore—or, if there has been no prior experience with questioning, infuse—faith in questioning itself.

Questioning is a self-authenticating activity. Questioning clears the mind. Uplifts the spirit. Creates community.

Obviously, these statements are not questions. The reader will have to inquire into whether questioning does these things—by asking a question. This chapter is not an argument. It is an invitation.

The reader has a right to know that this invitation really comes from a member of the Nazi Party—Martin Heidegger—at the time of his greatest mistake and closest connection to Nazi life.

The basic story about Heidegger's involvement with National Socialism is well known. A few months after Hitler was made chancellor of Germany in 1933, Heidegger was elected chancellor of the University of Freiberg. A week later, in May, he joined the Nazi Party. His inaugural address, on May 27, amounted to an enthusiastic endorsement of the party and its leader.

A year later, Heidegger resigned the chancellorship and it is clear that his hope to be the party's philosophical thinker had foundered. Eventually, though he never resigned from the party, his publication was forbidden and his teaching monitored.

This is not the place to discuss the relationship of Heidegger's thinking to this episode, which he later regarded as a mistake. It is very clear that Heidegger did not understand the militarized, dictatorial, racist, and indeed murderous aspects of the Nazi Party. But he was far from the only German to make that mistake in 1933.

It is also clear that Heidegger was looking for a radical transformation in German public life that is relevant here. Between his inaugural address and his resignation as chancellor, Heidegger taught a summer class entitled "The Fundamental Questions of Philosophy." In the course of these lectures, Heidegger addressed questioning and the German people. He said, "It is in itself that the German people is to ask the philosophical question, using those guides who lead it to the philosophical plane because the people itself has become this question."[2]

This is the questioning that is the task of a people on its way to becoming a people. Of course, a people in this formulation should not be heard racially or ethnically, but rather politically in the deepest sense. In its moment of spiritual crisis, the American collective must confront and engage what Tom Berry called its "Great Work," the essential issue of each historical period. In undertaking, rather than avoiding, its Great Work, a collective becomes a people.

The Great Work for the American people at this historical moment is to confront the catastrophic consequences of the Death of God for public life and to come to terms with its meaning. That is the only path to the renewal of American public life.

Heidegger is telling us that this engagement must take the form of a question. Not an argument, or an assertion, or a position, or a policy, or a direction, or an answer, but a question.

When we question, really question, that is, without restriction, we lay the groundwork for progress. We even question the significance of our questioning. That is a form of faith. It is the faith in inquiry itself. We are willing to face the consequences of our inquiring wherever they may lead.

A culture that does that is no longer in decline, whatever its answers turn out to be.

---

[2]   VICTOR FARIAS, HEIDEGGER AND NAZISM 133 (Joseph Margolis & Tom Rockmore eds., Paul Burrell & Gabriel R. Ricci trans., 1989).

It Must Be an Ultimate Question

When David Brooks wrote in February 2020 that the mythmakers in politics win, he said that such leaders "don't just tell a story. They tell a story that helps people make meaning out of the current moment; that divides people into heroes and villains; that names a central challenge and explains why they are the perfect person to meet it."[3]

This is why the gorilla teacher in Daniel Quinn's fable *Ishmael* tells the student that Hitler mesmerized the German people by telling them a story of how things came to be the way that they were (in that context, why Germany lost WWI and why Germany stood humiliated after the Versailles Treaty).

However, these particular stories are not answers to ultimate questions. That is why such limited stories are susceptible to resentments and scapegoats. An ultimate question is one that asks about the nature of the human experience and its relationship to ultimate reality.

This kind of ultimacy is what Heidegger meant by the philosophical question. In Heidegger's case, that question became, in different formulations, "What is the meaning of Being?"

For us, at this time, in our condition, the ultimate question comes from Bernard Lonergan's classic theological work, *Method in Theology*. In a section entitled "The Question of God," Lonergan put questioning, or as he called it, deliberating, into the largest possible framework. Lonergan said that to ask a question is inevitably also to ask whether the question is worth asking. To ask whether a question is worth asking is to ask whether the question is *ultimately* worth asking. To ask that is to ask whether there is ultimacy in reality:

> To deliberate about x is to ask whether x is worth while. To deliberate about deliberating is to ask whether any deliberating is worth while. Has "worth while" any ultimate meaning? Is moral enterprise consonant with this world? We praise the developing subject, ever more capable of attention, insight, reasonableness, responsibility. We praise progress and denounce every manifestation of decline. But is the universe on our side, or are we just gamblers and, if we are gamblers, are we not perhaps fools, individually struggling for authenticity and collectively endeavoring to snatch progress from the ever mounting welter of decline? The questions arise and, clearly, our attitudes and our resoluteness may be profoundly affected by the answers. Does there or does there not exist a transcendent, intelligent ground of the universe? Is that ground or are we the

---

[3] David Brooks, *Why Sanders Will Probably Win the Nomination*, New York Times (Feb. 20, 2020), https://www.nytimes.com/2020/02/20/opinion/bernie-sanders-win-2020.html.

primary instance of moral consciousness? Are cosmogenesis, biological evolution, historical process basically cognate to us as moral beings or are they indifferent and so alien to us?[4]

There is an enormous amount of content in this paragraph and we will be discussing its numerous aspects. However, in shortened form, the ultimate question for us is this: "Is the universe on our side?" This is the question that Bernard Lonergan sets for us to grapple with on the way to determining whether there is a form of meaning beyond the simple everyday of our existence.

That is what makes Lonergan's question an ultimate question.

An ultimate question has no politics. It has no policy prescriptions. It invites community.

The Question Must Really Be a Question

To be a question, there must be the possibility of at least a positive or a negative answer. Often, there will even be more than just two discrete possibilities.

Lonergan's question, "Is the universe on our side?," qualifies in this regard. As I said above, the question, in fact, has been answered in the negative very often.

Nevertheless, there are different sorts of ways for a matter to be presented formally as a question but actually not partake of genuine inquiry. For example, there is the issue of tainting an inquiry so that no question is really being asked. This is the "are you still beating your spouse" variety, in which the negative answer, *no*, actually implies a related positive response.

Then there is the kind of inquiry in which the historical experience with a certain term, or some other way in which a term is "loaded," taints the inquiry. Thus, the question "Should the United States adopt socialism?" is, in most contexts, not a genuine inquiry.

In Lonergan's message, set forth above, no restrictions on questioning are proposed. However, the very next sentence, "Such is the question of God," and the title of the section itself, suggest that in Lonergan's view, it is not possible to answer his question in the affirmative without also accepting that God in some sense exists.

But this objection is probably merely terminological. It might mean only that one of the ways of understanding the concept of God simply is that the universe is on our side. One could then take the question on its own terms, without accepting Lonergan's definition of God.

---

[4] BERNARD LONERGAN, METHOD IN THEOLOGY 102–03 (1971).

The final paragraph in the section raises the issue of restriction of the question in a different sense:

> The question of God, then, lies within man's horizon. Man's transcendental subjectivity is mutilated or abolished, unless he is stretching forth towards the intelligible, the unconditioned, the good of value. The reach, not of his attainment, but of his intending, is unrestricted. There lies within his horizon a region for the divine, a shrine for ultimate holiness. It cannot be ignored. The atheist may pronounce it empty. The agnostic may urge that he finds his investigation has been inconclusive. The contemporary humanist will refuse to allow the question to arise. But their negations presuppose the spark in our clod, our native orientation to the divine.

Lonergan is here asserting that human beings innately have a sense of the divine, of the infinite, that "cannot be ignored." In Lonergan's view, the negative answer to the question of the universe means that this innate sense is disappointed. Clearly, Lonergan grants that a sincere inquiry into our relation to the universe can yield the answer *no*. But it is impossible for the question not to arise, and it arises out of the human desire at our deepest level that the answer be *yes*. This is the "spark," "our native orientation to the divine."

In the next chapter, it will be necessary to ensure that Lonergan's assumptions do not preclude genuine inquiry. In Joseph Carter's case, for example, in Chapter 4, the human orientation to which Lonergan is pointing is accepted as a characteristic of human beings. That is, we want the universe to share our sense of purpose. Carter accepts that this feeling is present, but argues that it is bound to disappointment. Thus, Carter is not impeded in his inquiry by Lonergan's starting point.

Nevertheless, someone could argue that human beings do not intend the unrestricted, in Lonergan's sense, and that failing to do so is not harmful to us. So we do have to guard Lonergan's question against that supposed restriction.

One could also attempt to restrict inquiry into Lonergan's question by asserting that the existence of the human orientation toward the divine is itself evidence that the universe is on our side. But the counter to any simplistic question-begging in this way would be that the human orientation to the infinite arose naturally, through the undirected patterns of evolution, either as adaptive in some way or as a spandrel.

In any event, I believe that Lonergan's intellectual honesty is shown by the simple sentence, "The atheist may pronounce it empty." Lonergan's question is a real question.

How Does a Person Ask an Ultimate Question?

I have always admired the life of Orthodox Judaism. Until the fifth grade, I attended the New Haven Hebrew Day School, which was one of the schools created after WWII by the Rebbe, Menachem Mendel Schneerson, the leader of the Lubavitcher Hasidic movement. The Rebbe, as he was widely known even outside the movement, was a powerful spiritual presence. He created a school where a young child—at that time boys and girls went to school together—could experience genuine spirituality. The school was a wonderful expression of Orthodox Judaism.

I learned as a child that God was everywhere, in every place. I learned that every moment of existence has its proper blessing to recite, including going to the bathroom. I remember that this infused all of life with an aura of strangeness and holiness.

I could not get enough of this life, in which even the individual Hebrew letters of the Torah, the Hebrew Bible, seemed to dance, to be alive. Each letter seemed to be a door to a different world.

I have told the story before that I was removed from this life at the end of the fourth grade because I asked my mother why we did not keep kosher, a burden that she, as a modern, professional woman, was certainly not going to undertake.

But my mother's dissatisfaction was deeper than that. At that time, I seemed to be intoxicated with religious life. After spending the week in classes that extended into late afternoon, plus busing, I insisted on walking on Saturdays—you could not ride in a car on the Sabbath—to an additional Torah study that the school set up quite some distance from my house.

Part of this recounting is undoubtedly a trick of memory. But I had occasion to talk about all this with my mother in the months before she died. She confirmed at least the broad strokes of what I remember.

That intoxication is what it means to ask an ultimate question.

That is why Heidegger says that "questioning is the piety of thought."[5]

Questioning is how thinking achieves the life of transcendence. In our instance in this book, it means to keep the question "Is the universe on our side?" always before us. It means that all preconceptions, biases, and expectations must be banished. The question must be allowed its own space and time. We must in every minute be open to whatever the question reveals.

---

[5] Martin Heidegger, *The Question Concerning Technology*, in THE QUESTION CONCERNING TECHNOLOGY AND OTHER ESSAYS 35 (William Lovitt trans., 1977).

The comportment of one asking an ultimate question—and now it can be seen that all ultimate questions are really one question about the meaning of each of our lives—can be described as one of intensity, humility, gratitude, and compassion.

The intensity comes from the importance of the question. My life is at stake. Otherwise, questioning is merely curiosity.

Humility comes from understanding the question as not controlled by me but as something that has authority over me. Questioning comes to me from without, its insights unexpected.

Gratitude comes from the experience of questioning itself. The luminous quality of existence is revealed. A different way of life appears. The reader may remember the look of joy on the face of James Earl Jones in the movie *Field of Dreams*, when his character, Terence Mann, leaves the baseball diamond and enters the cornfield, amazed and transfixed by what he beholds. At that moment, he is grateful.

Compassion arises because the one asking the question is surrounded by others who are not questioning. They are actually not "woke," an important term that we mistakenly apply to certain political attitudes. These others are limited in what life can offer them. Their horizon, in Lonergan's sense, is constricted. The questioner is obligated to share with them what questioning has to offer. But this will often be a futile endeavor.

Since the questioner does not control the questioning, there is no danger of arrogance in such sharing, no hint of condescension. But there is also little direct communication, because the experience of questioning is alien if one is not in it. Instead, the experience of questioning can usually only be shared at the level of a model. The questioner becomes the model of genuine human life. This arouses the interest and curiosity of others.

Questioning is not a matter of withdrawal from life. Lonergan's question can be asked in a monastery. It can be asked at a race track. You don't have to leave the company or quit school. In fact, you may be more present in all the arenas of life than you were before.

Questioning does not keep you from earning a living. But it does put earning a living into a context.

There is no need for a certain education or preparation. Those are certainly helpful and once undertaken, questioning will lead to an exploration of the thought of others. But anyone can start questioning.

Questioning is what Pierre Hadot was pointing to in his book *Philosophy as a Way of Life*. But anyone can do philosophy.

Questioning requires only the question—is the universe on our side? We meet such a question in wonder and it teaches us its meaning.

Won't We Just Evade the Question?

Of course we will evade the question. I started evading it even as I was writing the previous section. Who lives that way?

Plus, we have the problem of a toxic culture that encourages, and even insists on, evasion. In Part I, I showed just how deep the hole in which we find ourselves is. We are filled with rage, unable to cooperate, unable even to discuss the plight we are in. We are rushing toward the destruction of what had been a wonderful human achievement: constitutional government. We see no way out of this horrible fate. All our explanations fall flat. Elections happen but nothing changes.

I tried to show in Part I that the reason that we cannot exhume ourselves from this hole is the fundamentality that brought it about—the Death of God. We are living with the consequences of no longer having a foundation under us. Our public life is therefore a tissue of lies and exaggerations. We are always acting in bad faith. Truth is dead.

Worst of all, because we are so stuck, we evade all the important questions. We cannot even constructively address the nature of our dilemma.

Given all this, what is the point of suggesting a new starting point, however helpful that starting point might be theoretically? Why wouldn't this culture evade Lonergan's question, just like it evades more immediate questions, like when human life begins or whether the Russians interfered with our presidential election?

Lonergan never suggested that "the culture" would do something to change itself in some way. He thought that redemption would come, but he called that "grace." It is not something that human beings do.

Fortunately, questioning does not start with the culture. Yes, there is a sense in which the collective asks a question and I will return to that below. But the first matter is not the culture. It is you and me.

It is true that questioning always begins in some form of community. You are reading this book. You meet a teacher. You have a friend.

But community is small scale. It does not require a movement. It does not engage at the level of culture.

Even at that small scale, however, the reader undoubtedly feels that the level of intensity that questioning requires is unattainable. You will feel, as I do every day, that this kind of activity is beyond your reach. Everyone will tell you, if you ask them, that this kind of life, the life of questioning, cannot exist in the modern world. These are all ways in which a toxic culture prevents health from occurring.

The potential response to such resistance, a resistance that Lonergan anticipated, is what I meant when I said that questioning is self-authenticating. If you can bring yourself to take the first step—this is, of course, the saying about how a long journey begins—you will experience this authenticity yourself. You won't have to take anyone's word for how beautiful it is. And you will be led onward.

There is one more block to questioning and it comes, ironically, from within the question. For if we already know the answer, we cannot ask the question.

Someone like me, for example, raised as I was, cannot shake the conviction, formed in religious school as a child, that the universe is on our side. I end up not questioning but looking for confirmation.

Or, someone else, raised in scientific materialism, already knows that the universe is not the kind of thing that can be on anyone's side. It is difficult for that person to summon the energy for the investigation.

That, by the way, is why the poet W. B. Yeats wrote in the poem *The Second Coming* that "the best lack all conviction." They don't. They have precisely the conviction that the universe is not on our side. That conviction just yields human beings who look like they lack all conviction, if it comes as an assumption rather than as the result of genuine questioning.

In order to prevent this kind of block, I present in the next two chapters examples of the *no* and the *yes* as answers to Lonergan's question. I want people like me to take the *no* more seriously than we would like to do. On the other hand, I want people who come from the *no* to see rational and scientific grounds for the *yes*, in Alfred North Whitehead, for example. In this way, I hope to help questioning go forward.

Yet, in the end, questioning is hard. There is no guarantee that it is even possible at this time.

There is one strange and unanticipated glimmer of hope in this dark time. In a way, we are fortunate that the conditions in America are as bad as they are. Years ago, none of this questioning would have seemed necessary. Things were not that bad and were getting better. There were still heroes. I could follow others. I did not feel the need to take responsibility on my own for saving my country. There was no reason for me to respond by changing my life, which is what questioning does.

But now, we can plainly see that unless we act individually to change something, catastrophe awaits us. No one would deny that something radical is needed. What could be more radical than changing your life? It requires a lot more of us than picking up a gun or going to a march.

Heidegger spoke to the difficulty of questioning in a culture apparently immune to it. Just before he ended his essay with the observation about piety and thinking, he addressed the stuckness of the culture and our inability to ask a question: "The closer we come to the danger, the more brightly do the ways into the saving power begin to shine and the more questioning we become."

So, maybe this is the only time to ask an ultimate question.

How Does a People Ask a Question?

Questioning does not operate at the level of the culture, but it does operate at the level of the collective. Both Heidegger and Berry are thinking beyond individual striving. With Heidegger, the "we" who question must become a people. For Berry, only "we" can undertake the Great Work. Similarly, for Unger, "we" have to retrieve the conflict over the basic terms of social life from the specialized disciplines and bring it back, transformed, to the larger life of society. For Camus, in the Introduction, the beginning of a hope was for French society and maybe the West.

And, of course, for this book, the aim is achieving health in American public life.

How can questioning apply to this larger scale? Questioning is always a small-scale activity. Questioning does not itself apply to the larger scale. Its effects do.

In his classic work, *Insight*, Lonergan developed a concept to translate healthy thought in a society mired in decline into renewal. He called it "cosmopolis."

Mark Miller, an interpreter of Lonergan in *The Quest for God and the Good Life*, describes cosmopolis as a kind of loose community. In terms of what we humans can do in a time of decline, Mark Miller notes Lonergan's reference to a "perhaps not numerous center" neither on the Right nor on the Left: "a redemptive community that would motivate people on a *cultural* level instead of attempting through economics or politics to impose new social structures."[6]

Contesting decline requires a response at the level of the human heart and mind. The need is to promote liberty and thus create an atmosphere that supports unbiased reflection. Renewal of a culture in decline in order to achieve this happens through the very activity of practicing liberty and thought. Or, perhaps it would be better to say here, liberty in thought—that is, questioning.

Lonergan used the term cosmopolis to describe the loosely organized, or maybe not organized, "social unit" that operates at the level of culture to reverse the cycle of decline and to promote renewal.

Miller explains that cosmopolis "is not one group that defines itself in opposition to other groups, nor is it a formal institution with enrolled members, a superstate ruling states, an academy endorsing ideas or a legal code." It is you and me, promoting, by our example of unbiased thinking, social change in the culture.

Lonergan writes that cosmopolis

is neither class nor state, that stands above all their claims, that cuts them down to size, that is founded on the native detachment and disinterestedness of every

---

[6] MARK MILLER, THE QUEST FOR GOD AND THE GOOD LIFE 177–78 (2013).

intelligence, that commands man's first allegiance, that is too universal to be bribed, too impalpable to be forced, too effective to be ignored. . . . Cosmopolis is above all politics. . . . So far from employing power or pressure or force, it has to witness to the possibility of ideas being operative without such backing. Unless it can provide that witness, then it is useless. . . . It is a dimension of consciousness.[7]

In 2017, the Duquesne University School of Law hosted a symposium entitled "Resurrecting Truth in American Law and Public Discourse." At that symposium, I talked about cosmopolis and our need for it. One of the participants said to me afterward that we had, as a group, created cosmopolis for a time in the symposium itself. All of us there, including the people in the audience, trying to understand how we had fallen into the state we were in, were practicing cultural renewal through reflection. While there was some political carping, we were not there blaming anyone. We were searching.

I hope that this book will be viewed as an outgrowth of cosmopolis. Even a recruiting brochure.

That is the point: recruitment, even though Lonergan warns that cosmopolis does not actually enroll members. The reader who finds in Lonergan's question about the universe a helpful starting point for questioning will be a part of cosmopolis, practicing cultural renewal. It is the old quote attributed to Gandhi— "Be the change you want to see." Reflection is promoted by practicing it. So is mutually beneficial exchange.

How Do We Ask Lonergan's Question?

In the formulation above, Lonergan begins with the concept of the "worth while." Questioning inevitably proceeds from the assumption that the "worth while" is real, is ultimate. It is from this perspective that human beings judge progress and decline. Some things are more worth while than are others.

As we will see in the next chapter, those who answer Lonergan's question with a *no* do not generally disagree with him here. They agree that human beings assume that there is ultimacy, assume that progress and decline are objective categories, and assume that we should seek progress.

Lonergan then asks whether, in these orientations, the universe is on our side, or if, instead, we are fools to struggle for authenticity and progress when decline is inevitable.

---

[7]   BERNARD LONERGAN, INSIGHT: A STUDY OF HUMAN UNDERSTANDING 238–41 (1957).

The persons who conclude that the universe is not on our side, like Joseph Carter asserting that the universe doesn't care about our purpose, are simply saying, in Lonergan's terms, that we are fools. If that sounds harsh, then let us say that we are foolish to believe these things.

The point is, though, that all this is within Lonergan's question.

Lonergan goes on to suggest that if the universe is on our side, then progress is real, values are real, and the universe is moral, that is akin to us as moral beings. It would then be the case that the universe and we, in the words of a character in E. L. Doctorow's novel *City of God*, "live in moral consequence."

We can reformulate Lonergan's question along the following lines. Is the universe like us in pursuing moral goals and purposes in its natural processes or is the universe merely a collection of forces and matter that may behave in predictable ways, but is ultimately meaningless? We are asking whether the universe is intelligible, has a direction, and contains a place for our participation. Or, more directly, "Is there a point to all this?"

That is what we need to know. These are the crucial issues for us.

Therefore, questioning along these lines, whatever the answer, is a rational, genuine endeavor for human beings.

Finally, Lonergan asserts that there are likely to be consequences in our lives in answering *yes* or *no*. That means we are to actually answer the question.

There is nothing in this questioning that presupposes or requires the supernatural. The question is not religious in that sense. Thus, the question is open to every person. In fact, the question inevitably arises. And part of the questioning will include the question of what counts as evidence. Lonergan is definitely seeking evidence. His question is not a stance or based on a presumption.

The person who refuses to allow Lonergan's question to arise, his "contemporary humanist," is evading the question through what we call in law an "irrebuttable presumption"—that the universe just cannot be on our side. Such a person does not even want to answer *no*.

The reason for that must be a desire to avoid the consequences of living in accordance with the *no*. I will return to that hesitance in the next section.

What then will count as evidence one way or the other about the universe and us? Certainly, the direction of history, if any. And the same about evolution. We will judge different paths of human life and whether there are better and worse ways to live. We will ask about the adequacy of materialism to account for and explain the universe and human experience. We will ask about the senses as the only reliable source of knowledge.

And we will ask about much else as we look at the thinkers who have engaged Lonergan's question or help us to do so.

A question deepens in the questioning. That is why questioning is rational, healthful, and satisfying. That is why it is self-authenticating—why it is a path to restoring faith, wherever the question leads.

Living by Our Answers

An ultimate question can only be answered provisionally and partially. We must be alert not to cement ourselves into a viewpoint.

Yet, we do come to answers. And these answers have consequences.

It is not clear to me why Lonergan writes that "our attitude and resoluteness may be profoundly affected by the answers." It seems to me that they *must* be so affected. What could be more important to our lives than the question of whether the universe is on our side?

Lonergan presumably meant that many of the people who ask about the universe are not actually putting themselves at risk. Therefore, their answers may not affect them very much. But, in the terms of this book, people like that are not really asking the question.

Real questioning means that I am willing to abide by the answer, notwithstanding how provisional and partial my answer may be. That means, for example, that if the universe is not on our side, I have to give up any unsubstantiated confidence in the future. It also means that if the answer is *yes*, I have to stop invoking casual nihilism and stop using the language of "my truth" and "your truth." Either way, I have to be willing to change my life.

These are high stakes. That is undoubtedly why the "contemporary humanist"—a title Lonergan is not using to indict the humanities—refuses "to allow the question to arise." This humanist is unwilling to live straightforwardly, like the atheist, with the answer *no*. The humanist is even unwilling to live with the uncertainty of inconclusive results, like the agnostic. Lonergan's humanist suppresses the question that is every human being's question for fear of any demand to change one's life.

That is the person we must not be.

The difference between the atheists and agnostics, on the one hand, and the humanist on the other—remembering that this appears to be a type of person, not a challenge to humanism itself—is the difference between Chapters 4 and 5 above. Honest questioning will not necessarily bring back faith in everything. So it is not necessarily a solution for the crisis in Chapter 4—"Faithless American Public Life." That depends on what our questioning reveals.

But honest questioning will resolve, by itself, the crisis described in Chapter 5, "The Age of Evasion." In the age of evasion, society is not serious. Once we begin asking Lonergan's question—really asking, so that the answer will matter—we will be a serious people. The Age of Evasion will then be over. That much we already know. We will not be cured, but we will be on the road to recovery.

7

No, the Universe Is Not on Our Side

In the previous chapter, I tried to show that asking Bernard Lonergan's question, "Is the universe on our side?," by itself, would begin the process of healing America's public life. In the next three chapters, we will see that answering the question, whatever the answer, moves that process of healing far along.

So, even the *no*, if thoughtfully pursued, could be a path to renewal of American public life. That is what I hope to show in this chapter.

Can I Be Fair to the No?

As the reader is already aware, my answer to Lonergan's question is *yes*, the universe is on our side. That is the title of this book. So, can my treatment here possibly be fair?

I acknowledge the likelihood that a more thoughtful and complete presentation both of the case for the negative answer and for its potential to renew American public life can and will be given by someone more sympathetic to it. The reason that I pursued the matter in this chapter is that many people will, at the very least, assume that the answer to Lonergan's question has to be *no*, even if further reflection might lead in a different direction. Therefore, if my goal is to begin to return American public life to health, it is necessary to show that even the negative answer will improve matters.

So, let us begin with the clear goal in mind to present the best possible form of American public life that can arise from the determination that the universe is not on our side. I will give counter illustrations about whether the universe is on our side in the next chapter.

Carl Sagan's Magnificent Gesture

Readers may be familiar with the "Pale Blue Dot" episode in Carl Sagan's original *Cosmos* series, which was repeated in the last episode of the 2014 remake of the series by Neil deGrasse Tyson.

In that final episode, Tyson reframed Carl Sagan's "pale blue dot" monologue from the first *Cosmos* series. Sagan had asked NASA to take one last picture of

The Universe Is on Our Side. Bruce Ledewitz, Oxford University Press. © Oxford University Press 2022.
DOI: 10.1093/oso/9780197563939.003.0008

Earth as the *Voyager 1* spacecraft passed Neptune. On February 14, 1990, just 34 minutes before *Voyager 1* powered off its cameras forever, a picture of Earth was taken, 3.7 billion miles away from the sun.

The viewer sees Earth fading to what Sagan calls the "pale blue dot." The following is part of Sagan's original commentary, played anew, as the audience watches:

> Our posturings, our imagined self-importance, the delusion that we have some privileged position in the Universe, are challenged by this point of pale light. Our planet is a lonely speck in the great enveloping cosmic dark. In our obscurity, in all this vastness, there is no hint that help will come from elsewhere to save us from ourselves.

In Sagan's 1994 book *Pale Blue Dot*, which was inspired by the photograph, he added to his commentary:

> Consider again that dot. That's here, that's home, that's us. On it everyone you love, everyone you know, everyone you ever heard of, every human being who ever was, lived out their lives. . . .
>
>   It has been said that astronomy is a humbling and character-building experience. There is perhaps no better demonstration of the folly of human conceits than this distant image of our tiny world. To me, it underscores our responsibility to deal more kindly with one another, and to preserve and cherish the pale blue dot, the only home we've ever known.[1]

Sagan was not consistent in answering *no* to Lonergan's question. In fact, in one famous instance, he gave what sounded like a resounding *yes* as his answer, referring to human beings as "a way for the cosmos to know itself."[2]

But Sagan's point with the pale blue dot photograph absolutely comes to us out of the *no*. We are alone in the vastness of space. Nothing in the universe will help us. We are on our own.

That status could be depressing. It should be terrifying. But Sagan also hopes that it will be softening. That is, since we are alone, we should be kind to each other.

This is the unexpected potential of the *no* to renew public life.

Matters may not go in that direction. Nietzsche had a similar vision, with a very different conclusion. Sagan presumably never read how Nietzsche also

---

[1]   CARL SAGAN, PALE BLUE DOT: A VISION OF THE HUMAN FUTURE IN SPACE 6–7 (1994).

[2]   Jonathan Cott, *The Cosmos: An Interview with Carl Sagan*, ROLLING STONE (Dec. 25, 1980), http://www.rollingstone.com/culture/features/the-cosmos-19801225 [https://perma.cc/67BM-T5T2].

described our cosmic aloneness. If he had, Sagan would have heard his own words with a far different resonance:

> In some remote corner of the universe, poured out and glittering in innumerable solar systems, there once was a star on which clever animals invented knowledge. That was the highest and most mendacious minute of "world history"—yet only a minute. After nature had drawn a few breaths the star grew cold, and the clever animals had to die.[3]

So, there is no guarantee about the *no*. In this chapter, we will search for its most generous possibilities, all the while understanding that despair is also a potential result if the universe is not on our side.

The Case for the No

It is not at all difficult to make the case for the *no*. We begin with the simple fact of death. In the Introduction, I quoted Sam Harris's observation that the universe sustains only to devour us. How could we regard such a universe as on our side?

Furthermore, not only do we die, but all those we love die. This is the point that the fictional detective Ulf Varg was making in Chapter 3, in describing life as a matter of regret.

One of the best-known examples of considering death as the ultimate betrayal is Peter Berger in the book, *A Rumor of Angels*. Berger describes a poignant scene from everyday childhood:

> A child wakes up in the night, perhaps from a bad dream, and finds himself surrounded by darkness, alone, beset by nameless threats. At such a moment the counters of trusted reality are blurred or invisible, and in the terror of incipient chaos the child cries out for his mother. It is hardly an exaggeration to say that, at this moment, the mother is being invoked as a high priestess of protective order. It is she (and, in many cases, she alone) who has the power to banish the chaos and to restore the benign shape of the world. And, of course, any good mother will do just that.... She will speak or sing to the child, and the content of this communication will invariably be the same—"Don't be afraid—everything is in order, everything is all right."

---

[3] Frederich Nietzsche, *On Truth and Lie in an Extra-Moral Sense*, OREGON STATE UNIVERSITY, http://oregonstate.edu/instruct/phl201/modules/Philosophers/Nietzsche/Truth_and_Lie_in_an_Extra-Moral_Sense.htm.

Berger then asks, "*Is the mother lying to the child?*"[4] Berger's conclusion is that if reality is entirely natural, so that the child will simply die, then the mother's statement is a lie. Everything is not in order. Everything is not all right. In the end, in the face of death, the child will once again find himself "in darkness, alone with the night," just as he had been many years before when he called to his mother for reassurance.

If this is the situation, says Berger, as it must be outside a traditional religious worldview, then we cannot trust reality. In Lonergan's terms, Berger is saying the universe is not on our side.

Nor is it just human beings who die. According to the popular understanding of entropy, the universe will move toward a state of inert uniformity over time, toward death and disorder. Whatever the details of its final state, it is not one in which human beings, or any form of life we can image, have an ultimate future.

So, even if human beings could somehow outlast the natural cycle of our sun, in which solar radiation will increase over time so that in one billion years, the oceans will evaporate and life will presumably end on Earth (if it has not before then), humanity is eventually doomed. Everything ends, including the universe.

Thus, the universe cannot be thought to be on our side indefinitely.

Then there is the narrower threat we face from the universe. In the relatively recent past, the Earth has been subject both to catastrophic impact events, such as asteroid hits, and longer-term disasters, such as ice ages. There are scientists who consider one or the other of these events to be inevitable at some point, despite the effects of climate change in raising global temperatures. Obviously, either event, considering its magnitude, would destroy human civilization.

In terms of the *no*, the point is not whether such events will happen, but the appreciation that there is nothing in the universe to prevent them. In terms of the scientific understanding of the universe, their occurrence is just a matter of chance—a wobble in the orbits of either a celestial object, in the case of an asteroid, or of our own planet, in the case of an ice age. Even if climate change and agricultural development over the past 5,000 years have permanently staved off the next ice age, as some scientists believe, we do not have the universe to thank for that.

Most of us believe that these events just cannot happen now, even though they have happened in the past. That is magical thinking, which is really just a relic of an earlier supernatural orientation. God could protect us from such events, but the natural universe will not. So, again, how can the universe be said to be on our side?

---

[4]   Peter Berger, A Rumor of Angels: Modern Society and the Rediscovery of the Supernatural 54–55 (1970) (italics in original).

Of course, nature is also threatening in terms of individual lives. Because nature is dynamic, humans face constant threats. The novel coronavirus of 2020, which killed half a million people worldwide by June 2020, was obviously one dramatic example. But there are many diseases that threaten us. And the next pandemic could be much worse.

We also face unpredictable natural harms on a regular basis. These disasters, including hurricanes and volcanic eruptions, do not threaten civilization as a whole, but they devastate and end individual human lives.

The same thing is true of things like birth defects. How can a nature that distributes such terrible effects, more or less at random, be considered on our side?

The cosmic story is part of the question of history. I have previously adverted to Martin Luther King Jr.'s inspiring formulation that the arc of the moral universe is long, but it bends toward justice. With this faith, legions of Americans courageously pursued racial justice during his lifetime.

But the philosopher John Gray, who belongs in the pantheon of thinkers of the *no*, asks in a review of the book *The Evolution of Moral Progress* why its authors should "believe anything like an 'arc of the moral universe'" exists? Gray points out that human societies can improve, but the ancient Greeks, for example, thought that any such improvement would inevitably be followed by decline. Perhaps history is cyclical, with "periods of civilization and barbarism and long periods of drift."[5]

No one denies that there has been material progress among human societies over time as scientific knowledge has increased. Poverty has been reduced. Large-scale famine is rare. People live longer, healthier lives in large part. All that is welcome, but it is not really a movement toward justice.

Furthermore, that same increase in human productive power rendered the 20th century uniquely bloody. Human beings were not previously technically capable of creating an Auschwitz or obliterating a Hiroshima.

A long period of recent history took the forms of colonialism and communism, both of which reduced large portions of the human race to forms of servitude. There is not much evidence there of an arc toward justice.

We are today in a better situation in terms of planetary governance than we have been in most of human history. But progress toward the recognition of human rights and the establishment of democracy, as well as the decline of international lawlessness, have stalled recently, and there is no guarantee that movement in those directions will continue. The Pax Americana is clearly ending.

[5] John Gray, *Getting Better All the Time*, NEW YORK REVIEW OF BOOKS (Dec. 19, 2019), https://www.nybooks.com/articles/2019/12/19/evolution-moral-progress-getting-better-all-the-time/.

At the same time, human beings are grossly harming life on the planet through extinctions and climate change, which is also a part of the arc of the moral universe and certainly does not seem to be bending toward justice.

And even calling history cyclical may be giving history more of a shape than is warranted. The author Ta-Nahesi Coates says the arc of history bends toward "chaos . . . that there is no order, there is no arc, that we are night travelers on a great tundra, that stars can't guide us."[6]

America does not believe in Dr. King's arc anymore, which is part of the lack of faith that I discussed in Chapter 4. When President Obama subtly changed King's formulation, stating that the "arc of the universe may bend toward justice, but it doesn't bend on its own," he was casting doubt on our relationship to the universe. If we human beings do the bending, the universe does not seem to have anything to do with it.

And even if it were so that there is an arc toward justice, and even if it were built into the fiber of the universe, would it be worth it? What about the millions of people who suffered under the slave trade before it was abolished? There is no justice for them in any natural understanding of the universe. So, how can we say that the universe is on our side when it operates in such a brutal fashion, even when it does bend toward justice?

Then there is the question of what justice is. The fact that Dr. King was talking about racism probably gives a false feeling of clarity around the nature of justice. What is justice for us today? Are we moving toward a greater individualism? More or less of an unregulated market? A renewal of the social welfare state? Toward socialism? All of these are possible futures for us. None of them has a total claim on justice.

In his review above, Gray was particularly lambasting arguments that give an evolutionary spin to moral progress, which was the topic of Allen Buchanan's and Russell Powell's book. This kind of evolutionary orientation, Gray points out, has been utilized in the past to justify collectivism, capitalism, scientism, racism, and all sorts of other views that presumably Buchanan and Powell would contemplate with horror. Gray says that in all such arguments, the universe inevitably ends up supporting whatever terminus the author happens to favor.

Far better, Gray argues, to follow the wisdom of T. H. Huxley, who, though he defended Darwin's theory of natural selection—Huxley was called Darwin's bulldog—also protested against identifying morality with anything in nature. In his famous 1893 lecture, "Evolution and Ethics," Huxley pointed out that the "thief and the murderer follow nature just as much as the philanthropist" and

---

[6] Ta-Nehisi Coates, *The Myth of Western Civilization*, ATLANTIC (Dec. 21, 2013), https://www.theatlantic.com/international/archive/2013/12/the-myth-of-western-civilization/282704/.

concluded that "ethical progress . . . depends, not on imitating the cosmic process, still less in running away from it, but in combating it."

So, not only is nature not on our side, nature may be our opponent in bringing about a better world.

Philip Kitcher, whom I discussed earlier, warned about the effect on humanity of living in a universe without God. But in his book *Living with Darwin*, Kitcher also made a narrower point—that evolution proceeds in such random and cruel ways that no one could believe that a beneficent God would have utilized it.

This is, of course, an argument against the existence of God. But it is also an argument against imagining that the universe is on our side. In Kitcher's view, it is cruel out there and we must not think of the universe as a friend.

There is another biological sense in which the universe is not on our side. Our natural tools, language, and the brain more generally, are quite imperfect. They lead us into both error and misunderstanding. Insofar as these capacities have evolved naturally, they have inculcated flaws that hinder us. Again, natural processes are not helping us.

There is also a sense in which we simply cannot consider the universe to be on our side. If we follow the tenets of materialism, with its atoms that are like billiard balls moving us around, there is no way for the universe to be on our side. The universe is just not the kind of entity that can be said to be on a side.

It is telling that Lonergan, in his question, moves from the universe being on our side in the sense of progress, to "intelligent ground" and "moral consciousness." For Lonergan, the universe cannot really be on our side unless it is the kind of entity that is "cognate to us as moral beings." You cannot get that in a materialist ontology—that is, an understanding of what is real that is purely material.

It is certainly true that the New Atheists mainly exhibited a simplistic view of materialism, as do most people. We are learning differently about matter. Those billiard ball-like atoms trail away into subatomic particles and end up in the weird probabilistic wave functions of quantum theory. Materialism isn't what it used to be.

But the fact that mechanistic materialism fails as an understanding of the universe does not necessarily support viewing the universe as on our side. For Albert Einstein, quantum theory made the alien quality of the universe worse. Einstein had a kind of theistic hangover in which, for him, there had to be an intelligence behind the universe. Einstein referred to this intelligence as Der Alte, "the old one," probably not a personal God, as Einstein later explained.[7] Some interpretations of quantum theory struck him as too random to function as a

---

[7] Kelly Dickerson, *One of Einstein's Most Famous Quotes Is Often Completely Misinterpreted*, BUSINESS INSIDER (Nov. 19, 2015), https://www.businessinsider.com/god-does-not-play-dice-quote-meaning-2015-11.

proper basis for reality. In a 1926 letter to Max Born, one of the progenitors of quantum theory, Einstein wrote, "Quantum theory yields much, but it hardly brings us close to the Old One's secrets. I, in any case, am convinced He does not play dice with the universe."[8]

Einstein's hostility strongly suggests that the end of mechanistic materialism will not necessarily bring us closer to a universe that is on our side.

And how would we know about the quality of such a universe even if it were on our side? Materialism as an ontology is half of the problem. But the other half is our commitment to sensation—the senses amplified by science—as the only basis for knowledge. If the universe is an entity cognate to us as moral beings, we might not be able to learn about it and know it. That would prevent us from embracing the universe as on our side.

The case for the *no* could easily go on forever. The reader can probably fill in other bases for thinking that the universe is not on our side.

I will conclude this short section with the phenomenon that so depressed Arthur Leff in his poem, set forth in Chapter 4: the inability to establish reliable grounds, outside of God, for values and judgments.

Leff began his poem, "As things now stand"—the word *now* signifying after the Death of God—"everything is up for grabs." There are two senses in which there are no binding standards. First, of course, we cannot agree on standards and values. This is obviously the case cross-culturally—cultures in which, for example, the worth of women is valued less than the worth of men—but it is also the case within our own culture, over the issue of abortion, most prominently. Who's to say who is right? As Leff puts it, "Sez who?"

The other sense of no binding standards is that even if we could agree on values, a foundation of mere agreement is not ultimately worthwhile in Lonergan's sense. Such agreement could be viewed as just a convention. The fact that human beings agree about something does not make the subject of that agreement ultimately right. This is obvious in the case of physical conditions—we might all believe there is water under the surface of Mars, but that does not mean there is such water. The same is true of values.

The reason everything is up for grabs is that, in Leff's understanding, the universe has not provided standards and measures for judgment. God did that, but without God, the universe does not and therefore is not on our side.

This leads Leff to anguish. He concludes, "God help us," all the while knowing that there is no longer a God to help us. This is a plea for help, in which no help is expected.

---

[8] Elisabetta Canetta, *Physics and Beyond: "God Does Not Play Dice": What Did Einstein Mean?*, St. Mary's University (Sept. 1, 2014), https://www.stmarys.ac.uk/news/2014/09/physics-beyond-god-play-dice-einstein-mean/.

What are we to make of this all-too-human cry for help in finding meaning, truth, value, ultimacy, and all the rest? You might imagine that this anguish is an indication that there is something present in the universe that calls forth these feelings in us. Perhaps Leff is resonating to something real, if only in his longing.

But even this glimmer of cosmic hope must be extinguished in the case for the *no*. This feeling that Joseph Carter identified in Chapter 4—the human need for sustaining and real purpose—is not connected to the universe. How or why this human need arose is not entirely clear. Any evolutionary response in that regard is fanciful. It could have been an accident, or it could be something that arises when brains get really big. We will never know. But the universe does not share in it. The universe is not a moral being like us.

Accepting the No

The point of this chapter is the renewal of American public life in the world of the *no*. This was Carter's goal, too. The Universe doesn't care about your purpose, but you do. And you care as well for the purposes of all those around you. And they care for your purposes and life. Carter was trying to get us to see that this reality need not lead to Leff's despair—just as Sagan tried to show that in the pale blue dot.

This is Simon Critchley's point as well in his book, *The Faith of the Faithless*. Critchley begins his book with Oscar Wilde's observation that "everything to be true must become a religion." Critchley says that "true" here is not logic or empiricism. And it cannot mean being in accordance with anything outside the self—not with divine commands and not with transcendent norms.

Nevertheless, Critchley says we can live truly—that is, faithfully. We can be true to our beliefs. If we do this, we will experience fidelity.

Critchley concedes that this is "seemingly contradictory," but he believes in the possibility of such a faith for the faithless—or in our terms, for those who do not have God and know the universe is not on our side.

Critchley would say to Leff, "Why don't you give it a try?"

And this was also Hilary Putnam's response to Richard Rorty. Just because we do not have metaphysical realism, we do not have to go all the way to breaking the connection of language to nature and breaking with all conceptions of reliability and truth.

Or, as Ludwig Wittgenstein might have put it, we can go on.

Lawyers go on. In *Law's Quandary*, Steve Smith calls law's quandary the gap between the traditional understanding of law that justice is real, on the one hand, and our ontology, which, as reflected above, has no place for objective norms.

But it need not be a quandary, in the sense of a difficulty. It just may be the way that we lawyers go on. Leff felt he could not go on, but he was unwilling to put the matter to the test. That feeling he had in the poem that the villains of history were really evil is not one that many persons would contest. That conclusion will certainly do as a working hypothesis, at least for going on.

We should not assume the worst. We should not assume that human civilization is incompatible with the *no*. In the spirit, if not the letter, of American pragmatism and the experimentalism of John Dewey, we should give civilization a try, even in the *no*.

Our model should be Julia Roberts's character Vivian Ward, in the movie *Pretty Woman*. Told by Richard Gere's character, the rich Edward Lewis, that Ward's gig as an escort participating in unimaginable material luxury would not be permanent—"Vivian, I will let you go"—Ward responds, aloud, but to herself, "But I'm here now."

We're here now.

What the No *Does Not Say*

The *no* tells us that the universe is not on our side. Progress is not guaranteed. In fact, decline may be inevitable, just as Lonergan described—an "ever mounting welter."

But here are some items that are also the case in the *no*.

We are adapted to life on this planet in this solar system, as a part of this universe. That universe may not be looking out for us, but it is also not hostile. We evolved here and we belong here.

Therefore, there is no reason to believe that it is impossible for us to live satisfying lives on the terms that this universe gives us.

That is what Daniel Quinn means in *Ishmael* when he has the gorilla teacher ask the student if there is any reason why, if sharks, tarantulas, and rattlesnakes can live harmlessly in the world, human beings cannot as well.

The universe may not be on our side, but neither are we out of step with it. At least not inherently.

Similarly, although the universe may be completely neutral with regard to our existence and our future, there is no reason that we cannot learn as a species what works for us and what does not.

Of course, we are learning that and we have been learning that all along.

So, communism did not work very well. The insane militarism and racism of the Third Reich brought only misery to its own people. The findings of science have proved fairly reliable. In these realms, and many others, humans have reached some pretty settled consensuses.

These conclusions are not merely conventional or arbitrary—we have learned from experience. On the other hand, these judgments are not ultimate. They are certainly subject to revision. The point is, though, that we can learn that some things work and some things do not work.

Does this observation extend to morality?

I believe it is fair to say that humanity has learned, in the sense of real knowledge, that chattel slavery was morally wrong. That is not inconsistent with Dallas Willard's view that moral knowledge, in the sense of its public presentation, has disappeared.

People who say that human trafficking continues slavery in another form are mistaking criminality for ignorance. People do not commit organized crimes for profit because they lack knowledge that what they are doing is wrong. Such criminals are not confused relativists. They commit their crimes knowing that they are wrong but preferring their self-interest to the welfare of others.

The conclusion that the end of slavery taught us something does not imply that history has a shape. It only means that sometimes humanity does learn. We don't need the universe to be on our side for that to be true.

Nor does a neutral universe condemn us to solipsism. It is more reasonable than not to assume that there is an outside world, that our knowledge about that outside world is often reliable and that our language about that outside world can be closer or farther away from the way that world actually is. This may be an area in which sophisticated philosophical doubts are just not worth it.

Finally, the absence of a universe that is on our side need not undermine all of our attempts at reason. The fear of unbridled subjectivity may be another exaggeration. While we certainly can fool ourselves, we can also be a check on ourselves. That is a strength of democracy, an issue to which I will return below.

In addition, just as in science, where nature can often serve as a corrective to runaway speculation, reality can serve the same function in public life. There are good policies and bad policies and eventually we find out which is which. And we can reason about that.

In the *no*, we don't have God. We don't even have a universe on our side. But we have something.

Voices in the No

There are a number of thinkers who can help us interpret the *no* in a way that allows for a renewal of public life. They do not necessarily answer Lonergan's question themselves. The following list of figures is not meant to be exhaustive, but representative. Here I will just give the basic outline of aspects of their thought relevant to the *no*.

First, we should note the potential of the *no* for genuine liberation. The philosopher Gilles Deleuze is definitely one of the freeing, and not despairing, voices in the pantheon of the *no*. Interpreting Deleuze is beyond the scope of this book. But in Todd May's interpretation of Deleuze, the absence of authority, even from a universe that could be said to be on our side, is a matter of liberation. We don't want ontology to dictate the possibilities of existence. In the *no*, we are free to investigate how human beings might live.

Deleuze's famous formulation that "behind everything is difference and behind difference there is nothing," means that when I face an oppressive social/economic/political context, and am told that it is inevitable because of some limit or other, I can now understand that such unjust arrangements are just part of the swirling difference and are in no sense inevitable.

Michael Shermer is a good example of a kind of faith in humanity that points directly opposite to the despair evidenced by Arthur Leff. In *The Moral Arc*, Shermer plays off the resonance of Dr. King's saying about history but does so without metaphysical foundations. The subtitle of the book telegraphs Shermer's position: *How Science and Reason Lead Humanity Toward Truth, Justice, and Freedom.*

Shermer does not really disagree with anything in Leff's poem. Everything is up for grabs in an ultimate sense. But, unlike Leff, Shermer concludes that, generally, human beings over time choose pretty well. And, insofar as we listen to science and choose reason as our foundation, we will continue to do pretty well.

Shermer agrees with Dr. King, in what could be called an empirical sense, that the arc of history bends toward justice, just not metaphysically. History can move away from justice, and does, when humans are in a period of unreason.

Shermer has some similarity to Sam Harris, except that Shermer does not share the depth of Harris's hostility to religion and does not seem to agree that science can determine our values. For Shermer, we use scientifically informed concepts in thinking our way to the meaning of truth, justice, and freedom, but these concepts remain in the arena of moral theory.

Anthony Kronman's 2016 book *Confessions of a Born-Again Pagan* attempts to set forth exactly what would seem to be needed to renew American public life under the *no*. His goal is to keep the good of the Christian faith in this post-Christian time. That good is our modern ideal of the "infinite value of every individual in the world."[9] But Kronman's paganism aims to do this while being at home in the world and not alienated from it. Kronman interprets the bad fruit of Christianity, including secularized versions of Christianity that also emphasize human autonomy and separation from the world, to have led to our homelessness and disenchantment.

---

[9] ANTHONY KRONMAN, CONFESSIONS OF A BORN-AGAIN PAGAN 24 (2016).

Kronman turns to the poet Walt Whitman as the embodiment of democratic faith in which God and the world are one, including "the uniqueness of every individual."[10] In this way, genuine diversity is maintained and the intelligibility of the world, far from a threat, becomes the bright promise of science, art, and politics.

The full political implications of Kronman's liberal paganism are not entirely clear. He certainly keeps the main parts of modern conceptions of freedom and liberty.

I am not certain that Kronman really belongs to the world of the *no*. I put him here because of his opposition to the Christian tradition and because Kronman's world is too much a part of us, and we of it, to be thought of in terms of being on our side or not. As the reader will see, in this sense Kronman shares some similarities with the thought of Alfred North Whitehead, who preeminently represents the *yes* in the next chapter.

The thinker who has thought in the most organized fashion about the implications of the Death of God for public life is John Gray. His book *Seven Types of Atheism* might even be thought of as a handbook to the potential of the world of the *no*.

Simon Critchley's thumbnail sketch of Gray's thought locates him perfectly: human beings are "killer apes . . . with metaphysical longing."[11] This longing makes us dangerous. Critchley quotes Gray from his book, *Black Mass*: "Nothing is more human than the readiness to kill and die in order to secure a meaning for life."[12]

This longing is delusional. There is no human action that can bring such meaning, which is why Gray is a thinker of the *no*.

Gray makes clear in *Seven Types of Atheism* that most forms of atheism today are just secularized versions of Christian thought. The zeal of the New Atheists to displace religion is a form of anti-religious religion. Other forms of atheism seek to replace God with surrogates, such as secular humanism, scientific rationalism, and political crusades. All of these retain forms of Christian thought in the categories of progress, universal values, and human exceptionalism.

According to Gray, the way to avoid the violence endemic to human beings is to renounce the search for meaning, and to practice forms of contemplation instead. There are types of atheism that move in this direction. One form, which Gray associates with George Santayana, is a practice of a kind of mystical materialism—"a transient awareness flaring up in matter itself." Again, there is here more than a little similarity to the process philosophy of Whitehead.

---

[10] *Id.* at 1025.

[11] SIMON CRITCHLEY, THE FAITH OF THE FAITHLESS: EXPERIMENTS IN POLITICAL THEOLOGY 109 (2012).

[12] JOHN GRAY, BLACK MASS 186 (2007).

The other atheism that moves in the contemplative direction Gray calls the "atheism of silence," which he associates with Arthur Schopenhauer. Schopenhauer viewed the nature of things as ineffable, which is perhaps also the case with Santayana, whom Gray describes as rejecting Spinoza's "belief that the world must be finally intelligible."

Finally, there is Peter Sloterdijk, a contemporary giant of continental thought. Sloterdijk's thought is much too overwhelming to summarize. But he does point to the *no* precisely in the Death of God: "If there is no transcendent god who confers shape and stands in solidarity with human beings, if this god has nothing in particular planned for us, then the world in and from which we exist is a hypermonstrosity that takes time and space for the display of its creations . . . an unstructured whole."[13] According to Marc Jongen, the monstrous for Sloterdijk "is unbounded, unconstituted, something that can no longer be located."[14]

The process of secularization, says Sloterdijk, "is the revelation of that monstrosity that leads to success and catastrophe, that endows and consumes us."

Sloterdijk sees in the pragmatism of William James a "shelter" for "individuals from the disturbance that must result from the revelation of the fullness of the world before mere human intellect." James's own word for this shelter is "chance." "Chance reconciles the individual with the monstrous by showing her where she should attempt anew to make the leap to success, even if she is surrounded by many failures."[15]

Sloterdijk's vision of the world is frightening. And yet, though differently from Wittgenstein, we can go on.

Public Life in the No

It might be assumed that there is, or should be, no concern for public life in the *no*, at least not in the political sense. That is certainly the view of John Gray: "Those who seek inner freedom do not care what kind of government they live under as long as it does not prevent them from turning within themselves."[16]

Gray's view is too individualistic for any sense of publicness. He does not simply relativize the political. He obliterates community.

---

[13] PETER SLOTERDIJK, AFTER GOD 215 (2020).
[14] Marc Jongen, *On Anthropospheres and Aphrogrammes, Peter Sloterdijk's Thought Images of the Monstrous*, HUMMA.MENTE J. OF PHIL. STUD. 199 (2011), http://www.humanamente.eu/PDF/Issue_18_Paper_Jongen.pdf.
[15] *Id.* at 225–26.
[16] JOHN GRAY, SOUL OF THE MARIONETTE: A SHORT INQUIRY INTO HUMAN FREEDOM 7 (2015).

So, although Gray may offer solace to some in the world of the *no*, he does not address the question of a healthier public life. Thus, we must leave Gray at this point. But he remains an option for individual seekers.

Both the Left and the Right today manifest Arthur Leff's despair at living in the *no*, without metaphysical foundation or values realism. They only differ in how they cope with this despair.

As I pointed out in Chapter 4 by reference to the *Casey* abortion case, the Left proceeds by an exaggerated deference to the wishes of the individual. That deference prevents any need for reasoning about moral issues, whether in abortion cases or same-sex marriage or related issues.

In terms of the Right, in the dissent in *Casey*, Justice Scalia actually repeated Leff's themes: there can be no reasoning in matters of value; it's all just a matter of opinion that we should vote on. You can hear Leff's lament that everything is up for grabs. Scalia also pointed out in his dissent that abortion practices, and for that matter acceptance of euthanasia, have differed over time and in various cultures.

This renunciation of rationality is the reason for the peculiar emphasis by Justice Scalia on not looking for purpose in interpretation, whether statutory or constitutional.

It is also the reason for textualism itself. For Justice Scalia, the fear is always subjectivity or, its equivalent in law, judgment. Interpretation solely through text, or through history in the case of the school of interpretation known as originalism, purports to avoid the need for reasoning.

The incapacity of American elites to defend reason and truth is a part of the general collapse of the foundations of Western democracy. It is part of the reason for the rise of authoritarianism.

But all of this is a misunderstanding of the implications of the *no*. It is the case in the *no* that the universe fails to provide reliable norms. But two things should be remembered.

First, the foundations of democracy have always been shaky. We should remember Winston Churchill's famous saying that "democracy is the worst form of government except all those other forms that have been tried from time to time." This is just as true in the *no*. There is absolutely no reason to think that any smaller or narrower human decision-making will be an improvement over democracy.

So, even if the universe is not on our side, democracy is still our best bet. For similar reasons, so is freedom of speech.

Second, as Randy Barnett convincingly demonstrates in his formulation of classic liberal/legal thought, *The Structure of Liberty*, natural law and natural rights can be derived through forms of if/then thinking, even without reliable normative foundations. Barnett introduces early in his book a parallel between natural law analysis and engineering: "*Given* the amount of force that gravity exerts on a building, *if* we want a building that will enable persons to live or work inside it, *then* we need to provide a foundation, walls, and roof of a certain strength."[17]

Similarly, given certain natural facts about human beings and the world we live in, if we want people to live together in peace and prosperity, then we should design our structures of governance in certain ways.

I am, of course, obscuring a lot of the difficulties. For example, which characteristics of human beings are malleable, what aspects of the world do we take into account, and how do structures of government work? And much else. But the basic idea is perfectly plain.

Even if we end up in permanent disagreement over proper ends, which I do not believe is actually the case, a lot of our arguments in public life are about means. We should be able to reason about them.

It should not be assumed that this form of natural law reasoning has an inherent conservative tendency. In *Ishmael*, Daniel Quinn utilized the very same kind of if/then thinking to derive a strong environmental ethic that he labeled in the book "the peace-keeping law."

So, it is simply not the case that everything is up for grabs. If we want certain ends for people, then we have to have certain kinds of laws and cannot have other types of laws. We already know that the forms of tyranny that Leff opposes are bad for people. If someone wants to contest that observation, then we can amass evidence and come to a conclusion.

The fact that there may be disagreements does not change this. As Barnett notes: "The mere existence of controversy does not render such principles nonexistent."

So, even if the universe is not on our side, it should still be possible to debate the norms that we want society to establish, with peace and prosperity certainly in the mix, and then very carefully to formulate the kinds of laws and structures that will tend to establish that type of society. Barnett's method does exactly that. He leaves out important matters, such as the social effects of private property, but no one conception will be perfect. The point is that political theory and reason can be employed even in the reign of the *no*.

But there is something deeper and more helpful at work here than even careful if/then thinking. In the Hart-Fuller debate about natural law in 1958, referenced in Chapter 4, Lon Fuller observed that it is easier to give reasons for a good result than for an evil one, "whatever standards of ultimate goodness there are."[18]

---

[17]   RANDY BARNETT, THE STRUCTURE OF LIBERTY: JUSTICE AND THE RULE OF LAW 4 (2d ed. 1998).
[18]   Lon L. Fuller, *Positivism and Fidelity to Law—A Reply to Professor Hart*, 71 HARV. L. REV. 630, 636 (1958).

To me, this is evidence that the universe is on our side. But that is not how Fuller put it. It could just be that giving reasons works this way. In other words, it could be so even in the world of the *no*. If that is the case, then we can have productive normative debate, and thus a healthy public life, even within a neutral universe.

The real problem in the world of the *no*, as Sloterdijk points out in his vivid way, is not the limit of reason, nor the objectivity of values, but the issue of motivation. As Sloterdijk writes, "Let's admit it: whoever is motivationally at the top has better chances of success. If Darwin had thought far enough, he would have spoken of the survival of the fittest believer."[19] The case for the *no* is dispiriting. The human hope for meaning is insurmountable, Gray's retreat to equanimity notwithstanding.

But here we can return to the wisdom of Carl Sagan and the pale blue dot. For Sagan, the fact that we are alone and adrift in the universe means that we should be kind to each other and to the planet.

Sagan's thought is similar to that expressed by Robert Harrison, reviewing a biography of the French intellectual Maurice Blanchot, who entirely accepted the *no*, but found it constitutive of human community:

> Blanchot believed that only by acknowledging the disaster that always already lurks in everyday human existence—disaster understood as the "necessary death" that precedes and awaits us in life, or as the endless movement of time that dissolves identity into difference—will we be able to found what he called an "unavowable community" whose members would relate to one another not as empowered citizens or egoic subjects but as fellow witnesses of a human condition predicated on disaster and impossibility. To bring some clarity to Blanchot on this crucial matter—I appreciate his reasons for wanting to resist such elucidations—I would say that only if and when human beings "reappropriate" their own mortality will they resolutely refuse to walk over the bodies of others to reach their own graves.[20]

In Harrison's view, as with Sagan, it is precisely the *no* that allows for human solidarity. We come together in suffering and death. When we recognize that this is what we have in common, we will have no reason to seek a precedence that cannot last or power that is only temporary.

But the *no* does not just bind us together in mutual compassion. Our mortality is more than tragedy. The *no* actually gives our lives meaning. This is the insight that Kronman voices at the end of his book. Speaking of human capacity,

---

[19]   SLOTERDIJK, *supra* note 13, at 223 (2020).

[20]   Robert Pogue Harrison, *The Nothing Beyond Nothing*, NEW YORK REVIEW OF BOOKS (Mar. 12, 2020), https://www.nybooks.com/articles/2020/03/12/maurice-blanchot-nothing-beyond-nothing/

he asserts that not only does death—the *no*—not rob us of meaning, it grants us our meaning:

> The meaning of everything that we do and experience with these powers is a function of the mortal limits within which we possess and enjoy them. If our mortality were somehow erased, the meaning of human life would vanish.
>
> In this sense, it is death that makes life wonderful.[21]

Surely the wonder, preciousness, and finitude of life are sufficient to found and sustain human civilization.

---

[21] KRONMAN, *supra* note 9, at 1068.

8

Yes, the Universe Is on Our Side

Before I can take up the *yes*, there are some preliminary matters to address.

The Danger of the Yes

Bernard Lonergan answered his own question with a resounding *yes*. But what did he mean by affirming that the universe is on our side? Patrick Byrne, director of the Lonergan Center at Boston College, summarized Lonergan's answer as follows: "The world of the natural sciences is intelligible and meaningful. . . . the totality of reality (being) is intrinsically and completely intelligible. . . . every event is purposeful and valuable. . . human striving is not at all in vain, but indeed a continuation of a dynamic, intelligible order which is the true and authentic implication of the modern natural science."[1]

For the moment, let us assume that when we interrogate the question, we come to similar positive conclusions. The first issue that must be addressed is whether such a *yes* is dangerous.

John Gray argues that the very idea of a normative order in the universe is a danger. He puts this argument in terms of religious thought in *Straw Dogs*, but the point can be generalized:

> The idea of "morality" as a set of laws has a biblical root. In the Old Testament, the good life means living according to God's will. But there is nothing that says that the laws given to the Jews apply universally. The idea that God's law applies equally to everyone is a Christian invention.
>
> The universal reach of Christianity is commonly thought an advance on Judaism. In fact it was a step backward. If there is one law binding on everyone, every way of life but one must be sinful.[2]

It is easy to see that Lonergan is not thinking in terms of something like laws of ethics in his answer about the universe, but of something closer to the

---

[1] LONERGAN WORKSHOP, VOLUME 24 2 (Fred Lawrence ed., 2013), https://lonerganresource.com/pdf/journals/Lonergan_Workshop_Vol_24.pdf.

[2] JOHN GRAY, STRAW DOGS: THOUGHTS ON HUMANS AND OTHER ANIMALS 90 (2003).

The Universe Is on Our Side. Bruce Ledewitz, Oxford University Press. © Oxford University Press 2022.
DOI: 10.1093/oso/9780197563939.003.0009

meaningfulness of intelligibility. But Lonergan does also specify that his question includes the matter of morality. He asks, is the universe "basically cognate to us as moral beings?"

That notion of morality could be enough to justify human violence because anything out of step with the universe would be wrongful. For Gray, any hint of universal standards, even the ideas of rationality and progress, can lead to bloodshed. Reason feels it must banish unreason. Progress is an enemy of the backward. As Gray puts it in *Black Mass*, "racial prejudice may be immemorial, but racism is a product of the Enlightenment."[3]

Gray's answer is to make no judgments. As Christopher Beha summarizes Gray's thought, there is no hierarchy of values, "there is just an endless variety of individual humans, going about fulfilling their wants and needs in much the same way as other animals do."[4]

This may sound Christ-like—judge not, that you not be judged—but it's not. People live in collectives and thus have to live together. Our needs and wants conflict. And there is that metaphysical longing, which somehow among all human needs, Gray is willing—indeed eager—to banish. That longing is expressed as a collective, not just a personal, push toward goodness. It would not be good for human beings to follow Gray's approach.

Gray is right, all the same, however, that the *yes* is dangerous. We always must keep that in mind. But that danger is not a good enough reason to live in the *no* or to refuse to ask Lonergan's question.

Religious Believers Already Know That the Universe Is on Our Side

Yes, they do. And as Alvin Plantinga suggests in *Where the Conflict Really Lies*, viewing something like Lonergan's question through the lens of faith is not going to be a matter of proof or argument. It is rational for the believer to perceive the presence of God, for example, in the ordering of biology without reference to something like "evidence." Plantinga calls this "design discourse."

But Plantinga does not mean that the religious believer, the Christian in this case, should not look at the universe and our relation to it. In fact, there is an obligation to look, and look closely. Referring to William Paley's argument about design in nature from the analogy of a watch, Plantinga considers what happens when we actually look at the watch:

---

[3] JOHN GRAY, BLACK MASS: APOCALYPTIC RELIGION AND THE DEATH OF UTOPIA 61 (2007).
[4] Christopher Beha, *The Myth of Progress*, NEW YORK REVIEW OF BOOKS (Feb. 21, 2019), https://www.nybooks.com/articles/2019/02/21/john-gray-atheism-myth-progress/.

The belief that a given object has been designed *is* a mental state-ascribing belief. If our other beliefs about minds, the mental of others, are formed in that basic way, it is not implausible to suppose that the same goes for this sort of belief. The idea would be, therefore, that when you are on that walk with Paley and encounter a watch, you don't make an *inference* to the thought that this object is designed; instead, upon examining the object, you form a belief in that immediate or basic way.[5]

Erkki V. R. Kojonen is right that, for Plantinga, "this arises in us as something like a perceptual belief."[6] The point is, though, that the belief that the object was designed is not a conclusion formed because it must be true, since God exists. The conclusion arises from an actual encounter with the object and thus with the universe. So, the believer should come along with the rest of us in asking Lonergan's question.

Don't Death and Destruction Give an Irrefutable No in Answer to the Question?

Lonergan is definitely not anticipating an afterlife or resurrection as an answer to his question, notwithstanding his own faith commitment. It is in that sense an entirely natural, rather than supernatural, inquiry. Thus, we die. The sun dies. The universe dies.

For many people, like Peter Berger, that would be the end of questioning. Obviously, then, the universe is not on our side.

Nothing so suggests the ambiguity of Anthony Kronman's position on Lonergan's question as his conclusion in the preceding chapter that it is death that makes life wonderful.

Yes, if we are sensitive, or when we are sensitive, we experience the fact of death all around us in everyone and everything. Leslie Jamison calls this feeling "pre-emptive grief."[7] But as she points out, this feeling can lead us to record or transcribe the world. Or, I would like to think, to attend to it.

My dog Maxine is thirteen years old. She is in good health. But she is obviously aging. My wife and I are acutely aware that she will not be with us for much

---

[5] ALVIN PLANTINGA, WHERE THE CONFLICT REALLY LIES: SCIENCE, RELIGION, AND NATURALISM 248 (2011).

[6] Erkki V. R. Kojonen, *Design Discourse: A Way Forward for Theistic Evolutionism?*, ACADEMIA (2018), https://www.academia.edu/38492346/Design_Discourse_A_Way_Forward_for_Theistic_Evolutionism?email_work_card=view-paper.

[7] Leslie Jamison, *Other Voices, Other Rooms*, NEW YORK REVIEW OF BOOKS (May 14, 2020), https://www.nybooks.com/articles/2020/05/14/private-lives-other-voices-other-rooms/.

longer. We are experiencing Jamison's "pre-emptive grief." It is leading us to cherish every moment we have with her.

But, of course, my wife and I are aging too. Every time we consider Maxine, we think of ourselves and our time together.

These are individual events. To understand what Kronman is looking at, you have to imagine, as occasionally is portrayed in science fiction, that we and everything we value would live forever.

What kind of beings would we be then? We would be the kind of beings who never experience the tenderness occasioned by the knowledge of loss. Of course, that would mean that we would not be the beings who we are.

It might mean, though, something much darker than that. It might mean that we would be something hideous. This may be why the gods of the Greeks, who seem to be like us, but immortal, are not portrayed as wiser or more compassionate than we are. In a way, the Greek gods are less than human.

Peter Berger is mistaken. The mother in the scene he drew could have said to her child, with all sincerity, "Everything is all right. You are safe now. Eventually you and I will die. And that is also a part of everything being all right."

We Are Looking for Something

It is not only the religious believer who comes to Lonergan's question with presuppositions. We all do. We try to question honestly, despite our preconceptions. In order to do that, or even to try to do that, we have to know what those preconceptions are. Since this chapter is in a way a record of my answering Lonergan's question, I should set forth my preconceptions, insofar as I know them.

I come to Lonergan's question with an almost unshakeable faith in the unity of the universe, including us. Lonergan understands that position, should it be borne out in the questioning, as essentially a *yes*. That is why he adds at the end of his question the alternative that the universe is "alien" in some senses to us. That would mean that there is no unity. That conclusion would be a *no*.

The way Tom Berry puts this in the documentary *The Great Story* is, "I'm a part of everything. I'm not myself without everything else."

This unity ties together the true and the beautiful. As the Nobel Prize–winning physicist Frank Wilczek once said of an equation, "It was just so pretty that I knew it had to be correct."[8]

It also ties each of these to the good and the just.

[8] Krista Tippett and Frank Wilczek, *Why Is the World So Beautiful?*, ON BEING (July 25, 2016), http://www.dailygood.org/story/1343/why-is-the-world-so-beautiful-/.

This perceived unity is a powerful attractor. I want to be a part of this harmony. I want to contribute to it. I know that, as a human being, I introduce disharmony into that cosmic unity to some extent. That seems inevitable. In a way, that capacity for discord is what makes humans unique.

My hope is to come to understand the unity of the universe better and to be less of an impediment to its expression.

I know whence this faith derives. It comes from my childhood experience of the Jewish prayer, the Sh'ma. That prayer proclaims that God is One—it ends, "Adonai Echad." The oneness of God translates into the unity of everything.

This is not pantheism, because God in the Jewish tradition was the ground of the universe rather than the universe itself. Thus, elements of reality "resist" this unity, including human beings.

As I say, this is a presupposition that I find in myself. It is by no means an answer to Lonergan's question.

Process Philosophy Renders the Yes Plausible

For a long time, I could not ask Lonergan's question. I was held captive by a restricted understanding of the limits of any form of naturalism, by which I just mean an analysis without recourse to the supernatural.

I was like Dr. McCoy in the "Shore Leave" episode of the original *Star Trek* series. Not realizing the nature of the planet that they had encountered—it was a kind of theme park for an advanced civilization—McCoy decides that a knight on a horse charging him, lance in hand, must be a hallucination. As a man of science, McCoy therefore stands his ground, saying, "These things cannot be real." But the knight is real and McCoy is killed. (The advanced technologies of the caretakers of the planet restore him.)

Like McCoy, even when I actually had experiences of a spiritual nature— forgiveness of sin, Sigmund Freud's oceanic feeling of oneness with all things, personal renewal from surrender to the divine and even visions—I could not accept them as real, and therefore could not allow conversion based on them. I had prior commitments to mechanistic materialism as what was real and to evidence of the senses as the only source of knowledge. With those precommitments to ontology and epistemology, I said along with Dr. McCoy that these experiences, although wonderful, inspiring and helpful, could not be real.

It was only when I encountered the process philosophy of Alfred North Whitehead and, to a lesser extent, Charles Hartshorne, that I could begin to accept such experiences as corresponding to something real in the universe, as opposed to something only in my imagination or psyche.

My interpretation of process philosophy is guided by the able process com-
mentator, David Ray Griffin, especially in two books, *Reenchantment Without
Supernaturalism* and *Panentheism and Scientific Naturalism.*[9] The quotations
below are from these books.

Griffin distinguishes two forms of naturalism: naturalismsam, which is the
predominant view today, and is the one that held me captive, and naturalismppp,
which Griffin presents as the process alternative. SAM in this formulation stands
for sensationism, atheism, and materialism, while PPP stands for prehensive,
panentheist, and panexperientialist.

We will return to the issue of God in Chapter 10. Here we will concentrate on
epistemology and ontology—sensationism and materialism versus prehensive
and panexperientialist. I do have to add, however, that both of these naturalisms
are genuinely non-supernatural. That is, the process God that Griffin introduces
in the concept of panentheism—"God is the soul of the world"—does not, and
indeed inherently cannot, "interrupt the most basic causal patterns of the world."
The God of traditional theism—omniscient and omnipotent—is still dead in
process theology.

The process critiques of the dominant view are devastating. Sensationism,
which is the doctrine that perception is limited to the senses, cannot account for
induction and causation. For that matter, it cannot give knowledge of an external
world, "that is, actual things beyond our own minds." Nor do the senses grant
knowledge of the past or time more generally. Griffin quotes Whitehead on these
points: "Pure sense perception does not provide the data for its own interpretation."[10] Even Hume's attribution of seeing to the eye is not knowledge granted
by the senses. To ignore all this, which is what modern scientists tend to do, is to
build irrationalism into science.

The conventional notion of materialism, in which physical things are the only
real entities, treats matter as "vacuous actualities," entirely devoid of experience.
Bits of matter can only have external relations with one another. Or, as we might
say today, matter is dead. This is essentially Weber's disenchanted world.

Whitehead argues that materialism in this sense is inadequate for physics and
biology. It cannot adequately account for induction, causation, time, life, evolution, the emergence of mind in animals, including human beings, mind's relation
to everything else, human freedom, and rationality. It cannot even account for
the emergence of science.

---

[9] Some readers will be familiar with Griffin only through knowing about the 9/11 controversy.
I do not endorse Griffin's views about 9/11, but will not comment further for fear of distraction. No
one doubts Griffin's bona fides when it comes to process philosophy.

[10]   DAVID RAY GRIFFIN, REENCHANTMENT WITHOUT SUPERNATURALISM: A PROCESS
PHILOSOPHY OF RELIGION 37 (2001).

Griffin does not rest with these criticisms, which are not unknown, but introduces Whitehead's complex alternatives.

In place of the vacuous actualities of mechanistic materialism, Whitehead argues that all individuals—which is a term of art including atoms, but not sticks and stones—have some degree of experience and spontaneity. Griffin says that bacteria make decisions. All living cells have what could be called experiences. At the quantum level, there is responsiveness to information, which is why Whitehead's thinking is considered hospitable to quantum mechanics in a way that traditional materialism is not. For Whitehead, the universe's most basic units are momentary spatiotemporal events—happenings. This is entirely compatible with quantum reality.

The rejection by Whitehead of mechanistic materialism has special resonance for the possibility that the universe is on our side because process philosophy may reconcile quantum theory and human purpose. As Michael Epperson explains,

> Whitehead's repudiation of fundamental mechanistic materialism is also a repudiation of its correlate characterization of the universe as a cold realm of mechanical accidents from which our purportedly illusory and sheerly subjective perceptions of purpose and meaning are, by certain views, thought to derive.... In sharp contrast, by Whitehead's cosmology as exemplified by the decoherence interpretations of quantum mechanics, the universe is instead characterized as a fundamentally complex domain with an inherent aim toward an ideal balance of reproduction and reversion—a balance formative of a nurturing home for a seemingly infinitely large family of complex adaptive systems such as ourselves.[11]

In addition to, but not instead of, sensation, Whitehead propounds a nonsensationist doctrine of perception that provides a natural explanation of knowledge of matters like our bodies, causation, and the past, which we inevitably presuppose in practice, but could not know if the senses were our only source of knowledge. Whitehead's general term for perception is "prehension."

In this way of non-sensation perception, human beings gain real knowledge from religious experiences, mathematical and logical principles, and cognitive moral and aesthetic ideals.

In other words, my spiritual experiences could have been matters of genuine perception and knowledge.

---

[11]   MICHAEL EPPERSON, QUANTUM MECHANICS AND THE PHILOSOPHY OF ALFRED NORTH WHITEHEAD 17 (2004).

But what truth could be provided by these types of spiritual experiences? First, religious experience, which is as good a term as any in this context, as well as other forms of experiences, such as ethical and aesthetic, deal with values. Like other forms of perception, they reveal truths about reality. In turn, truths about values provide clues about the nature of the cosmos. Griffin quotes a saying of Whitehead's, "that the universe contains a 'character of permanent rightness'"[12] that we intuit in much the same way that we apprehend the character of our friends. But in the case of the universe, the intuition goes to the basic nature of things.

It is not that everything in the universe corresponds to this character of rightness. There is some measure of conformity and some measure of diversity. Griffin again quotes Whitehead: "So far as the conformity is incomplete, there is evil in the world."[13]

We do not experience our own existence in the world as a succession of bare facts. Instead, Griffin writes, we experience the "world as oriented toward the production of value." We intuit our own existence in terms of freedom and responsibility.

Obviously, Whitehead answers *yes* to Lonergan's question about the universe being on our side. But it is not my purpose in introducing process philosophy to provide direct support for the *yes*. Rather, I simply wish to show that the *yes* is possible, plausible, and credible.

After this short exposure to process thinking, one need not be embarrassed by the *yes*. One need not think of the *yes* as supernatural or even "religious" in the sense of institutional religion. Nor as anti-scientific. Nor as anti-rational. In Whitehead, the *yes* is actually supportive of science and rationality.

How Does One Decide Whether the Universe Is on Our Side?

Plantinga is undoubtedly right about the inapplicability of proof in matters like this. For what would such a proof look like? The reason that religious believers have even been troubled by the need for proof is their own commitment, overwhelmingly supported and demanded by the culture, to sensationism and materialism. The problem is that within those constraints, belief in God is nonsense.

Once liberated from those constraints, questions of proof do not arise. To decide, for example, whether history bends toward justice, one would not count each death by cruelty and each life saved by beneficence and then add up which sum is larger.

[12] GRIFFIN, *supra* note 10, at 87.
[13] *Id.*

Instead, we present our experiences to the larger community for contemplation. No one is (or should be, anyway) trying to coerce consent by constructing arguments. Advance in matters like this does not work that way.

But there are some rules of exchange.

First, there should at least be hesitance before invoking the concepts of illusion and accident in considering human experience and the history of the universe. If large numbers of human beings throughout recorded history report certain experiences, such as spiritual ones and, more formally, religious ones as well, it is not reasonable to just shrug them off. I don't mean that everyone is bound to accept my report of my experience as corresponding to something in the universe if that would be impossible. But barring such impossibility, we should take seriously the possibility that such experiences correspond to something real.

The same is true of the concept of accident. The course of the universe has taken a certain path, with certain consequences. We should not assume, especially not irrebuttably, that this course was purely contingent.

It was my purpose in introducing process philosophy to limit this tendency to invoke concepts like illusion and accident, which often are invoked when certain conclusions would be impossible under sensationism and materialism.

Second, the logical limit of non-self-contradiction should apply. As will be seen in what follows, I believe that some of the case for the *no* does in fact violate the principle of non-self-contradiction.

Finally, as Griffin explains, a primary criterion for evaluating any theory, whether philosophical, theological, or scientific, is that the theory must do justice to what Whitehead referred to as "the inevitable presuppositions of practice."[14] Griffin calls these matters of hard core common sense. Since these presuppositions are inevitably invoked in practice, denying them or ignoring them is irrational.

What Is Our Side?

The final preliminary matter has to do with an ambiguity in Lonergan's question. What does it mean for the universe to be on our side? What is our side?

Certainly Lonergan did not mean that the universe sides with us, no matter how destructive or unsustainable our activities are. The universe is responding to our runaway numbers and profligate practices by an increase in global temperature that is likely to cause humans enormous harm in the future and is already beginning to do so. So, in some sense, the universe can serve as a barrier against our wishes.

---

[14] *Id.* at 29.

Insofar as we make of nature a "standing reserve," as Heidegger said in his essay "The Question Concerning Technology," human beings will suffer. The universe is not always in our favor.

For that matter, we can create conditions, like a nuclear winter after a full-scale nuclear exchange, in which humans become extinct.

I'm sure Lonergan was well aware of considerations like these.

It would be more helpful to think of the question as actually asking whether the universe has its own side that corresponds to human flourishing. After all, the question does not ask whether the universe is on our side in general, but asks, is the universe on our side when "we praise progress and denounce every manifestation of decline" and when we are "individually struggling for authenticity and collectively endeavoring to snatch progress from the ever mounting welter of decline?" Lonergan wants us to decide whether the universe is on our side then.

We could reinterpret the question in the following terms:

In pursuing progress, is the universe on our side?
In creating beauty, is the universe on our side?
In working for justice, is the universe on our side?
In living a good life, is the universe on our side?

In these formulations, if we answer *yes*, it is the universe that is primary. The universe is actually on the side of progress, beauty, justice, and the good. The question really is, are we?

As Patrick Byrne explained above, Lonergan thought that the universe was on the side of intelligibility and meaningfulness. For Whitehead, the universe is on the side of value realization, particularly beauty: "Beauty, moral and aesthetic, is the aim of existence."[15]

The question of the *yes* is whether Lonergan and Whitehead are right that the universe is on our side in these pursuits.

In terms of the breakdown in American public life, we can turn Lonergan's question in one final direction. Griffin sets forth ten core doctrines of process philosophy. This is the ninth principle: *"The provision of cosmological support for the ideals needed by contemporary civilization as one of the chief purposes of philosophy in our time."*[16]

This formulation assumes that there are ideals needed by civilization and that these ideals are in jeopardy because of the lack of their perceived support in the universe. This was, in fact, Whitehead's view. In the 1930s, Whitehead saw the

---

[15] *Id.* at 302.
[16] *Id.* at 7.

likelihood of the wreckage of civilization and sought through philosophy "to re-create and reenact a vision of the world, including those elements of reverence and order without which society lapses into riot."[17]

We can now ask whether the universe is on the side of reverence and order. If the answer is *yes*, there is a good chance of restoring faith in American public life.

Now we are ready to proceed. We begin with attributes of the universe and, although the categories overlap, we then move on to consider ourselves as representatives of, and participants in, cosmic process.

Creativity/Emergence/Possibility

Tom Berry calls these moments of grace:[18] These are moments of great cosmological, or religious and historical, transformation. These moments in the story of the universe that we know, and the parts of that story that most concern us, are numerous. The beginning of the universe. The supernova that collapsed and thus provided the materials for our solar system. The Earth in its life-sustaining orbit. The emergence of life. The beginning of photosynthesis. The awakening of human intelligence. And on and on.

All of these moments, individually unpredictable and unexpected, form a beneficent pattern for humanity.

In the language of theology, but appealing to this same cosmic power of the new, the theologian Karl Barth wrote, "The truly creative act by which men become the children of Abraham, by which stones are transformed into sons, does not lie in the possible possibility of the law, but in the impossible possibility of faith."[19]

Everything important that we rely on would once have seemed impossible.

Science has a term for this creativity: emergence. Emergence can mean simply that an entity has traits that its separate components do not. Thus, emergence is a quality of most complex systems.

But in evolutionary theory, emergence includes the sense of the unpredictable and the unanticipated. Life on Earth is a series of such emergences—from life itself, to the living cell, to sexual reproduction, to sentience, to cognition. As Brian Swimme asks in the *Journey of the Universe* documentary, what is the creativity that could bring forth all this?

We human beings are an example of this cosmic creativity, both in our own emergence, and in the creativity of which we are capable.

---

[17] GRIFFIN, *supra* note 10, at 288.

[18] Thomas Berry, *Moments of Grace*, YES! MAGAZINE (Apr. 1, 2020), https://www.yesmagazine.org/issue/issues-new-stories/2000/04/01/moments-of-grace/.

[19] KARL BARTH, THE EPISTLE TO THE ROMANS 138 (1933).

We overlook this. In the view of the psychologist Alison Gopnik, the human adult in engaging in adult pursuits—basically goal-oriented getting and spending—loses the capacity of the baby and the child to be open to the spaciousness and richness of the world. Caring for a child can help recover that openness, as apparently certain drugs also can, by, in a sense, reproducing the younger brain. The universe is filled with potential for discovery.[20]

The Telos of the Universe

Toward the end of the fable *Ishmael*, Daniel Quinn puts this thought in the words of the student: "There is a sort of tendency in evolution, wouldn't you say? If you start with those ultrasimple critters in the ancient seas and move up step by step to everything that we see here now—and beyond—then you have to observe a tendency toward . . . complexity. And toward self-awareness and intelligence."[21]

But Quinn does not stop there. The student then observes that "all sorts of creatures on this planet appear to be on the verge of attaining that self-awareness and intelligence." The Earth may have been on its way to being filled with creatures of intelligence and self-awareness. The tragedy so far is that humans have been unable to make room for this continuing evolution, but are thwarting it.

Obviously, science founded on sensationism and materialism must strenuously insist that this apparent tendency in evolution is an illusion and a misunderstanding. But this stance is driven by those prior commitments and not by disinterested observation.

Griffin is clear that unlike naturalismsam, naturalismppp, "is not embarrassed by the directionality of evolution."[22] In that sentence, Griffin captures both the sense that the apparent directionality of evolution is pretty obvious and that atheistic scientists fear admitting it because this might reintroduce forms of medieval, God-dependent science.

Another form of the telos of the universe is the debate over whether the emergence of life is built into the nature of matter and its tendency of self-organization. It had been assumed by orthodox Darwinian thought that the emergence of life was an unlikely and contingent event. And this was Sagan's at least unconscious assumption in his pale blue dot monologue.

[20] Alison Gopnik, *The Evolutionary Power of Children and Teenagers*, ON BEING WITH KRISTA TIPPETT (Jan. 23, 2020), https://onbeing.org/programs/alison-gopnik-the-evolutionary-power-of-children-and-teenagers/.

[21] DANIEL QUINN, ISHMAEL: AN ADVENTURE OF THE MIND AND SPIRIT 241–42 (1992).

[22] DAVID RAY GRIFFIN, PANENTHEISM AND SCIENTIFIC NATURALISM: RETHINKING EVIL, MORALITY, RELIGIOUS EXPERIENCE, RELIGIOUS PLURALISM, AND THE ACADEMIC STUDY OF RELIGION 34 (2014).

But there is a growing view that matter's self-organizing tendency, when combined with energy and the proper conditions, will generally produce life. In *The Origin and Nature of Life on Earth*, Eric Smith and Harold Morowitz are suitably subdued and careful in their pronouncement. Perhaps they chafe at the popular idea of life arising inevitably. But they do say, "As the extent, complexity, and structure of geodynamics become a part of the frame through which we understand the living state, it becomes much more difficult to see life as a singularity, and more seemingly inevitable that it is an elaboration within an ongoing process of planetary maturation."[23] We can conclude, at the very least, that life arises naturally.

And if life does arise, the biologist Simon Conway Morris has argued for years that the human evolutionary path would basically be followed. There is nothing unique about the way that humans evolved on Earth.

This life-friendly universe is entirely natural. And that is the point. The universe can be viewed as on the side of the emergence of beings like us.

The telos of the universe is not just revealed in physical properties like complexity, or even mental properties like self-awareness. In *Primates and Philosophers*, Frans de Waal traces the evolution of morality. We come from a long line of animals that gradually developed capacities for empathy and sympathy. As Brian Swimme puts it in *The Journey of the Universe*, we are descendants of a fish that, contrary to the practice of other fish, did not eat her young.

All of this is suggestive in its individual parts. But when you put it all together, you end up with a universe that favors life, complexity, intelligence, and morality. What more do you need to see that the universe is on our side?

Of course, as noted in the previous chapter, the criminal is also natural. In addition, the fascist and the racist may be entirely motivated by moral concerns, such as protecting one's family and culture from perceived threats.

But that is not an objection to the idea of the universe being on our side. The criminal is exercising freedom that is also built into the universe at higher levels of organization. And I certainly don't mean that evolution has made humans good. But it has given us the capacity to do good, to act with compassion, and when we do not, there is also the power of reason and truth to correct ourselves. I will come back to that in the section below on history.

The Friendly Universe

Albert Einstein is generally credited, probably falsely, with saying that "the most important decision we make is whether we believe we live in a friendly or hostile

---

[23]   HAROLD MOROWITZ & ERIC SMITH, THE ORIGIN AND NATURE OF LIFE ON EARTH 106 (2016).

universe." But students of Lonergan, reflecting on the question, often use this formulation. The theme, for example, of the 2009 annual Lonergan workshop was "Reversing Social and Cultural Decline in a Friendly Universe."

It could be that Lonergan's question itself is aimed at determining whether this is a friendly universe. But the phrase could also have a much simpler meaning. The universe could be considered friendly because its laws favor us.

In one sense, this is obviously so. As I noted in the previous chapter, even if we answer Lonergan's question with a *no*, that is, that the universe is not on our side, the current scientific laws that govern our planet are easy for us to live with. We need oxygen and the planet produces oxygen in abundance. We need food and the planet produces food. Just about everything about life on Earth is good for humans, which is why we are here.

But there are two more significant possible meanings of this simple phrase. First, why are these laws that favor us stable and apparently universal? John Gray, who takes the *no* with the utmost seriousness, argues against both stability and universality in *Seven Types of Atheism*. Here is his comment about the laws of science:

> It is asserted that science is the exercise of discovering the universal laws of nature. But unless you believe that the human mind mirrors a rational cosmos . . . science can only be a tool the human animal has invented to deal with a world it cannot fully understand. . . . the order that appears to prevail in our corner of the universe may be local and ephemeral, emerging randomly and then melting away. The very idea that we live in a law-governed cosmos may not be much more than a fading legacy of faith in a divine law-giver.[24]

You have to admire such unflinching honesty and consistency. But Gray's observations just show that if the universe is rational, and if we can come to understand the universe (in part, anyway), and if our minds do mirror the universe, and if its laws are stable and universal, then these conclusions by themselves are persuasive that the universe is on our side. Gray came to his contrary conclusions not by observation but by precommitment. There is no reason to believe that he is right about any of his suppositions.

But there is yet one more, even stranger, sense of the universe as on our side. All those horrible events that occurred before the advent of human civilization, such as an asteroid strike, have not happened since. Granted, the sample size is small. There have only been at most 10,000 or 15,000 years of human organized society. And even if we go back to the emergence of our strain of energetic apes,

---

[24] John Gray, Seven Types of Atheism 13 (2018).

even a million years is not very long. There could be an asteroid or other terrible event around the corner.

But the fact that it has not happened, however mysterious, is something to think about.

Furthermore, there is also the fact that although the solar radiation reaching the Earth has substantially increased over the past four billion years, the Earth's temperature has remained mostly stable and within a favorable range for life. The mechanism through which this has occurred, the reduction of carbon in the atmosphere, is clear, but why it happened is not.

Lewis Owen and Kevin Pickering explain this result as the Gaia hypothesis: "the Earth's organisms collectively have an innate ability to self-regulate the external environmental conditions necessary to support and sustain life."[25]

I'm not sure that calling this the Gaia hypothesis accomplishes anything besides pointing out that it happened. You could just as well say that the universe is on our side.

Process philosophy even has an answer for the unfavorable aspects of the universe. Unlike the omnipotent God of traditional theism, any organizing principle of process theory, including those process theorists who argue for a divine entity, take the nature of the universe as a given. There is no creation ex nihilo. Furthermore, there is no power to intervene coercively in physical processes. For this reason, there can be tendencies but not miracles. Given those parameters, any dynamic system like the Earth is going to yield violence and pain in unpredictable ways.

We Participate in the Unfolding of the Universe

The concept of the friendly universe casts humans as passive. The universe is good to us, which is true. But we are not just recipients and observers. We are participants.

Conway Morris has a lovely phrase for this participation. His book *The Runes of Evolution* has this subtitle: "How the Universe Became Self-Aware." Of course, we, in our imaginations, are a pre-eminent aspect of the self-awareness of the universe. We share what Conway Morris calls "cognitive architecture" with other animals, but our way of understanding is unique. We appreciate the deep beauty of the universe in a way other animals do not seem to. This may be our most significant participation in the universe.

---

[25] LEWIS OWN & KEVIN PICKERING, AN INTRODUCTION TO GLOBAL ENVIRONMENTAL ISSUES 29 (1997).

In an episode of the original *Cosmos* series, Carl Sagan not only pointed to our participation in this way, but rooted it in our biological and physical oneness with everything else—the carbon of which we are composed: "We are a way for the universe to know itself. Some part of our being knows this is where we came from. We long to return. And we can, because the cosmos is also within us. We're made of star stuff."

Quantum mechanics is probably the best known, and strangest, example, of human interaction with the universe. It appears that human observation of a particle collapses its wave function and fixes its position. In fact, as Bob Henderson observed in a *New York Times* article about a major controversy in quantum theory, because particles only behave like particles when we observe them, it isn't clear "how much the word 'particle' is apropos to the unobserved world."[26]

On one level, the controversy in the article is over the role of human observation. The physicist Angelo Basi is conducting experiments attempting to demonstrate that there are physical laws behind the observations of quantum theory that can be stated without reference to human action.

But on another level, the controversy is over whether the physical universe is really knowable and whether physics is about knowledge or simply prediction.

Certainly, if it turns out that the universe is fundamentally unknowable, Bernard Lonergan's view of its intelligibility will suffer and John Gray's position will be strengthened. That conclusion would counter an important aspect of the view that the universe is on our side.

But we don't know this yet. And, at the moment, even the strange world of quantum physics, in which, again in the words of Henderson, it appears that we humans are "conjuring the reality we experience out of a murky netherworld that quantum mechanics implies is unknowable," is itself a reminder of how connected with everything we really are.

On the other hand, if it turns out that the universe is something that we can know, it will be Lonergan's ultimate vindication. He felt that "[t]he immanent source of transcendence in man is his detached, disinterested, unrestricted desire to know."[27]

History Bends Toward Justice

Dr. Martin Luther King Jr., described history as "the arc of the moral universe." In this way, he pointed to larger forces—for him, of course, the actions of God—that

[26] Bob Henderson, *The Rebel Physicist on the Hunt for a Better Story Than Quantum Mechanics*, NEW YORK TIMES (June 25, 2020), https://www.nytimes.com/2020/06/25/magazine/angelo-bassi-quantum-mechanic.html.

[27] BERNARD LONERGAN, INSIGHT: A STUDY OF HUMAN UNDERSTANDING 636 (1957).

explain the movement toward justice. His description was carefully crafted to allow the nonbeliever to look for such trends apart from God.

So, there are two aspects to Dr. King's claim. One is that this trajectory toward justice is the case and the other that it is the result of something reliable, rather than a happy accident.

John Gray presents two objections to the first aspect. One is that without God, there is no standard by which to judge better and worse outcomes. Improvement could only be in terms of "the standards of the time."[28]

But Gray is not that interested in relativism and nihilism. Most people are willing to grant that something like the chattel slavery system was objectively evil. And if it was, then, we should by analogy find other things to be objectively evil, or at least to be able to discuss their evil aspects in comparison to slavery.

Gray is more interested in a different, second objection—that it isn't the case that history bends toward justice, even if justice is understood in some conventional, common sense way. And there are two parts to his argument. One is that, insofar as the idea of progress implies that human beings morally improve over time, the claim is "meaningless" outside the structure of monotheistic religion. The other part is that the only reason that people believe in historical progress is because the claim is never presented as a "falsifiable hypothesis." If it were, Gray says, it would have been abandoned long ago.

Again, the overwhelming example of the abolition of chattel slavery undermines Gray's position. That abolition is a one-way street. Short of a catastrophe that destroys civilization, the Middle Passage will never return.

Chattel slavery was not a crime committed by particular evil men. It was the commercial center of economic life. Slavery was enforced by police, navies, governments. Its abolition was a great moral achievement.

It is true that people do not change. But we do learn. And we do not just learn physical lessons that add to our productivity. Humanity learns moral lessons as well.

Learning a moral lesson suggests that one of the engines of the movement of history toward justice is the power of reason and truth. Racial inferiority was a necessary foundation of chattel slavery because otherwise slavery's injustice would have been too awful for its defenders to bear. And that claim of racial inferiority was untrue. That untruth inevitably led to slavery's destruction.

This does not imply that the arc of the moral universe bends because we bend it. Rather, we bend it because the moral power of reason and truth are overwhelming in our being. And we are that way because the universe made us that

---

[28] GRAY, *supra* note 24, at 24.

way. The universe is on our side. The trajectory of history is no accident. It is reliable.

Human beings are drawn to the good. We are many things, including selfish and violent. But there is no such thing as a human society that understands itself as evil. We always tell a story in which we are doing something good. That means that reason and truth can serve as corrections to our falsehoods.

We should not think of Dr. King's formulation as a hypothesis, as Gray does. We should think of it as an experiment in which we are both the subject and the observer. If we look with the eyes of commitment, we will see the trajectory. And seeing it will help make it so.

That is the wisdom of Mahatma Gandhi, who surely knew the evils in history: "When I despair, I remember that all through history the way of truth and love have always won. There have been tyrants and murderers, and for a time, they can seem invincible, but in the end, they always fall. Think of it—always."

We Are Filled with Longing

Gandhi's faith is connected to something else about us that shows the universe is on our side. We strive to make a better world in history because we are filled with longing for a connection to something larger and more beautiful than we experience in our day-to-day lives.

Here is how Fred Rogers connected these thoughts in his last graduation address, in 2002, at Dartmouth College, his alma mater: "When I say it's you I like, I'm talking about that part of you that knows that life is far more than anything you can ever see, or hear, or touch. That deep part of you, that allows you to stand for those things, without which humankind cannot survive. Love that conquers hate. Peace that rises triumphant over war. And justice that proves more powerful than greed."[29]

This longing also explains our connection to truth. In the remake of the *Cosmos* series, Neil deGrasse Tyson was not above making fun of humanity's "hunger for significance, for signs that our personal existence is of special meaning to the universe." Admittedly, the feeling in people that we are uniquely significant might be considered the *yes* run amok.

But on the issue of ultimate meaning, Tyson sang a different tune. In the final episode of the series, he asserted that human beings engage in scientific inquiry "because it matters what's true."

---

[29] Office of Communications, *Revisiting Fred Rogers' 2002 Commencement Address*, DARTMOUTH NEWS (Mar. 27, 2018), https://news.dartmouth.edu/news/2018/03/revisiting-fred-rogers-2002-commencement-address.

This longing to understand what's true is a part of what Griffin presents as the ultimate religious motivation in Whitehead's thinking—"the desire to correspond with the general harmony" in the universe.[30]

This is not the longing for longing that I criticized previously. The general harmony that we wish to embrace is foundation, and the clearest indication, that the universe is on our side.

We Act Collectively with Purpose

John Gray was also insistent there was no such thing as humanity. He wrote in *Straw Dogs*: "If you believe that humans are animals, there can be no such thing as the history of humanity, only the lives of particular humans. If we speak of the history of the species at all, it is only to signify the unknowable sum of these lives. As with other animals, some lives are happy, others wretched. None has a meaning that lies beyond itself."[31]

In this insistence, Gray echoed an earlier comment by Margaret Thatcher: "You know, there is no such thing as society. There are individual men and women and there are families." Of course, the whole notion of family presumably would strike Gray as hopelessly romantic and a striving for social meaning that is an illusion. Thatcher was not nearly hard-headed enough for Gray.

This insistence that collective human purpose is unreal is an aspect of the *no* that has seeped deeply into Western thought. As Lon Fuller explained, it is at the heart of positivism, which refuses to engage the meaning of purposeful human action. It is the peculiar reason that American judges interpret statutes without regard to their purposes.

It is also an insistence that there is, in effect, no "our" for the universe to be on the side of. We are alone in the universe, not just because the universe is indifferent, but because we are essentially indifferent to, and alienated from, each other.

This view is part of the self-contradiction of the *no* that I will describe in the next section. Gray, for example, though insisting that there is no humanity, considers humanity to be composed of killer apes with metaphysical longing. That description is, of course, part of the history of humanity that Gray insists cannot be told.

The view is also false on a deeper level. The truth of human beings is that we can and have acted collectively in united purpose. We have difficulty doing this now, in America specifically, because we have lost faith in ourselves. That lack of faith

---

[30] Griffin, *supra* note 10, at 11. The quote is from the historian Carl Becker.
[31] GRAY, *supra* note 2, at 48.

is a part of the breakdown in American public life that I hope will be addressed by the activity of asking Lonergan's question and healed by answering *yes*.

The No *Is Self-Contradictory and Arbitrary*

I wanted to illustrate aspects of the *yes* without attacking the *no*. As I have explained, any questioning will be an improvement over the current breakdown and the *no* itself has important features that can serve as correctives to human striving.

Nevertheless, it is important at least to note the tendency in the *no* to self-contradiction and arbitrariness.

Some of these self-contradictions are very specific. So, the author who tells us that reality is just matter in motion through forces, will not explain how such matter and forces wrote a book.

Or, the author who argues that everything is determined, will try to convince us without apparently realizing that our assent or disagreement is already determined.

But the fundamental problem for the *no* is its need to restrict the human frame of reference. For example, the *no* always treats aspects of human experience as illusory. But it never gives any criteria for determining which aspects are illusory and which are not. This is because the *no* aims to disconnect us from the larger whole of the universe. That position will always require that humans represent an absolute uniqueness in the universe, a uniqueness that the *no* at other points rejects.

So the *no* will assert both that humans are nothing special and that we are especially alienated. The truth is that everything else is connected to the universe, so why should we not be?

In contrast, the *yes* results from the most robust inquiry in search of the greatest unity. Nothing is left out because the quest is for wholeness. Once that wholeness is achieved, once that unity is reached, the path to social health lies open. If the universe is on our side, the breakdown in American public life is only temporary and can be healed. The next chapter asks, "What would such health look like?"

9

Restored Public Life

What happens next in American public life? That depends on which chapter in Part II most inspires the reader. I have had the experience of engaging in questioning, as set forth in Chapter 6. When I first met my friend and mentor Robert Taylor in 1980, I was introduced to questioning as a way of life. That experience changed me. I no longer considered it a defeat if my students remained conservatives. I had not realized how one-sided my early classes had been.

I can imagine a reinvigorated public life in America in which investigation would be pursued with honest intensity and without hint of partisanship. This one change would begin our healing and it must occur in any form of restored public life.

Nevertheless, I did not address public life in Chapter 6. If we ask Bernard Lonergan's question about the universe, we are going to move beyond investigation into forming some conclusions. Questioning must always be at the forefront because our answers always remain provisional. But there will be provisional responses. So, while a reader may remain at the questioning phase, society probably will not.

The most immediate likely response by most people to Lonergan's question is *no*, the universe is not on our side. After all, as shown in Chapter 5, that is already this society's default position. The unwillingness to face that reality is why America is currently in the Age of Evasion.

I hope that after reading Chapter 7, the reader who engages in questioning and concludes that the universe is not on our side will have a path for going forward. I suggested at the end of Chapter 7 that American public life could become healthier if the *no* were forthrightly endorsed. It would be painful to live in such a universe, but if that is the way things are, we must accept it and move on. And there are paths to pursue, and thinkers to follow, in moving on.

Nevertheless, my treatment of public life in the *no* in Chapter 7 is nothing like the attempt to describe public life in this chapter. That is because my answer is *yes*, the universe is on our side, and I hope that American public life will come to agree with my commitment. So, this chapter is about public life in the *yes*. Or, more helpfully, public life as we begin to embrace the *yes*.

This chapter proceeds in three levels: the individual reader, cosmopolis (that is, groupings of readers), and finally public life as a whole.

But, before proceeding, one potential misunderstanding must be addressed.

The Universe Is on Our Side. Bruce Ledewitz, Oxford University Press. © Oxford University Press 2022.
DOI: 10.1093/oso/9780197563939.003.0010

What Is the Role of Nature in the Yes?

The universe is on our side. Does that mean we are in the realm of natural law thinking that argues that there are direct policy implications from nature? That is the kind of natural law thinking that argues that nature prescribes certain forms of life, such as heterosexual life.

I doubt that is the case, although it is impossible to rule it out. This chapter is certainly not going to proceed by isolating certain traits in human beings that are said to be more proper than others, or more necessary, and then conclude that these traits are more natural and, therefore, for example, same-sex marriage is to be accepted, or prohibited, or immigration policy should be loosened or tightened. That is how some natural law thinking goes, but it is not my intention to proceed that way.

Everything we do is natural in the sense that we are part of nature. But not everything we do is right, not everything we do is sustainable, not everything we do is good for us or good for other forms of life, including human generations yet unborn. There are obviously policy implications in all that. The content of what is right or good, however, is something to be filled in through learning, not something to use in support of policy positions that someone already has. This book is not about natural law in that way of thinking.

The primary effect of the Death of God in American public life has had nothing to do with pursuing bad policies. It has had to do with the way that policies are pursued. The Death of God left us fearful, hopeless, and aggressive. That is the level at which the *yes* heals us.

Back from the Brink

Independence Day, 2020, was a dark time in American life. President Trump delivered a divisive and incendiary Independence Day address, more like a campaign rally, promising to defeat "the radical left, the anarchists, the agitators, the looters . . . the angry mob" and to "protect and preserve the American way of life, which began in 1492 when Columbus discovered America."[1] Every racist dog whistle was sounded, every angry instinct provoked, despite the fact that the demonstrations had been mostly peaceful and, anyway, had mostly melted away by July 4. Mobs defacing statues were certainly not a national problem by that time.

---

[1] *Remarks by President Trump at the 2020 Salute to America*, WHITE HOUSE (July 5, 2020), https://www.whitehouse.gov/briefings-statements/remarks-president-trump-2020-salute-america/.

But it was not just President Trump that represented an American crisis. The pandemic caseload was spiking despite months of total or partial economic and social shutdown. Deaths had not yet caught up, but it was expected that they would. People were frightened and frustrated. Physical fights were breaking out in grocery and convenience stores over wearing a mask. It was also expected that the new surge in cases would interrupt, if not end, the budding economic recovery. At the same time, Russia was suspected of paying a bounty for the deaths of American soldiers. China had just ended Hong Kong's partial independence, which no international coalition seemed prepared to contest. Two American aircraft carriers were on their way to the South China Sea, signaling a new and dangerous level of confrontation with China.

And it was hot. Really hot. And dry. Over most of the country. Climate change had not taken a break with the pandemic.

It was at this moment that the *New York Times* columnist David Brooks wrote what might have been the bleakest July 4 message ever: *The National Humiliation We Need.*[2] The column began with the American failure to rein in the virus. Because of that failure, Brooks noted, Americans were depressed and many important economic and social institutions were about to go under.

No matter what the upcoming election result in November—and Brooks thought the American people had already decided not to re-elect President Trump—the economic future looked bleak, political division appeared to be permanent, racial discrimination remained, despite progress, and social capital was crumbling, including family formation.

The core problem, wrote Brooks, is that a lot of Americans refuse to think of the social whole, the common good. We think, instead, in terms of what's best for us and we believe we know what that is. This radical individualism stems from a long-term crisis in legitimacy that involves both meaninglessness in individual lives and amorality in the distribution of social and economic benefits.

Brooks hoped that, down deep, we have a shared love of our nation and that we would find that faith in our common lives together.

Let's leave aside the fact that history suggests national humiliation does not improve things. Brooks knew this and actually admitted that the pandemic, rather than bringing us together, had made everything worse.

Brooks's failure to offer any positive program or amelioration was like Ross Douthat's book *The Age of Decadence* in implying, in effect, that it's the times. A lot of observers feel that everything is bad and there is no path to national

---

[2] David Brooks, *The National Humiliation We Need: July 4th and America's Crisis of the Spirit*, NEW YORK TIMES (July 2, 2020), https://www.nytimes.com/2020/07/02/opinion/coronavirus-july-4.html.

reconciliation—nothing to be done—which was highlighted in Chapter 1 as part of the breakdown in American public life. The American elite has lost faith in the American future.

At the same time, however, there was a glimmer of something hopeful in the world of commentary. A few days before the Brooks column appeared, another *New York Times* columnist, Nicholas Kristof, wrote that the "'Hispanic paradox' could offer a model for civil society."[3]

The paradox is that, despite poverty and discrimination, Hispanic Americans do better on numerous social metrics—life expectancy, crime rates, suicides, etc.—than do white or black Americans. The "paradox within the paradox," as Kristof put it, is that this effect wears off in the second generation and as people leave ethnic enclaves for more mixed neighborhoods.

Generally both of these phenomena are explained by reference to what are called traditional family values—ties to faith, family, and community. These ties fade as later generations assimilate.

Kristof referred to "faith and church" in particular. Religious beliefs not only reduce risky behavior, but church attendance and prayer correlate to greater life satisfaction.

It might be asked why there is no African-American paradox, if religious faith is a factor in welfare. After all, the black community is much more religious by any measure than is the white community.[4]

Kristof's article indirectly gives a suggestion for that as well—there is in fact an African-American paradox. It is just hard to see given the enormous history of oppression, the destruction of black family life in slavery, and the continuing legacy of racism. When Kristof compares the Hispanic experience to his own, largely white, hometown of Yamhill, Oregon, in which a quarter of the kids from his old school have died from deaths of despair, the reader can hear a comparison to black communities, which probably show much greater resilience than Kristof's white hometown.

But Kristof did not consider the content of faith and how to renew it. It is time to stop thinking about faith and religion as primarily non-cognitive social glue—like bowling leagues, in Robert Putnam's account of social decline in *Bowling Alone*. In that view, church life is social and social life is good for people. In terms of content, however, all that view can say is that something called faith exists and it has good effects on the people who have it.

This idea that religion has nothing to do with knowledge is a holdover from materialism and sensationism. Actually, religions tell a story about our

---

[3] Nicholas Kristof, *Now Is a Time to Learn from Hispanic Americans*, New York Times (June 27, 2020), https://www.nytimes.com/2020/06/27/opinion/sunday/hispanic-americans.html.
[4] *Racial and Ethnic Composition*, Pew Research Center (2014) https://www.pewforum.org/religious-landscape-study/racial-and-ethnic-composition/.

connection to the universe. That connection is good for us. Unfortunately, the connection that religious stories tell is unavailable to many because of the Death of God.

The purpose of this book is to tell a different story of connection, one in which the universe, though entirely natural, is on our side. That is our new story. That will be good for us.

We now turn to the effect that the realization of this new knowledge would have on public life. We begin with the effect on the individual reader.

The Reader Who Discovers That the Universe Is on Our Side

The reader I am envisioning is one who never had God, or perhaps no longer has God, thus, not a religious person. Nor am I assuming any prior philosophical experience. Such a person might have been feeling, as David Brooks was feeling, a strong sense of disappointment and disillusionment at where America is and where we seem to be headed.

How might such a person react to her own conclusion, after careful consideration, that the universe is on our side?

This question, though personal, is important for public life. We are dealing here with what Lonergan called the development of "a personal depth" that can yield a "public opinion."[5]

First, the reader may have a feeling of celebration. We are not alone. The universe is not indifferent. Our strivings have ultimate meaning. The reader's own striving in particular has meaning. We are part of something larger, and more beautiful, than we had imagined. We are participants in an ongoing cosmic process and we can help it along if we act rightly. We can act rightly if we practice keeping a clear and reasonable consciousness. This is all incredible news. Good news, you might say.

The Death of God cast a shadow over the West. It cast thunderclouds over America. Because we relied more on God, America suffered more than most. Now, in the words I quoted from Camus, there is the beginning of a hope.

Within this celebration of a friendly universe, it feels much easier to regard my fellow citizens with respect, compassion, and affection. If they act in wrongful ways—if they are racist or hate religion or are prejudiced in other ways on either political side—it now seems that the reason is that they lack the knowledge that the reader has gained. Genuine evil is fairly rare. More common is the distortion that the Death of God has brought. My fellow citizens may act the way

---

5   BERNARD LONERGAN, INSIGHT: A STUDY OF HUMAN UNDERSTANDING 241 (1957).

they do because so many of us find the disenchanted universe unbearable and we lash out.

As opposed to defeating them, I now can envision a reconciliation. This insight will begin at a small scale in terms of numbers, but it will grow.

Second, the reader might experience gratitude. Granted, this gratitude should not be called prayer because of possible misunderstanding. But we should be grateful to be part of this stupendous event. It is not something that could have been expected after the Death of God. We did nothing to deserve our place in the universe. Yet, here we are.

Third, there might be confession. In so many ways, we have been profligate. We have not lived up to our place in the universe. At the very least, we have hated our political opponents and have not seen the very same errors in ourselves that we have denounced in them.

Confession is not just about looking backward. We should now be open to correction from the universe in the future. There can be no more of the thinking that I am the master of my fate. Not entirely anyway.

What such correction from the universe might mean and what form it might take, I have no idea. But we should now regard the universe as, in its own ways, normatively binding on us. Very much is now not up for grabs.

Our conclusions will be our own. I am not referring here to any institutional authority that can tell us with certainty what the universe is about. On the other hand, we are not free to ignore indications that the universe takes a certain stance. We are not the final judge—the universe is.

Those indications might well come from other voices and from other traditions. This is not coercion. This is openness.

Obviously, these first three responses would improve American public life on a personal level. They would improve our own lives and our interactions with others. This secular society has not had any place, nor any reason, for celebration, gratitude, and confession. Perhaps that is why we have been so unhappy. Now we do have a place and a reason.

These are just the immediate and personal responses to the realization that the universe is on our side. But how is this insight to be propagated?

The Role of Cosmopolis in Restored Public Life

It might appear that I can only be using Lonergan's concept of cosmopolis in propagating the *yes* as a kind of analogy. Cosmopolis would seem more appropriate as a description of the loose community of inquirers that I described in Chapter 6. This group takes no position on the question of the universe. It inquires. Its members are "representative of detached intelligence that both appreciates and criticizes."[6] John Gray is just as much a member as Whitehead or Lonergan.

But, as these thinkers demonstrate, inquiry leads to insight. The participants in cosmopolis are not detached in the sense that they have no commitments. The point of inquiry is to learn.

It is appropriate to use the concept of cosmopolis here because of the situation in which the Death of God has put us. As shown in Chapters 4 and 5, the Death of God has rendered us, in Lonergan's terms, an "uncritical culture" captive to human aberration. In such a context, practicality is all that matters. That is why our political struggles are only about which group, or side, or race, or coalition of these, will dominate. We are in what Lonergan calls the "longer cycle of decline."

Lonergan says that what is needed to break such a cycle is a "higher viewpoint," one that is more comprehensive. That viewpoint in our case is that the universe is on our side. That insight is not the kind of program that cosmopolis abjures. Instead, it is the notion upon which cosmopolis rests—that ideas matter.

So, I am now anticipating that persons in America who practice Lonergan's four transcendental precepts—people who are attentive, intelligent, reasonable, and responsible—have, upon reflection, come to the conclusion that the universe is on our side. What do they do? How do they comport themselves? If Chapter 6 asked how a people asks a question, I am now asking, how does a people propagate an insight?

The role of cosmopolis in our uncritical culture is not to confront the no. After all, the no has also come about because of disinterested inquiry. It is false but only in the sense of being incomplete. That is why the thinkers in Chapter 7 have such an honored place.

The point of cosmopolis is to confront un-criticalness itself. So, the participants in cosmopolis confront the breezy nihilism of an Arthur Leff and ask, how can you say that everything is up for grabs when your own longing for justice is in no sense up for grabs?

Leff is just one example. I hear Leff's breezy nihilism all the time, everywhere. It is the assumption that truth is just a word for someone's opinion. It is the view that all hierarchies of value are power plays. It is the suspicion that all claims of expertise are tricks. It is the denigration of the possibility of objectivity. All this is the mantra of America today.

When I say "confront," I am not suggesting that there should be more anger and assertion in public life. The confrontation by cosmopolis is always disinterested. That is what I meant above when I said that Robert Taylor taught me not to judge the success of a class by whether students came to agree with me.

---

[6] *Id.* at 237.

Confrontation by cosmopolis is always an invitation to deeper reflection. But no instance of nihilism should go unchallenged.

Our current lack of faith is not based on careful thought. It is more like a reflex. Upon deeper reflection, it will begin to fade away.

Cosmopolis will confront forcefully, however, all instances of bullying. Conservatives are right that today a noxious orthodoxy is enforced throughout much of liberal thought. But it was not very long ago that communists were being fired from university faculties. That was bullying on the Right. Progress for Lonergan depends on intelligence, but also on liberty. Any restriction on inquiry must be earnestly resisted, wherever it originates.

Cosmopolis will confront fear. Fear is the engine that drives bullying. Fear is the basis of the refusal of insight. In this case it is the fear of what inquiry will reveal. Cosmopolis must first reassure that the universe is friendly.

Cosmopolis will confront all instances of illogic. It cannot be said that nothing matters, if saying so obviously matters to the person saying it.

Cosmopolis will confront fatalism. This is the attitude that human endeavors cannot change things fundamentally. Fatalism is the ground of the lack of hope that even activists in America demonstrate through their anger. If we believed that things really could get better, we would not be so angry.

But cosmopolis also will confront the illusion that everything can change, that there are no essences or natures. Some things are fixed, some things are not and some things are relatively fixed. Discernment comes from learning which is which.

Cosmopolis will confront cynicism. Not everything is self-interest. Not everything is lies. Some people are trying to do the right thing.

Finally, although the list is meant to be suggestive, not exhaustive, in all these endeavors, cosmopolis will be even-handed. It cannot be the case that my political opponents are not really people; that they have lost their minds; that they are not worth engaging.

What do participants in cosmopolis look like when they are so engaged? They must model the faithfulness that they say the universe manifests. In this sense, cosmopolis has faith and is positive about our problems and our future, even though it has no program.

There must be wholeness in viewpoint. All evidence must be taken into account. Nothing excluded a priori.

Cosmopolis must be logical. In particular, no aspect of what David Griffin calls hardcore common sense can be violated. It must not itself be self-contradictory.

Because this book is primarily about the political side of public life, it sounds like participants in cosmopolis appear every week on *Face the Nation* or Fareed Zakaria's *Global Public Square*. But for Lonergan, as Mark Miller says, society changes through culture, through a set of meanings and values that are transmitted intersubjectively, artistically, symbolically, linguistically, and in all these ways together.[7] So, I certainly mean to include more than just our political and policy selves. There are many ways to renew a society.

Restored Disciplines

There is not much intellectual excitement today in going to college. The reason for that is the absence of a desire to learn anything new. That is not a criticism of the young. They have no reason to believe that there is anything really important for them to learn. They certainly expect to gain skills. They know this will involve the transfer of information. They may even anticipate entry into a different way of life. But they don't expect transformation.

Unfortunately, the idea that there is genuine knowledge to be learned about how to live, about how to become a better, fuller, and deeper human being, is rarely present in students. That idea is rare among faculty also.

But if the universe is on our side, then there are important matters to learn. We need to know the universe and all its ways in order to enter into this greater harmony. If we believe that, we then would expect both learning and transformation at a university. University would then again be a journey and an adventure in education.

There are several ways to look at the transformed role for the university in the world of the *yes*.

First and foremost, universe and university both root in the notion of the whole. The universe is the whole of things. The university is where the whole of things is studied.

This means a new emphasis on the "uni" in both cases. There are not completely different courses of study. There are only differing approaches to the various manifestations of the unity of all things. All these studies must be connected by an inner harmony.

I don't mean that these studies "should be" connected, as if this is something humans create. I mean the harmony is there and it is our job to find it.

In law, that inner harmony corresponds to order and lawfulness. Classically, this idea was misinterpreted in the natural law tradition, and the common law that was founded on it, to mean that all human law should be same because it all corresponds to one eternal law. As Cicero put it, "there will not be one law in Rome and another in Athens, one now and another in the future, but all peoples at all times will be embraced by a single and eternal unchangeable law."

---

[7] MARK MILLER, THE QUEST FOR GOD AND THE GOOD LIFE 180–81 (2013).

Instead, what should be thought of as in common is not the content of a law, but lawfulness itself, which then corresponds to the order that we see in nature and in the cosmos. That order may, and in fact does, manifest differently in different human societies. But it never represents injustice.

Or, in another example, if, as Whitehead thought, the universe is engaged in the cultivation of beauty, then physics and art are aspects of one study.

Ironically, this unity would be manifested in much more variety than we usually practice in the university. This is the issue of reappraising the canon. It is known as the problem of the dead white men. European thought is treated at Western universities as the norm and a male perspective is treated as the norm of norms.

This book, of course, is no exception to that narrow view. It is overwhelmingly based on a very limited set of sources, though it claims to be about the universe.

In my case, the problem is simple ignorance. But in the disciplines, the problem has proved more fundamental. Only three resolutions of the issue of the canon have emerged. Either the canon is left exactly as it had been, or it is enlarged through edict, or it is abolished.

The reason for this impasse is simple—it represents the disintegration of faith in a hierarchy of value. It is in that sense a legacy of the Death of God.

But if the universe is on our side, then, in every field, although difficult, it should not be impossible to rank the sources, and the wisdom that they represent, in terms of the insights they yield. If this is done honestly, it will lead to a new canon.

In turn, this effort to rank wisdom will require a reappraisal of what knowledge is and a reestablishment of judgment. When Dallas Willard wrote about the disappearance of moral knowledge, he did not mean that there was no moral knowledge to be had. He clearly thought there was. He meant that the public institutions that convey moral knowledge had ceased to do so.

This is true to varying extents in every field. Because we operate on certain assumptions—that only matter is real, that matter is dead, in the sense of disenchantment, and that we can gain knowledge only through the senses—there is a strict limit as to what can be regarded as knowledge, including moral knowledge. In this view, morality cannot be a subject of knowledge.

Sadly, in my own field of law, it is currently irrebuttably presumed that judgments in politically sensitive areas are always and only matters of power rather than matters of thought. It follows that we can never consider a judgment of law to be true or false. All we can say is that this judge followed this school of law and that judge followed some different school of law. This will sometimes be referred to as following different philosophies of law, but never with the expectation that there might be some unified viewpoint underlying all such approaches to interpretation. This is why we have come to refer to Obama judges and Trump judges, rather than to able judges and incompetent judges.

But assuming that this kind of strict materialism and this kind of limited epistemology are jettisoned, it will become possible to widen the field of knowledge. We will then be in a better position to judge which sources in the disciplines have added to our knowledge and to what degree.

Even with a new epistemology and ontology, there will be disagreements. These disagreements will not be easily resolved. They may not be resolved at all. But if the universe is on our side, then in principle, and in important disputes, it will usually be the case that some views are closer, and other views farther away, from the way things actually are.

To put this in perspective, think of slavery. Whatever the issue, it will often seem like the equivalent of the 1850s: there will be competing arguments and no one will be able to prove indisputably that the other side is wrong.

Nevertheless, we must not give up the ideal of truth. Eventually, that truth will reveal itself, as it did with regard to slavery. It does not remain the 1850s forever.

The harmony of the universe will also simplify and broaden the disciplines. It will reopen what the disciplines are about and how they relate to the question of our connection to the universe.

As we saw in Chapter 6, Roberto Unger referred to this as the conflict over the basic terms of social life. That is how the matter will appear in economics, for example, or political theory. But in ecology, the very same kind of question will have a different aspect.

These conflicts over the basic terms of social life will require investigation into the meaning of justice and freedom, as well as consideration of concepts like efficiency and productivity. In other words, the matters that we already study will be reframed as basic questions that both unite the disciplines and express the deepest human longing for connection and truth. This means that the disciplines will be re-founded in terms of their contributions to learning about our connection to the harmony of the universe.

A perfect illustration of reopening a discipline and re-founding its subject matter is the treatment by Robert Vischer of the moral role of the lawyer in his book, *Martin Luther King Jr. and the Morality of Legal Practice*. Vischer describes the role of the lawyer as always expressing a substantive understanding of human nature and the requirements of justice. Law simply cannot be practiced without reference to these matters. We now can see that this same statement means that law cannot be practiced without a conception of the nature of the universe and our relation to it.

So, the questions that law seeks to answer, and thus its subject matter, take on a new and broader form: that of human nature and justice.

Even in the natural sciences, a broader, more humanly oriented subject matter will emerge. Mechanistic materialism and sensationism have kept science back, as Whitehead saw. This is obvious in the case of something like the mind-body problem. But as we have seen, it is the case even in quantum theory. When something like climate change affects people, science inevitably becomes intertwined with human interest. If the universe is on our side, that intertwinement will always be the case.

Does all of this respond to the problem of a lack of faith that I introduced in Chapter 4? Would these changes restore faith or would not the opposite happen since we disagree over fundamental issues of meaning, morality, and values? Am I suggesting that the university should be rededicated to certain political outcomes, and the only question would be whether these outcomes favor the Left or favor the Right?

In our current divided and hopeless state, I understand that it will sound that way. But I mean exactly the opposite. If the universe is on our side, then the universe has a nature and so do we. We then can study both. That realization is obviously subject to abuse. It has been utilized to suggest that women's roles in public life should be restricted, for example.

But the reason for such abuse is that the study was previously restricted and was not pursued honestly. Because the universe is on our side, we have nothing to fear from a forthright investigation into the nature of all things, which is what the university should be. When we do that, and when it is seen that we are doing that, without preconception and limitation, and with a healthy regard for the variety and freedom of human experience, we will not be viewed as partisan, partial, or discriminatory. Instead, we will be on the road of restoring faith in the disciplines. Those in the disciplines will begin again to have faith in them. And those outside, in the public, will begin to have faith in them, as well.

Restored Policy Debate

This section is just a sketch of how people might approach policy in the world of the *yes*. In a range of issues, we will see just how alienated our ways of thinking had become in the breakdown in public life. That insight also suggests what a better public life might be like.

We have to start with race, America's great unfinished business. Coming to terms with the historical crime of slavery is absolutely necessary. The romance of the Confederacy for many white people has to end. I say that as one who revered Robert E. Lee as a boy.

The question is, however, what is the ultimate goal? It is clear that the goal for Martin Luther King Jr., was a society in which race was insignificant. The dream of Dr. King, as he said in his "I have a dream" speech, was that his "four little children will one day live in a nation where they will not be judged by the color of their skin but by the content of their character." In other words, the ultimate goal is not addressing the heritage of slavery, violence, and discrimination, but transcending it.

Acknowledging this ultimate goal would help us see that statues of George Washington and Thomas Jefferson do not come down with statues of Stonewall Jackson and renaming Fort Hood in Texas. Even in the case of Lee, a statue commemorating his calls for national unity after the Civil War would be in a different category than one honoring his military career.

Identity politics is what happens when our identities are not universal. Only universalism can renew us. That universalism comes from our common relation to the universe. All men are created equal. And, of course, that has to be universalized as well.

Another basic flash point currently in American public life is what U.S. Attorney General William Barr calls the "war on religion." This war has two sources. One is a very real hostility on the part of some secularists toward religion on the basis of its supposed irrationalism. The New Atheists believed that religious irrationalism was a major cause of world violence. I will return to the issue of supposed religious irrationality in the final chapter.

The other source of popular hostility against religion is the discrimination in religious doctrine and practice. Major examples of such discrimination are the prohibition of birth control coverage for employees of religious institutions and enterprises, various forms of anti-gay discrimination, and discrimination against transgender persons, whether practiced by individuals, companies, or churches.

Because religious teachings change slowly, these problems are not going away. But they are all made worse, and thus harder to compromise, because the feeling on both sides is one of warfare. These issues would feel very different if we understood ourselves as sharing a certain form of faith, even though we do not share religious commitments. In the world of the *yes*, faith in the unseen, such as in beauty, is not so different from faith in God. That starting point of shared faith would assist in creating new and healthier forms of disagreement.

Of course, the same intractability pertains to the issue of abortion in particular. But surely even here the debate would be different if its starting points were gender discrimination and early human life. Seeing abortion as a necessary evil, given the injustices of society toward women, feels very different from treating abortion as some kind of good.

Public life in the *yes* is also healthier in terms of its more generalized approaches to matters. Bernard Lonergan's transcendental precept of being responsible, as well as the return of faith in expertise, would help with mundane, but important, issues like the national debt. They would also help with existential threats such as climate change.

In contrast, we are not responsible now. We have difficulty thinking about anything but ourselves.

Being responsible means a commitment to the common good. It means a willingness to look beyond my own interests or those of my group. David Brooks was right in his column that a lot of our problems stem from an inability to think about the common good. Progressives think this is only a problem for the Right—the refusal to wear masks to prevent the spread of the virus, for example. But the dominance of my rights and interests is just as present in abortion issues and identity politics.

The absence of consideration of the common good can be really extreme. We saw in Chapter 4 that, when Harvard Law Professor Adrian Vermeule wrote that we needed a constitutionalism of the common good, both the Right and the Left were absolutely horrified.

The Left was apoplectic at Vermeule's conception of what the common good is:

> respect for the authority of rule and of rulers; respect for the hierarchies needed for society to function; solidarity within and among families, social groups, and workers' unions, trade associations, and professions; appropriate subsidiarity, or respect for the legitimate roles of public bodies and associations at all levels of government and society; and a candid willingness to "legislate morality"—indeed, a recognition that all legislation is necessarily founded on some substantive conception of morality, and that the promotion of morality is a core and legitimate function of authority. Such principles promote the common good and make for a just and well-ordered society.[8]

But the Left was never willing to debate Vermeule on the nature of the common good. Micah Schwartzman and Jocelyn Wilson, for example, criticized Vermeule for rejecting John Rawls' liberal conception of citizens as equally capable of forming rival conceptions of the good,[9] as if all conceptions of the good are valid, as long as they accept citizens as free and equal. In restored public life, that actual debate about the common good will have to take place.

The reaction on the Right was, if anything, even more hostile to substantive values. Vermeule was attacking originalism as a method of constitutional interpretation. In response, Randy Barnett argued that judges using any

---

[8] Adrian Vermeule, *Beyond Originalism*, ATLANTIC (Mar. 31, 2020), https://www.theatlantic.com/ideas/archive/2020/03/common-good-constitutionalism/609037/.

[9] Micah Schwartzman & Jocelyn Wilson, *The Unreasonableness of Catholic Integralism*, 56 SAN DIEGO L. REV. 1039 (2019).

non-originalist approach to interpretation would just decide "results that they like,"[10] as if reason about the common good is always just a power play. But I think Justice Scalia, if confronted with Vermeule, would have said that his form of originalist constitutional interpretation, which Scalia called "textualism," already served the common good by limiting the power of judges and enhancing democracy. That was why he used it. Justice Scalia already practiced common-good constitutionalism.

Fundamentally, America needs a conception of the common good. But there is no common good without a story in common. The universe on our side is the story that we need—a unifying story that applies to all of us.

Then there is the matter of hope. Our policy debates are narrow and dispirited because we have no hope for the future. We cannot respond to the call of Roberto Unger, for example, to imagine new institutional arrangements that would replace our current form of capitalism. Our imagination is broken because we don't believe in the future.

We cannot even imagine what the post-war generation could imagine—a world of prosperity, democracy, and peace. A world of trust, not a world of walls.

When the nationalist populists came in 2016, all over the world, the post-war liberal order surrendered without even attempting to defend itself. It was exhausted.

The fires of that first wave of populism are now burning out. Of course, it did not deliver anything. But what will replace it? All we have at present are different forms of groupings as our politics. That is what both anti-racism and Making America Great Again are about.

The post-war consensus wasn't wrong. It just could not be sustained without God. As the ripples from the Death of God finally arrived in full—came home to roost—there was no universal dream to take its place. Now, perhaps, there is, in a universe that is on our side.

Restored Politics

In a way, this is the easiest change to understand. We already know what politics looks like when you believe that the arc of the moral universe is long, but bends toward justice. Politics with that viewpoint looks like the politics of Martin Luther King Jr.

It will be pointed out, correctly, that Dr. King was a Christian first. The source of his faith in the future lay with Jesus Christ. That is absolutely right.

---

[10]   Randy E. Barnett, *Common-Good Constitutionalism Reveals the Dangers of Any Non-Originalist Approach to the Constitution*, ATLANTIC (Apr. 3, 2020).

Without disputing Dr. King's Christian commitment, he spoke of the moral universe for a reason. Dr. King knew how to preach the Gospel. He was not preaching the Gospel when he spoke of the universe. He was very intentionally reaching out to all of us, using a vocabulary that we have in common. He was creating a common good in his very language.

The politics of Dr. King is not our only model. When Tom Berry spoke of the universe as a communion of subjects and not a collection of objects, he meant that a communion of subjects is what the universe actually is. Berry was not speaking idealistically. If we think that the universe is a collection of objects, we are not just callous and shortsighted, we are also incorrect. Politics based on Berry's understanding would not just be better, it would be more truthful.

The reason that the other conception—that the universe is a collection of objects for our use—leads to politics that make us miserable is that it is untrue.

Whitehead explains how we come to understand Berry's truth about the universe. We apprehend our connection to everything else. It is as much a part of knowledge as other aesthetic and moral truths. It is not as exact as knowledge gained through the senses. But it is knowledge all the same. Whitehead gives us the architecture behind Berry's pronouncement. He is the philosopher for Berry's theological orientation.

We have tried to go down this road of substantive values before. In the 1990s, Bill and Hillary Clinton adopted for a time the framework of the "politics of meaning" from the Jewish thinker Michael Lerner, who saw a spiritual crisis at the heart of American public life. In 1993, Hillary Clinton gave her famous "politics of meaning" speech in which she reportedly said, "We need a new politics of meaning. We need a new ethos of individual responsibility and caring. We need a new definition of civil society which answers the unanswerable questions posed by both the market forces and the governmental ones, as to how we can have a society that fills us up again and makes us feel that we are part of something bigger than ourselves."[11]

You can add here Rick Warren's *Purpose Driven Life*, although Warren has said that he has " 'no political aspirations' " and " 'no aspirations to even influence public policy.' "[12] Progressives dispute this, but accepting Warren at his word, there certainly are public policy implications in his church renewal movement.

But Warren's staying power, as compared to the ephemeral quality of the politics of meaning, illustrates why any form of spiritual renewal for American

[11] Hillary Clinton, *Hillary Clinton's Politics of Meaning Speech: University of Texas, Austin April 6, 1993*, Tikkun Aug. 1, 2016, at 24, 25, https://read.dukeupress.edu/tikkun/article-abstract/31/3/24/10354/Hillary-Clinton-s-Politics-of-Meaning?redirectedFrom=PDF. Because no actual transcript of the speech exists, *Tikkun* magazine published a partial, reconstructed version. But no one has disputed its essential accuracy.

[12] Wendy Kaminer, *The Pastoral Is Political*, Atlantic (Dec. 7, 2009), https://www.theatlantic.com/national/archive/2009/12/the-pastoral-is-political/31354/.

public life has thus far failed at its goal of renewal. Either the effort is grounded in God, as in the Warren example, in which case it cannot reach a nonbelieving culture, or it is not grounded in anything but a vague hope for better feelings, as in Lerner's case. But then it just dwindles away over time.

In a series of books, and in an entire academic career, Christian Miller has shown how a better understanding of our character can improve our lives individually and collectively. But his work is premised on the implicit idea of a good person—that it is better, for example, to be willing to help someone in an emergency than to turn away. This culture will not be able to teach such moral knowledge and character formation until we have confidence that our efforts are objectively and demonstrably grounded in the sort of beings we are and the sort of entity the universe is.

America needs restored faith. But that can only come as knowledge. As truth. It must be based on inquiry and not just in feelings and character. Improvements in feelings and character are necessary to improve public life. But exhortation in that regard is not enough.

When we actually see that the universe is on our side, then it will be obvious that we need to be on each other's side. Politics will then not be about my winning at your expense, as it was not for Dr. King. Politics will about the realization, partial but in the right direction, of the care that the universe shows for us.

I wrote above that faith in the unseen is not so different from faith in God. But is that so? And if it is so, then has this book just been a roundabout way of attempting to reverse the Death of God that I have asserted is irreversible for us at this time? We turn to that question in the last chapter.

10

Does This Bring Us Back to God?

It was certainly not my intention in writing this book to bring us back to God. For one thing, as I have said repeatedly, that is not a cultural possibility at this time.

But that could change. One effect of the realization that the universe is on our side might be to reawaken interest in the question of God. People might be drawn to ask how it has come to be that the universe is on our side. Remember, Lonergan's question was put in a chapter entitled "Religion," in a section denoted "The Question of God." And in that section, prior to asking whether the universe is cognate to us as moral beings, Lonergan asked, "Does there or does there not necessarily exist a transcendent intelligent ground to the universe?" Lonergan always thought that we would end up asking: what is behind the universe, if anything?

So, as Lonergan knew, the question of God has a strong tendency to arise once we begin to think about reality in a serious way.

But this chapter will not attempt to fully answer the question of God. This chapter will be different from the rest of the book. It will be shorter and it will not reach a conclusion. Not only am I not prepared to answer the question of God, but, in the context of this book, it is premature to do so. America is a society in disarray, with a public life that has broken down. The realization that the universe is on our side is what we need to know right now to address the breakdown. A full-scale argument about God would distract us from that realization.

Nevertheless, the unrestricted investigation that I have invited will include, for some readers, the question of God. So, even though for me questioning about God is only beginning, I will provide some of the materials for that inquiry. That is my purpose in this chapter, though I will make my own preliminary thoughts clear.

In a way, then, this chapter is both a conclusion to where we have been and the new beginning that Camus hoped for.

Process thought, which I have heretofore relied on in this book, is a God-based system. As Griffin explains, for Alfred North Whitehead, and his student Charles Hartshorne, God was a necessary element in process philosophy. That is why Griffin labeled the naturalism of process thought naturalismppp. The second P stands for panentheist, which means essentially God in the world.

Panentheism is a theological position between the God of traditional theism, who transcends the world, and the conception of God *as* the world, which is

The Universe Is on Our Side. Bruce Ledewitz, Oxford University Press. © Oxford University Press 2022.
DOI: 10.1093/oso/9780197563939.003.0011

called pantheism. In panentheism, divinity interpenetrates the world in some way but is not identical with all of the world's processes.

Process thought understands itself as both panentheistic and still thoroughly naturalistic. Griffin refers to God as the soul of the world. That image of the soul is meant to suggest the way God works naturalistically in the world.

In process thought, unlike traditional theism, God cannot interrupt, even in principle, the normal causal relations in nature. There is thus no hint of supernaturalism. In that sense, process philosophy is naturalistic, while traditional theism is not.

The other important difference between process thought about God and traditional theism is that, in process thought, God is not omnipotent in the traditional sense. In process thought, God does not create ex nihilo—from nothing. God must work with the existing material of the world, both at the beginning, that is, in creation, and throughout all time. In the beginning, there was chaos, not nothing.

To see the effect of this limit on God, consider the words of the Reverend George V. Coyne, S.J., director of the Vatican Observatory and thus a traditional theist. In 2006, Reverend Coyne came to Duquesne University, where I teach, to lecture about intelligent design. He said it was not science.

In the course of his remarks, one observation he made was unforgettable for me. He said—and this is from my memory and not an exact quote—that he did not know why God chose to use carbon in the creation of life. But, having made that decision, God had to wait until the advent of a generation of supernovas, which would create carbon.

This is how traditional theism must talk about the interaction of God with the laws of nature. God's decision to follow the laws of nature must always reflect some kind of divine choice.

In process thought, in contrast, God is limited intrinsically in the way that matter can become life. If carbon is a necessary element of life through the laws of nature, then our universe cannot contain life until it contains carbon. God can do nothing about it.

Similarly, the actual entities and true individuals who act in the universe in process thought also cannot just be ordered around by God. In process thought, every finite individual embodies at least some slight power of self-determination and has causal effects that cannot be overridden by God. The God of process thought can only give initial aims and then provide influence. That is all the process God can do.

Nevertheless, this God does have an effect. That is why, for example, though evolution takes a long time—God cannot just issue an order for sentience—evolution has a direction. God has issued the initial aim of the process of evolution and continuously influences it.

At the highest level of organization in the universe—that is, in human beings—God's influence is at its weakest. We have minds of our own. But, again, we are nevertheless influenced by God. And we encounter that divine influence in every action that we take.

On the other hand, at the beginning of creation, because matter was unorganized, God's influence was much more powerful. God could then in large part direct, though even then there was resistance from the chaos that God had to work with.

In many ways, the God of process thought is a much more satisfactory God for modernity than is the God of traditional theism. The God of process thought, for example, is not responsible for the natural evils of the world—for its viruses, volcanoes, and birth defects. Those natural evils are inevitable because of the dynamic processes of the universe. In process thought, the question never can arise as to why God did not create a universe with a different fundamental capacity, one in which natural evil would not arise. There was no divine choice involved.

Reflecting on all this, it is not clear to me what God is like in process thought. Early in his thinking, in *Science and the Modern World* in 1925, Whitehead described God as "merely a principle" and as "'not concrete.'"[1] Later, in 1929 in *Process and Reality*, Whitehead changed his view and considered God to be "a single, everlasting actual entity."[2]

The problem with that conception of God, however, was that in several ways, God as an actual entity conflicted with the nature of actual entities elsewhere in Whitehead's thought. Since Whitehead had also written that "'God is not to be treated as an exception to all metaphysical principles' but instead as 'their chief exemplification,'"[3] this inconsistency was a serious flaw.

According to Griffin, it became clear to "many process philosophers and theologians" that this problem had to be dealt with, and the concept of God made "coherent with the basic principles" of process thought, by reconceiving God as a "living person—that is, as an everlasting personally ordered society of divine occasions of experience." This is much more in keeping with the basic way in which enduring individuals are treated generally in process thought. So, God is a person.

This reconception of God allows Griffin to keep the God of process thought more or less within the generic idea of God in traditional theism. So, for example, the God of process thought is a "personal, purposive being" just as is the God of traditional theism.

---

[1] David Ray Griffin, Reenchantment Without Supernaturalism: A Process Philosophy of Religion 174 (2001).

[2] *Id.* at 155.

[3] *Id.* at 140.

To illustrate what it means to keep God within the tradition, Griffin presents a list of thirteen traditional attributes of God—no relation to the thirteen Middot, or attributes of God, in the Jewish tradition from Exodus 34:6–7. The only differences in the process conception of God are that the power of God only operates within certain parameters—creation is not ex nihilo, for example—and God's acts are never coercive.[4] Otherwise, Griffin implies, the God of process philosophy is what we usually think of as God.

However, the differences that Griffin notes are much more significant than he seems to think. While I can imagine what the traditional God of theism might be like, it is hard for me to do so with regard to the purposive but restricted God of process thought. Does the God of process thought become frustrated at only being able to work with existing material? Does God long for a different situation?

Furthermore, these carefully imposed restrictions on God seem more designed to allow the process system to function than to be the outcome of attentive reflection on how things actually are. These careful distinctions about God seem arbitrary.

In addition, and to some extent the other side of the coin, the process conception of God also seems to violate Griffin's fundamental insistence that process thought is a form of naturalism. As Jerome Stone observes in *Religious Naturalism Today*, "the God of process theology, while deeply immersed within this world, is so ontologically distinct and superior as to fall outside of naturalism" altogether.[5]

Perhaps because of the rickety quality of the process conception of God, and the fraught aim of staying within naturalism, an approach to process thought has emerged known as "Whitehead Without God," associated originally with Donald Sherburne. Sherburne dispenses with divinity altogether.

Griffin describes Sherburne as affirming that the basic metaphysical order of the universe—that is, in the terms of this book, that the universe is on our side—does accord with the principles of process philosophy. Thus, Sherburne is a process theorist. But Griffin goes on to say that in Sherburne's approach, this metaphysical order "*just is*, without needing to be instantiated in a primordial actuality." That is, there is no God behind the universe's order.

That description—that the basic order of things *just is*—seems right to me. This conception is not so different from Heidegger's oft-used phrase, "Es gibt"— it gives. Heidegger is pointing to the radical givenness of everything.

---

[4] *Id.* at 166.
[5] JEREMY STONE, RELIGIOUS NATURALISM TODAY: THE REBIRTH OF A FORGOTTEN ALTERNATIVE 8 (2014).

Griffin is critical of Sherburne's position because Griffin, like John Gray, does not think it can account for the universality of the laws of nature. That universality, however, does not seem to me to be outside the realm of the *just is.*

More difficult for me is describing, even to myself, how the influence of the universe in favoring life, complexity, intelligence, and morality comes to bear on events, without the involvement of a purposive being like God.

Perhaps we can think of the influence of the ideals of the universe in terms of force or structure, instead of a person. Analogies like that are, admittedly, only partial, and can be misleading, but they are often helpful for understanding. I hope that my use of "perhaps" here is not the same as the surrender of thought that I was criticizing in Chapter 5.

So, perhaps the divine influence of which process thought speaks is like the blueprint from which a medieval cathedral will be built over centuries. That is, divine action is a kind of inherent force, influencing our actions and those of other entities.

That blueprint, although not complete, gives the initial aim of the cathedral— a form of building that serves holiness. Every action, the laying of every stone, encounters and participates in that initial aim. Furthermore, that initial aim manifests differently, and comes to be understood differently, as the cathedral takes shape over the years.

In other words, the workers and builders come to new and maybe fuller understandings of that initial aim over time. The same is true of us and the ideals of the universe.

Or, we might think, instead, of divine influence as a structure. We might think of those science museum demonstrations of the curvature of Einsteinian space-time. Like gravity, the ideals of the universe might create wells in reality by their attraction. We humans may be deflected from our straight paths by the attraction of goodness, truth, beauty, and justice—and love. The advantage of this structural image of curvature is that it replicates Dr. King's message about how history bends toward justice.

As opposed to structure, however, the advantage of an image of divine action as a force is that some of our most intense experiences of the goodness of the universe take the form of personal response. Process thought insists that these sorts of intense, personal, religious experiences—for example, prayers for forgiveness, help, or clarity that are answered—are real and represent a form of truth about things. A force, as opposed to a structure, can operate in that kind of active way.

But an inherent force, like a blueprint, can only go so far in explaining our experiences of the divine. These experiences can be so personal that the notion of a divine being who is a friend is almost impossible to deny. In other words, the holy reality that in mainstream process thought underlies everything often has a personal aspect in its interactions with human beings. So, must there not be a personal, loving God, just as Griffin suggests?

I don't have an answer for this deep question. Like Stone, above, given the assumptions of naturalism, I just do not understand how such a being could exist. But I admit that it is difficult for me to assert that the love and caring that I have experienced from the universe, *just is*. That does not seem to correspond to my experiences. At the moment, this is my impasse.

Assuming that Sherburne is right that we can have a godless process philosophy—that is, Whitehead Without God—another issue arises. Would that understanding be enough to validate our relation to the universe? Up to this point, I have treated the idea that the universe is on our side as sufficient by itself to bring healing to American public life. Given how broken things are, that is undoubtedly correct to some extent.

But God functions in a very particular way in process thought. By remembering the past, God is said to confer indestructible meaning on all of our striving. God is thus the ultimate guarantor of worth, of value. And that real worthwhileness, said Lonergan, is the beginning of his question about the universe. Losing that could undermine the positive message for the culture that the universe is on our side.

When I discussed this issue above, in a different form, the question was, how could the universe really be on our side if we and everything else, including everything we love, dies? The answer to that concern was not difficult. We could not love unless we ourselves were finite and unless everything else was finite as well.

But that answer does not address the issue here. The question here is whether our striving has to be worthwhile forever to be really worthwhile. Must value be guaranteed permanently? Without God, it is not.

Sherburne takes this issue on directly: "If one were the type to be depressed at the thought that the sun will run out of energy some day and our planet become an empty chunk of rock, then I should think one would derive cold comfort in the thought that even at that time God will prehend the present as objectified in his consequent nature!"[6]

In other words, if I can accept my own mortality, and still maintain with Whitehead that my actions participate in the "permanent rightness" of the universe, then it must be the quality of my actions now, their objective goodness now, that has ultimate significance. According to Sherburne, the fact that my actions will not be remembered does not detract from that objective quality of rightness.

---

[6] Donald Sherburne, *Whitehead Without God*, *in* PROCESS PHILOSOPHY AND CHRISTIAN THOUGHT (Delvin Brown, Ralph James, & Donald Sherburne eds., 1971), https://www.religion-online.org/book-chapter/chapter16-whitehead-without-god-by-donald-w-sherburne/.

To return to the story of Abraham in the Bible, Abraham is promised that his descendants will be a blessing to all the people of the world. That satisfies Abraham even though he will himself die.

What Sherburne is adding here is that this satisfaction should remain for Abraham even if Abraham realizes that this blessing will come to a finite end with the end of the peoples of the Earth. Abraham has still lived an objectively proper life and has still reaped his reward for it.

Is this enough? That depends on what we think we need. Peter Berger felt he needed to be guaranteed that he would live forever. That turns out not to be what we need.

The debate among the process thinkers is about something else. It is about vindication. Do we need permanent vindication?

The resurrection is considered the vindication of Jesus against the government authorities who murdered him. In the words of Gregory Beale, professor of New Testament and biblical theology at Westminster Theological Seminary: "Jesus's own resurrection was an end-time event that 'vindicated' or 'justified' him from the wrong verdict pronounced by the world's courts. The vindication of God's people against the unjust verdicts of their accusers was to happen at the eschaton, but this has been pushed back to Christ's resurrection and applied to him."[7]

In the mainstream of process thought, God's permanent memory of the rightness of my actions serves a role similar to that of the resurrection. God's memory of me vindicates the goodness of my good actions forever. Can we do without that?

No one knows the answer to that question of course, but we can note that Jesus himself did not need the resurrection. Yes, Jesus did call from the cross, in Matthew and Mark, "Eli, Eli, lama sabachthani?" which is the opening of Psalm 22: "My God, my God, why hast thou forsaken me?"

But this should not be taken as Jesus's last word on the matter of justification. In the first place, as the Jewish readers of the Gospels would have known, Psalm 22 only begins in despair. It ends in triumph.

In addition, the accounts in Mark and Matthew should be read along with Jesus's words in the Gospel of Luke—"Father, into thy hands I commend my spirit." This saying, from Psalm 31:5, would have been known to end as follows: "Into thine hand I commit my spirit: thou hast redeemed me, O LORD God of truth." Again, triumph.

---

[7] Gregory Beale, *Resurrection as Christ's Vindication (and Ours)*, WESTMINSTER THEOLOGICAL SEMINARY (Oct. 25, 2016), https://faculty.wts.edu/posts/resurrection-as-christs-vindication-and-ours/.

Jesus says all of this from the cross. Yes, Jesus is vindicated by the resurrection. But Jesus did not know that would happen. It is on the cross that Jesus is the personification of faithful human life.

So, why cannot a human being, knowing the universe is on our side—that is, on the side of life, complexity, intelligence and morality—be willing to die without anything more than that? If we actually believe that the universe is like that, we are already vindicated.

Maybe that is the problem. Maybe we just do not have the same kind of faith that Jesus had. But, if we did, we would not need the prospect of God remembering us forever.

Clearly, we crave the ultimate vindication that God is said to supply. But perhaps we do not need it.

There is another desire that we have that is related to our craving for ultimate vindication. We want those who have done wrong to be punished or at least to be denounced. Although neither Sherburne nor Griffin refers to this desire, it is, as Beale recognized above, the other side of the resurrection. In the resurrection, Jesus is vindicated and, at the same time, his false accusers are in effect unmasked as wrongdoers. God will also remember that for all time.

Jesus demonstrates, however, that we do not need this either. Jesus's word on the matter of punishment is the parable of the elder brother and the prodigal son in the Gospel of Luke.[8] When the father welcomes home the prodigal son, the elder brother's complaint is not that he has been mistreated by his father, but that the prodigal son has been treated well by their father and does not deserve it: "Look! All these years I've been slaving for you and never disobeyed your orders. Yet you never gave me even a young goat so I could celebrate with my friends. But when this son of yours who has squandered your property with prostitutes comes home, you kill the fattened calf for him!"

The father's response is reassuring: " 'My son,' the father said, 'you are always with me, and everything I have is yours.' " In other words, all that the elder brother has a right to hope for is the proper reward for his life of good deeds, which the elder brother has always received. Jesus is insisting that we don't have the right to demand that the guilty be punished. Thus, there is nothing for God to remember.

So, I believe that Sherburne is right. We can have process thought without God and not lose the essence of its insight that the universe is on our side. Lonergan's question, properly considered, can lead to the healing of American public life even without God.

How important is the question of God? Obviously in one sense, it is of ultimate significance. Other than the question about the universe, what could be

---

[8] Luke 15:11–32.

more important than the question of whether God exists? It is another ultimate question.

But in the terms of this book, once we are living in the *yes*, the answer to the question of God may eventually be seen as a continuum, rather than a simple matter of God's existence or not.

Lonergan's question about the universe was for him the question of God. The very next sentence after the paragraph we have been examining is, "Such is the question of God." It did not occur to Lonergan that one could conclude the universe is on our side and yet conclude as well that God does not exist.

This is not shocking. There are probably many believers who understand the word 'God' basically to mean that the universe is on our side, although Lonergan was not one of them. The distinction between God as the universe on our side and God as a being goes to the nature of God. There have always been many different ways of thinking about the nature of God.

Aside from theology, how important is the question of God to the breakdown of American public life? This whole book is a proposal that the breakdown was caused by the Death of God. In that sense, the question of God is everything to the breakdown.

The question of God in this chapter, however, is different. Griffin explained the two approaches to God that are relevant here in a book entitled *God Exists But Gawd Does Not*. The God who died was the supernatural, omnipotent creator of the universe. That is the God who grounded Western civilization and in whom America believed. His death led to the breakdown in public life that we see today.

The question in this chapter is different. It is whether there is a God who is a part of the universe that is on our side. In that context, the question of God is not actually a separate question. In fact, the connection of the question of God to Lonergan's question about the universe is one of the ways that Lonergan's question can heal us. We can all become fellow seekers exploring the deepest nature of the universe.

That would be very different from the situation we have now. Currently, the division between religious believers and non-believers is one of the worst aspects of the breakdown in American public life. In the courts and in politics, religion and anti-religion are crucial parts of the coalitions on both sides—religious people favor the Republicans and anti-religious people favor the Democrats.

I am exaggerating, of course. There are pious Democrats and atheistic Republicans, but overwhelmingly religion in America is partisan.

This is a disaster for both public life and for religion. No one really believes religion is supposed to favor a political party.

One reason for the division between believers and non-believers is the view that religion is some sort of special realm, separated from all forms of reason.

Obviously, the New Atheists believed this, but it was also a prejudice of the Enlightenment generally.

What is not well known is that religious believers have been pushing the same idea of religion as irrational in constitutional litigation. Their goal has been to expand the areas in which religious believers cannot be questioned in court.

I mentioned in Chapter 5 that the claimed irrationality of religion lay behind the decision in *Employment Division v. Smith* in 1990 that religious practices were not protected by the Free Exercise Clause because no judgments could be made about the importance of religious claims. Since we could not reason about religion, it would have to be all or nothing. And since religion could not be accepted as a justification for disobeying all laws—that would lead to anarchy, asserted Justice Scalia—religion would have to receive no protection at all from generally applicable laws.

In *Smith*, the irrationality of religion led to a restriction on religious liberty. But a similar argument succeeded in 2020 that no judgment could be made about whether a teacher at a religious institution was a minister.[9] That had to be left to the religious institution to decide. And all the Obamacare contraception litigation was premised on the argument that the severity of a burden for a religious believer could only be judged by that believer herself. So, a notice requirement that a religious entity did not want to cover contraception in its healthcare benefits plan was treated as if it had resulted from a dire threat to conscience.[10] The government was not allowed to argue that this position was absurd.

In contrast, Lonergan was a rationalist. He believed that religion was part of a rational universe. His question about the universe arises out of that rational commitment.

Once we conclude that we can question and reason about whether the universe is on our side, the separation of religion from the rest of life will be at an end. There will then be, in Whitehead's sense, a unified viewpoint on reality. Within that unified viewpoint, the question of God is just a part of questioning the nature of reality.

You could say at that point that we are all religious, that there really is no such thing as a nonbeliever. We all are seekers inquiring about the universe and asking ultimate questions. To paraphrase the great constitutional theorist of religion Douglas Laycock, all answers to ultimate questions are religious.[11] I have no objection to saying we are all religious since we all ask these questions.

---

[9] *Our Lady of Guadalupe School v. Morrissey-Berru*, No. 19-267, 2020 WL 3808420 (U.S. July 8, 2020).

[10] *Little Sisters of the Poor v. Pennsylvania*, 140 S.Ct. 1292 (2020).

[11] The actual quote is, "for constitutional purposes, any answer to religious questions is religion." Douglas Laycock, *Religious Liberty as Liberty*, 7 J. CONTEMP. LEG. ISSUES 313, 329 (1996).

But I believe there is a better and holier characterization that arises out of the same common seeking. You can say at that point that we are all human.

Our divisions are at an end.

That ending point of restored unity is a fitting place for us to stop. In Part I of this book, we began with the terrible breakdown in American public life today. We saw that none of the usual explanations could really account for its depth and breadth. This led to the conclusion that we are witnessing the working out of the Death of God that has been unfolding for a long time. The Death of God left Americans without faith in anything and evading serious questions.

In Part II, we looked at raising an ultimate question—whether the universe is on our side—as a way of beginning the path back from the breakdown. In questioning, we renew faith, if only in questioning itself. The society that questions is already serious again.

Whether we decide the question of the universe as a *no* or a *yes*, we can build from our answer to a healthier and more satisfying American public life. Nevertheless, the *yes* seems to me to more fully answer Lonergan's question and to lead to a public life of restored faith.

But questioning does not end. Not only will Lonergan's question never be finally answered, it will lead to what is the ultimate mystery: the nature of holiness. We know in Whitehead's sense of knowing that there is holiness in the universe. But we do not know its nature. We do not know its name.

We must leave that question unanswered for now. Restored public life today does not require its answer. But in the end, the human desire to know is going to insist on a response to this question also.

Afterword

I wrote a version of this Afterword right after the election. Joe Biden was president-elect, baseless claims that the election was stolen were proliferating, weak legal challenges to the election were pending, Democrats were weakened in the House and were probably going to fail to flip the Senate in two January elections in Georgia, and President Trump was refusing to concede. There was even talk of Republican legislatures in battleground states like Michigan reversing the will of the voters and appointing the presidential electors themselves.

I knew that reality would eventually set in over the election result. But I anticipated that Biden would assume office facing a hostile Republican majority in the Senate and a frustrated Democratic majority in the House.

Meanwhile, there were 202,138 new Covid-19 cases and 2098 deaths on November 20. Hospitalizations nationally were at an all-time high. Numbers of cases and deaths were climbing.

The political situation changed dramatically on January 5 and 6. On January 5, the voters of Georgia, undoubtedly in part because of relentless attempts to subvert the November presidential election result, voted for the two Democratic Party Senate challengers, thus giving control of the Senate to the Democrats, along with the House and the presidency.

On January 6, during the debate over the formal certification of Biden's victory, an ugly mob stormed the Capitol building and disrupted the counting for hours. It is not clear whether they, and for that matter the lawful protestors also present, believed they could change the election result, but they plainly believed that the election had been stolen by Biden and the Democrats.

These events, even the riot, had the potential to improve our politics. The narrow Democratic Party majorities in Congress ensured both that there would not be endless conflict in the next two years over actually running the government—nominations to the Cabinet, for example—and that any Biden legislative agenda with the support of the moderate center would probably pass.

The attack during the election certification seemed to me at the time likely to diminish any future influence of President Trump. Presumably the event would give some pause to America's relentless partisan division.

Unfortunately, however, these events did not change the underlying context, which readers of this book know predated President Trump's arrival on the political scene. Though his malign influence will recede, the frayed fabric of American public life will not spontaneously mend. Our partisan differences will continue as Republicans aim to retake the House and Senate in 2022. There is not going to be bipartisan cooperation on any fundamental matter.

Worse than that, millions of Americans will remain convinced that the presidential election was stolen through fraud. It is hard to imagine a worse result for constitutional democracy. If you really believe that, why would you not support a military coup or an assassination?

There is in January 2021 some unambiguously good news. The vaccines that have been developed show every sign of effectiveness and safety. Thus, by mid-2021, Americans will probably be resuming a more normal life. The current darkness will lighten. It will be a time of hope for a new beginning.

Prior to the election, the prevalent mood of nihilism on both sides of our political and cultural divide, described in Part I of the book, was on full display. In a *New York Times* review of Katie Mack's book about the end of the universe, *The End of Everything*, James Gleick concluded that the book refutes Dr. King's view that the universe bends toward justice:

> It seems safe to say, though, that any meaning and purpose will have to be found in ourselves, not in the stars. The cosmic end times will bring no day of judgment, no redemption. All we can expect is the total obliteration of whatever universe remains and any intelligence that still abides there.

At about the same time, Josh Blackman, a very influential conservative law professor, rendered the same judgment, without mentioning Dr. King by name, on a popular legal blog in an entry that he entitled "There Is No Court of History":

> In general, when I hear the phrase "court of history" or "arc of history," I simply presume that a liberal is trying to shame a conservative into reaching a liberal result. These phrases no longer have any meaning for me. Alas, the Chief bought into this mythology.

The reference was to Chief Justice John Roberts overruling *Korematsu*, the WWII Japanese-American internment case. For Blackman, the widespread condemnation of that case as objectively wrong, as an evil that constitutional democracy should never have countenanced, "no longer has any meaning." That kind of historical judgment is mere "mythology." Justice John Harlan weeps over this descent of law into nihilism.

We were reminded how far we have fallen by the 75th anniversary of the Nuremberg trials on November 21. Just compare the above with Justice Robert Jackson's opening. Jackson assumed there would be universal agreement that law is founded on reason:

That four great nations, flushed with victory and stung with injury, stay the hand of vengeance and voluntarily submit their captive enemies to the judgment of the law is one of the most significant tributes that power has ever paid to reason.

Our nihilism prevents us from addressing the crisis of American public life. We don't believe there can be an answer.

You can see the paralysis in David Brooks. In October, he published a long piece in the *Atlantic* about the loss of social trust. The current crisis, he wrote, is a manifestation of our loss of faith in our institutions and in each other.

But when it came time in the article to suggest a remedy, Brooks was not hopeful. He wrote that the experts—psychologists and political scientists—are not much help when it comes to restoring social trust.

What Brooks was certain about is that there will no future American ethos:

If you think we're going back to the America that used to be—with a single cohesive mainstream culture; with an agile, trusted central government; with a few mainstream media voices that police a coherent national conversation; with an interconnected, respected leadership class; with a set of dominant moral values based on mainline Protestantism or some other single ethic—then you're not being realistic. I see no scenario in which we return to being the nation we were in 1965, with a cohesive national ethos, a clear national establishment, trusted central institutions, and a pop-culture landscape in which people overwhelmingly watch the same shows and talked about the same things. We're too beaten up for that. The age of distrust has smashed the converging America and the converging globe—that great dream of the 1990s—and has left us with the reality that our only plausible future is decentralized pluralism.

I guess in this decentralized pluralism every geographic entity gets to decide on right and wrong. Brooks does not understand that you cannot get to public health from this starting point. You need to take truth much more seriously.

I did see one small step before the election in the direction of truth about reality as an antidote to our crisis. In a review of Anne Boyer's book about her experience with cancer, *The Undying*, Nellie Hermann pointed to an important moment in the book when Boyer tells the nurses who have been saying that the chemotherapy injections would not hurt, that they do hurt. This inspires other patients in the room to speak up in the same way.

Saying this does not lessen the pain, of course. The point of "joining together to say that what appears to hurt actually *does hurt*," is, according to Boyer, "so that no one would ever again say while they were hurting us that what really hurt us—hurt all of us—never did."

As Hermann put it, the patients were joining together "to expose a lie."

You would hope that the book and/or the review would then conclude that the truth—large and small, about cancer treatments and the universe—might make us free. That would be the right next step. Then we would be moving toward a foundation in the real.

The reader of this book already knows that in this culture, that step was not likely to occur. We don't dare to assert that truth is our goal.

Here is how the review actually ended, and it is a fitting epitaph for our time:

> Though there is a quest here, Boyer's seems to be not for meaning but instead for a narrative that reveals the chaos all of our narratives are a part of. A work about breast cancer, Boyer concludes, "will be judged by its veracity or its utility or its depth of feeling but rarely by its form, which is its motor and its fury, which is a record of the motions of a struggle to know, if not the truth, then the weft of all competing lies."

To be fair, it's a start. When we realize that lies are somehow at the root of our problem, we have begun to ask questions about the truth of things. Maybe, in what I hope will be our post-pandemic yearning for a new beginning, we will be ready for the kind of questioning about the universe, and our place in it, that can provide a truthful foundation for our lives together. Maybe it will be the right time for this book.

One last word. I mentioned in the book that our dog Maxine was getting older and that we could foresee her end. Since then, she has had serious health problems and we have spent a lot of time with the vets. She does not now walk as well as she did, nor see as well as she did.

But she is not in pain. She still enjoys life. And we are determined to enjoy her as long as that is so.

Maxine is a daily miracle. Our love for her, and hers for us, is a truth about the universe. It is a truth of eternal significance. It will endure after she is gone. After we are gone. And after this universe is gone.

Yes, that is a faith. I hope I have shown in this book that it is a faith that can be investigated and evaluated. And held. Now it is time for the scoffers to give up their unthinking assumptions to the contrary and to engage. Their lives are at stake, as are ours.

Bibliography

Barnett, Randy. *The Structure of Liberty: Justice and the Rule of Law*. Oxford, UK: Oxford University Press, 1998.

Barth, Karl. *The Epistle to the Romans*. London: Oxford University Press, 1933.

Bealer, George, and Robert C. Koons, editors. *The Waning of Materialism*. Oxford, UK: Oxford University Press, 2010.

Becker, Adam. *What Is Real?* New York: Basic Books, 2018.

Berger, Peter. *A Rumor of Angels: Modern Society and the Rediscovery of the Supernatural*. New York: Anchor, 1970.

Berman, Morris. *The Reenchantment of the World*. New York: Cornell University Press, 1981.

Brooks, David. *The Second Mountain: The Quest for a Moral Life*. New York: Penguin Random House LLC, 2019.

Brown, David. *Paradise Lost*. Cambridge, MA: Belknap Press, 2017.

Brown, Delwin, Ralph James, and Donald Sherburne, editors. "Whitehead Without God." In *Process Philosophy and Christian Thought*. Indianapolis: Bobs-Merrill Company, Inc., 1971.

Buchanan, Allen, and Russell Powell. *The Evolution of Moral Progress: A Biocultural Theory*. New York: Oxford University Press, 2018.

Buhner, Stephen Harrod. *The Lost Language of Plants: The Ecological Importance of Plant Medicines to Life on Earth*. White River Junction, VT: Chelsea Green Publishing, 2002.

Carney, Timothy. *Alienated America: Why Some Places Thrive While Others Collapse*. New York: HarperCollins Publishers, 2019.

Casanova, Jose. *Public Religions*. Chicago: University of Chicago Press, 1994.

Chua, Amy. *Political Tribes: Group Insight and the Fate of Nations*. New York: Penguin Press, 2018.

Chua, Amy. *World on Fire: How Exporting Free Market Democracy Breeds Ethnic Hatred and Global Instability*. New York: Random House, 2004.

Critchley, Simon. *The Faith of the Faithless: Experiments in Political Theology*. New York: Verso Books, 2012.

Dawkins, Richard. *The God Delusion*. New York: Houghton Mifflin, 2006.

Dawkins, Richard. *The Magic of Reality: How We Know What's Really True*. London: Bantam Press, 2011.

De Caro, Mario, and David MacArthur, editors. "Artisanal Polymath of Philosophy." *Philosophy in an Age of Science: Physics, Mathematics, and Skepticism*. Cambridge, MA: Harvard University Press, 2012.

Deneen, Patrick. *Why Liberalism Failed*. New Haven, CT: Yale University Press, 2018.

De Waal, Frans. *Primates and Philosophers: How Morality Evolved*. Princeton, NJ: Princeton University Press, 2006.

Doctorow, E. L. *City of God*. New York: Random House, 2000.

Douthat, Ross. *The Decadent Society: How We Became the Victims of Our Own Success*. New York: Avid Reader Press, 2020.

Epperson, Michael. *Quantum Mechanics and the Philosophy of Alfred North Whitehead.* New York: Fordham University Press, 2004.

Fackenheim, Emil L. *To Mend the World: Foundations of Post-Holocaust Jewish Thought.* Bloomington: Indiana University Press, 1994.

Farias, Victor. *Heidegger and Nazism.* Philadelphia: Temple University Press, 1989.

Fernbach, Philip, and Steven Sloman. *The Knowledge Illusion: Why We Never Think Alone.* New York: Riverhead Books, 2017.

Fisher, Mark. *Capitalist Realism: Is There No Alternative?* Hampshire, UK: O-Books, 2009.

Frank, Thomas. *What's the Matter with Kansas?: How Conservatives Won the Heart of America.* New York: Henry Holt and Company, 2005.

Fukuyama, Francis. *The End of History and the Last Man.* New York: Maxwell Macmillan International, 1992.

Gane, Nicholas. *Max Weber and Postmodern Theory: Rationalization versus Re-enchantment.* New York: Palgrave, 2002.

Gilens, Martin, and Benjamin I. Page. *Democracy in America? What Has Gone Wrong and What We Can Do About It.* Chicago: University of Chicago Press, 2017.

Ginsburg, Tom, and Aziz Huq. *How to Save a Constitutional Democracy.* Chicago: University of Chicago Press, 2020.

Gorsuch, Neil M. *A Republic, If You Can Keep It.* New York: Crown Forum, 2019.

Gray, John. *Black Mass: Apocalyptic Religion and the Death of Utopia.* New York: Farrar, Straus and Giroux, 2007.

Gray, John. *Seven Types of Atheism.* New York: Farrar, Straus and Giroux, 2018.

Gray, John. *Soul of the Marionette: A Short Inquiry into Human Freedom.* New York: Farrar, Straus and Giroux, 2015.

Gray, John. *Straw Dogs: Thoughts on Humans and Other Animals.* New York: Farrar, Straus and Giroux, 2003.

Griffin, David Ray. *Panentheism and Scientific Naturalism: Rethinking Evil, Morality, Religious Experience, Religious Pluralism, and the Academic Study of Religion.* Claremont, CA: Process Century Press, 2014.

Griffin, David Ray. *Reenchantment Without Supernaturalism: A Process Philosophy of Religion.* New York: Cornell University Press, 2001.

Hadot, Pierre. *Philosophy as a Way of Life: Spiritual Exercises from Socrates to Foucault.* Hoboken, NJ: Wiley-Blackwell, 1995.

Harris, Sam. *The End of Faith: Religion, Terror, and Future of Reason.* New York: W. W. Norton & Company, 2004.

Harris, Sam. *The Moral Landscape.* New York: Free Press, 2010.

Heidegger, Martin. *The Fundamental Concepts of Metaphysics: World, Finitude, Solitude.* Bloomington: Indiana University Press, 1995.

Heidegger, Martin. *The Question Concerning Technology and Other Essays.* New York: Harper Perennial, 1997.

Hitchens, Christopher. *God Is Not Great: How Religion Poisons Everything.* New York: Hachette Book Group, 2007.

Hochschild, Arlie Russell. *Strangers in Their Own Land: Anger and Mourning on the American Right.* New York: New Press, 2016.

Hunter, James Davison, and Paul Nedelisky. *Science and the Good: The Tragic Quest for the Foundations of Morality.* New Haven, CT: Yale University Press, 2018.

Jaffa, Harry. *Original Intent and the Framers of the Constitution: A Disputed Question.* Washington, DC: Regnery Gateway, 1994.

Judt, Tony. *Ill Fares the Land*. New York: Penguin Random House, 2010.

Kakutani, Michiko. *The Death of Truth*. New York: Tim Duggan Books, 2018.

Kang, Han. *Human Acts*. New York: Hogarth, 2016.

Kelly, Lynne. *The Skeptic's Guide to the Paranormal*. Crows Nest, Australia: Allen & Unwin, 2004.

Kitcher, Philip. *Living with Darwin: Evolution, Design, and the Future of Faith*. New York: Oxford University Press, 2009.

Klein, Ezra. *Why We're Polarized*. New York: Simon & Schuster, Inc., 2020.

Kronman, Anthony. *Confessions of a Born-Again Pagan*. New Haven, CT: Yale University Press, 2016.

Krugman, Paul. *Arguing with Zombies: Economics, Politics, and the Fight for a Better Future*. New York: W. W. Norton & Company, 2020.

Ladin, Joy. *The Soul of the Stranger: Reading God and Torah from a Transgender Perspective*. Waltham, MA: Brandeis University Press, 2019.

Ledewitz, Bruce. *American Religious Democracy: Coming to Terms with the End of Secular Politics*. Westport, CT: Praeger Publishers, 2007.

Ledewitz, Bruce. *Hallowed Secularism*. New York: Palgrave Macmillan, 2009.

Lessig, Lawrence. *America, Compromised*. Chicago: University of Chicago Press, 2018.

Lessig, Lawrence. *Republic, Lost: How Money Corrupts Congress—and a Plan to Stop It*. New York: Twelve Books, 2011.

Levitsky, Steven, and Daniel Ziblatt. *How Democracies Die*. New York: Broadway Books, 2018.

Lewis, Michael. *Moneyball*. New York: W. W. Norton & Company, 2004.

Lewis, Michael. *The Undoing Project*. New York: W. W. Norton & Company, 2016.

Lilla, Mark. *The Stillborn God: Religion, Politics, and the Modern West*. New York: Vintage Books, 2008.

Lind, Michael. *The New Class War*. New York: Penguin Random House LLC, 2020.

Lonergan, Bernard. *Insight: A Study of Human Understanding*. New York: Philosophical Library, 1957.

Lonergan, Bernard. *Method in Theology*. New York: Herder & Herder, 1973.

May, Todd. *Gilles Deleuze: An Introduction*. New York: Cambridge University Press, 2005.

McCall Smith, Alexander. *The Department of Sensitive Crimes*. New York: Pantheon Books, 2019.

McKibben, Bill. *Falter: Has the Human Game Begun to Play Itself Out?* New York: Henry Holt and Co., 2019.

Michaels, David. *The Triumph of Doubt: Dark Money and the Science of Deception*. New York: Oxford University Press, 2020.

Micklethwait, John, and Adrian Wooldridge. *God Is Back: How the Global Revival of Faith Is Changing the World*. New York: Penguin Press, 2009.

Miller, Christian. *The Character Gap: How Good Are We?* New York: Oxford University Press, 2017.

Miller, Mark. *The Quest for God and the Good Life*. Washington, DC: Catholic University of America Press, 2013.

Morowitz, Harold, and Eric Smith. *The Origin and Nature of Life on Earth: The Emergence of the Fourth Geosphere*. Cambridge, MA: Cambridge University Press, 2016.

Morris, Simon Conway. *Life's Solution: Inevitable Humans in a Lonely Universe*. Cambridge, MA: Cambridge University Press, 2004.

Mounk, Yascha. *The People vs. Democracy: Why Our Freedom Is in Danger and How to Save It*. Cambridge, MA: Harvard University Press, 2018.

Murthy, Vivek. *Together: The Healing Power of Human Connection in a Sometimes Lonely World*. New York: HarperCollins Publishers, 2020.

Nietzsche, Friedrich. *The Gay Science*. New York: Vintage Books, 1974.

Noah, Timothy. *The Great Divergence: America's Growing Inequality Crisis and What We Can Do About It*. New York: Bloomsbury Press, 2012.

O'Connell, Mark. *Notes From an Apocalypse: A Personal Journey to the End of the World and Back*. New York: Penguin Random House LLC, 2020.

Owen, Lewis, and Kevin Pickering. *An Introduction to Global Environmental Issues*. Milton Park: Routledge, 1997.

Pinker, Steven. *The Better Angels of Our Nature: Why Violence Has Declined*. New York: Viking, 2011.

Pinker, Steven. *Enlightenment Now: The Case for Reason, Science, Humanism, and Progress*. New York: Viking, 2018.

Plantinga, Alvin. *Where the Conflict Really Lies: Science, Religion, and Naturalism*. New York: Oxford University Press, 2011.

Postman, Neil. *Amusing Ourselves to Death: Public Discourse in the Age of Show Business*. New York: Viking, 1985.

Putnam, Hilary. *The Collapse of the Fact/Value Dichotomy and Other Essays*. Cambridge, MA: Harvard University Press, 2002.

Putnam, Hilary. *Words and Life*. Cambridge, MA: Harvard University Press, 1994.

Putnam, Robert. *Bowling Alone: The Collapse and Revival of American Community*. New York: Simon & Schuster Paperbacks, 2000.

Quinn, Daniel. *Ishmael: An Adventure of the Mind and Spirit*. New York: Bantam/Turner, 1992.

Rawls, John. *A Theory of Justice*. Cambridge, MA: Belknap Press, 1971.

Rorty, Richard. *Philosophy and the Mirror of Nature*. Princeton, NJ: Princeton University Press, 1979.

Sagan, Carl. *Pale Blue Dot: A Vision of the Human Future in Space*. New York: Ballantine Books, 1994.

Sasse, Ben. *Them: Why We Hate Each Other—and How to Heal*. New York: St. Martin's Press, 2018.

Scalia, Antonin. *A Matter of Interpretation: Federal Courts and the Law*. Princeton, NJ: Princeton University Press, 1997.

Shermer, Michael. *The Moral Arc: How Science and Reason Lead Humanity Toward Truth, Justice, and Freedom*. New York: Henry Holt and Co., 2015.

Sitaraman, Ganesh. *The Crisis of the Middle-Class Constitution: Why Economic Inequality Threatens Our Republic*. New York: Alred A. Knopf, 2017.

Sloterdijk, Peter. *After God*. Cambridge, MA: Polity Books, 2020.

Smith, Christian. *Atheist Overreach: What Atheism Can't Deliver*. New York: Oxford University Press, 2019.

Smith, James K. A. *Awaiting the King: Reforming Public Theology*. Grand Rapids, MI: Baker Academic, 2017.

Smith, Justin. *Irrationality: A History of the Dark Side of Reason*. Princeton, NJ: Princeton University Press, 2019.

Smith, Steven D. *Law's Quandary*. Cambridge, MA: Harvard University Press, 2004.

Stone, Jeremy. *Religious Naturalism Today: The Rebirth of a Forgotten Alternative.* New York: State University of New York Press, 2014.

Sykes, Charles. *How the Right Lost Its Mind.* London: Biteback Publishing Ltd, 2017.

Taylor, Charles. *A Secular Age.* Cambridge, MA: Belknap Press, 2007.

Unger, Roberto. *What Should Legal Analysis Become?* London: Verso, 1996.

Vance, J. D. *Hillbilly Elegy: A Memoir of a Family and Culture in Crisis.* New York: HarperCollins Publishers, 2016.

Vischer, Robert K. *Martin Luther King Jr. and the Morality of Legal Practice: Lessons in Love and Justice.* New York: Cambridge University Press, 2013.

Warren, Rick. *Daily Inspiration for the Purpose Driven Life: Scripture & Reflections From the 40 Days of Purpose.* Grand Rapids, MI: Zondervan Publishing House, 2010.

Weber, Max. *Economy and Society: An Outline of Interpretive Sociology.* New York: Bedminster Press, 1968.

Weber, Max. *The Protestant Ethic and the Spirit of Capitalism.* New York: Scriber, 1948.

Weber, Max. *Science as a Vocation.* New York: Oxford University Press, 1946.

Whitehead, Alfred North. *Process and Reality: An Essay in Cosmology.* New York: Free Press, 1978.

Willard, Dallas. *The Disappearance of Moral Knowledge.* New York: Routledge, Taylor & Francis Group, 2018.

Wright, N. T. *The Resurrection of the Son of God.* London: SPCK, 2003.

Index